SLIDES FOR STUDENTS

The Effective Use of
Powerpoint in Education

GARY D. FISK

SLIDES FOR STUDENTS

The Effective Use of Powerpoint in Education

GARY D. FISK

UNIVERSITY of
NORTH GEORGIA™
UNIVERSITY PRESS

Blue Ridge | Cumming | Dahlonega | Gainesville | Oconee

Copyright © 2019 by Gary D. Fisk

All rights reserved. No part of this book may be reproduced in whole or in part without written permission from the publisher, except by reviewers who may quote brief excerpts in connections with a review in newspaper, magazine, or electronic publications; nor may any part of this book be reproduced, stored in a retrieval system, or transmitted in any form or by any means electronic, mechanical, photocopying, recording, or other, without the written permission from the publisher.

Published by:
University of North Georgia Press
Dahlonega, Georgia

Printing Support by:
Lightning Source Inc.
La Vergne, Tennessee

Book design by Corey Parson.

ISBN: 978-1-940771-43-4

Printed in the United States of America
For more information, please visit: http://ung.edu/university-press
Or e-mail: ungpress@ung.edu

Contents

0　Introduction　vii

1　Presentation Software　1

2　Powerpointlessness　14

3　Educational Effectiveness and Student Perceptions　32

4　Avoiding Death by Powerpoint　53

5　Design for Emotion I　67

6　Design for Emotion II　84

7　Design for Sensation　100

8　Design for Perception I　117

9　Design for Perception II　135

10	Design for Attention	156
11	Design for Cognition I	170
12	Design for Cognition II	190
13	Design for Behavior	213
14	Technology Choices	232
15	Tips and Tricks for Slide Presentations	247
16	A Classroom Presentation Example	264
17	The Bright Future of Powerpoint in Education	292
A	Appendix A	307
B	Appendix B	310
C	Appendix C	314

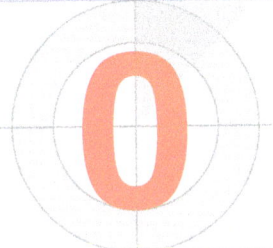

INTRODUCTION

The creative spark that motivated this book was the observation that powerpoint presentations sometimes fail to produce a positive impact on student learning. There seems to be a strange, somewhat curious disconnect between an amazing technology and a mediocre or poor student learning experience. Discussions with other college faculty reinforced the idea that powerpoint presentations often fall short of expectations in the classroom. The initial curiosity about this disconnection became a personal journey to learn more about presentation technology and how it was used—or misused—in the classroom. My overall conclusion is that powerpoint presentations are often used in ineffective ways. This is not entirely the fault of the technology. Rather, the main problem lies in how humans use the technology. If we want to unleash the full potential of powerpoint presentations, we must do a better job of creating presentations that fit the educational needs of our students.

My exploration of the use of powerpoint in education suggested a need for definitive guidelines that would inform educators about the best practices for its use. Many educators have written specific studies of powerpoint in the classroom, but clear-cut recommendations based on this evidence were missing. The present book addresses this need by synthesizing information across psychological research areas, such as sensation, cognition, and behavior. Other evidence comes from classroom-based studies conducted by educational professionals across a wide range of academic disciplines. A third body of evidence was the recommendations made by professional designers who aim to improve the quality of powerpoint presentations. The present book was synthesized from these widely varied sources into recommendations that should help education professionals connect with their students and get better learning outcomes from their powerpoint presentations.

This book is not meant to be a software manual or a how-to guide for using a particular software application. Many such books are available for Microsoft's PowerPoint or Apple's Keynote software applications. Instead, this book's emphasis is on the design of educational presentations. The ideas behind these design concepts focus on general principles of human learning rather than a specific technology, so these ideas should work well for any particular kind of presentation software. Another feature that sets this book apart is the emphasis on an evidenced-based, scientific approach. This evidence focus leads to a substantively different way of designing presentations, one that provides a true educational benefit rather than emphasizing the construction of pretty slides.

A small but important challenge in the writing of this book was how to handle the term "PowerPoint." At first, it seemed best to avoid using this term because it represents a proprietary product that is trademarked by the Microsoft Corporation. On the other hand, my attempts to write about presentations without using the term "PowerPoint" resulted in awkward writing. The heart of the issue is that the term "PowerPoint" has taken on multiple meanings and, therefore, can be used in more than one manner. Hubert Knoblauch, a sociologist who studies PowerPoint as a cultural phenomenon, suggests an elegant way to delicately treat this ambiguous term (Knoblauch, 2012, p. 3). He uses "PowerPoint" (note the capitalization) to refer specifically to the Microsoft Office software application. This capitalization is appropriate given that Microsoft's PowerPoint software is a proper noun. In contrast, the term "powerpoint" (all lower case) is used to describe a modern presentation style that is characterized by some form of multimedia supplement to the speaker's voice. This broad use of the term can refer generically to many modern presentations, regardless of the technology that was used. This book will follow Knoblauch's suggested usage of these terms to make this important distinction between a specific software product (PowerPoint) and the more general uses of multimedia to support presentations (powerpoint).

The writing of this book was a large and somewhat audacious project that was supported by many people. In particular, I thank Ellen Cotter, my wife, for her support of this project and her great proofreading skills. This book would not have been possible without her. From my department, I thank Jamie MacLennan for giving feedback on the manuscript and Chuck Huffman for his support of this scholarly activity. More broadly, I would like to thank the faculty of Georgia Southwestern State University (GSW) for their encouragement and enthusiasm. These GSW colleagues reinforced my initial impressions that powerpoint presentations can be problematic and are worthy of greater scientific attention. My colleagues also suggested numerous ideas that have been incorporated into this book. The Interlibrary Loan librarians at GSW were instrumental for obtaining the numerous articles that formed the basis of this book. Their support is greatly appreciated. I thank Stephen Snyder, Director of University Relations at GSW, for taking high-quality pictures of the powerpoint displays in the classroom. Finally, I would like to thank the University of North Georgia Press for believing in the vision of this book and the potential benefit that it might have for educational professionals. I thank the editors and peer-reviewers for their work, which greatly strengthened the book.

PRESENTATION SOFTWARE

The Revolution and the Dilemma

The PowerPoint program is like the weather: Everyone likes to complain about it but nobody does anything about it. (Kosslyn, 2007)

Picture the following scenario: A modern college class begins with an introductory title slide that displays a topic title and a few bullet points. The class begins with a warm greeting from the professor, who then walks the classroom of 200 students through a progression of twenty-five slides. The presentation is very orderly, with the slides being delivered in a carefully-planned sequence. Each slide has a neat hierarchy of information laid out in a bullet point list. A few slides have graphs or diagrams that support an important idea. Once in a while, a student asks a question. At the end, the professor shows a conclusion slide and asks the class if there are any further questions. One student asks a question, which the professor answers. The class is dismissed.

Now, consider your reaction to this scenario. It's likely that your initial response is that this imaginary class sounds a bit dull. This scenario fits our modern standards for education, but it doesn't seem to be dynamic or student-centered. It describes a rather passive approach to learning that places too much emphasis on the slide show. Somewhat mysteriously, the state of the art powerpoint technology has led to a mediocre educational experience. This humdrum result occurred even though the professor had good intentions and put a significant effort into giving the students a first-rate education.

The above scenario, with some slight variations, is repeated in university and K12 educational settings numerous times each day all over the world. Of course, the exact number of educational presentations is not precisely known, but the number must be rather high. Microsoft once estimated that 300 million PowerPoint presentations of all kinds are given daily (I. Parker, 2001). Another estimate is that 350 powerpoint presentations are being given each second (Parks, 2012). These high numbers illustrate the importance of powerpoint presentations in modern culture. Slide presentations are found in business, education, government, and the sciences. Even churches have adopted this technology to assist worshippers during church services. The ubiquity of powerpoint presentations shows that powerpoint is taking a central role in everyday modern life (Knoblauch, 2012). The current cultural standard is that every presentation must include a slide show. For educators, the classroom experience often focuses on the slide deck (an antiquated term for a powerpoint presentation), which makes powerpoint the center of the modern classroom.

A Brief History of Visual Presentation Aids

The use of visual aids to supplement presentations emerged in the early part of the twentieth century as a movement towards making business management more scientific. An early example is from the Du Pont chemical company, which had a special "chart room" that was designed for business meetings (Yates, 1985). Large charts with financial information were moved in and out of the conference room on tracks to support the process of making business decisions. The use of visual displays for presentations was slowly adopted and imitated by other companies throughout the twentieth century. Early proponents of this visually-focused approach to presentations included scientists, engineers, and the military. By the 1960s, the practice of supplementing presentations with visual aids had become the presentation standard in many technical fields.

Important technical innovations that fostered is practice are the introduction of the overhead projector in 1962 (3M, 2002) and the introduction of the microcomputer in the 1980s. Microsoft's PowerPoint software, which is the industry standard for presentations, began as a commercial product called "Presenter" in 1987 (Gaskins, 2007). The initial purpose of the software was to facilitate the creation of transparencies (version 1.0) and 35-millimeter slides (version 2.0) for use in business presentations. In 1990, the software became a component of the Microsoft Office business software suite and was rebranded

"PowerPoint." The distribution of PowerPoint software as a part of the Microsoft Office product suite helped PowerPoint to quickly become the standard presentation software in the field of business, which was then followed by its adoption in government, schools, and other institutions.

The use of visual aids for supplementing a presentation is a twentieth century technology revolution in the way that presentations are given. In the 1800s, it would have been unusual to supplement a presentation with a visual aid. At most, educators used chalkboards to provide a visual supplement to their lectures (May, 1855; as cited in S. C. Parker, 1912, p. 92). In the 1960s through the 1980s, educators occasionally used transparencies on an overhead projector to supplement a lecture. Now, it is almost unthinkable to give a presentation without supporting visual materials. It would feel unnatural and wrong. In the past 100 years, our cultural standards for what constitutes a good presentation have changed from purely verbal speeches to presentations supplemented by multimedia visual aids.

Microsoft's PowerPoint software has enjoyed a near monopoly on presentation software for almost thirty years, which is an unusually long period of market dominance compared to other computer-based technologies. Just think of the technologies that were popular a decade or two ago—film cameras, WordPerfect, My Space—but have disappeared or been replaced by newer and better technology. Educational professionals are not immune to these rapid technology changes. Given this ever-changing technology environment, it seems appropriate to ask the question of whether or not powerpoint is still relevant in the contemporary classroom. Perhaps powerpoint technology is nearing the end of its lifespan.

So, is PowerPoint obsolete? If we focus on PowerPoint, the Microsoft product, then the answer might be "maybe," although obsolescence seems unlikely given the decades of market dominance that this product has enjoyed. A better question is to shift to a broader focus: Is powerpoint (the multimedia presentation form) obsolete? The answer to this question is a resounding "no." Educators have been using visual aids to complement the teacher's voice since chalkboards became common classroom equipment in the 1800s. Furthermore, our current cultural standard has an expectation that a speaker's words will be accompanied by a visual event for the audience to watch. Multimedia presentations that supplement the speaker's voice with text and images clearly have much to offer for educators and students. Research efforts in this area are still making significant progress in understanding the best multimedia methods for teachers to use in their classrooms. Altogether, multimedia presentations are clearly valuable for teachers and students, and so powerpoint, the multimedia presentation style, will continue to be an important educational tool well into the future.

The instructional recommendaations given in this book will not become quickly obsolete like last year's iPhone model. A strong effort has been made to avoid providing a simple "how-to" book for using Microsoft's PowerPoint software application, although in some situations references will be made to specific PowerPoint features given that this software is widely used. In contrast, the overall aim of this book is to focus on the design of visual aids or multimedia presentations that are effective for education. The principles outlined in this book will help the reader to become proficient in assembling text and images in multimedia presentations in a manner that promotes student learning. These ideas should work regardless of the software product or vendor (Microsoft PowerPoint, Apple Keynote, and others) because the emphasis is on how students learn from multimedia instruction. The principles of how students learn will not go obsolete like so many technology products.

The Powerpoint Paradox

Powerpoint technology clearly offers some strong advantages for presentations. Professional-looking graphics can be easily and quickly created, even by people who have limited experience with the software. The visual display of information makes text and graphics more accessible to the audience. For example, words projected on a powerpoint presentation are much more legible than hand-written words on a chalkboard. Presenters can also use graphics to support their main points in ways that were difficult to accomplish before the powerpoint revolution.

Although the modern powerpoint presentation has some clear advantages, the very real downside that accompanies the use of presentation technology is apparent to anyone who has watched enough presentations. Powerpoint seems to be a double-edged sword. It can make good presentations better, but it also has the potential to make bad presentations become worse. Powerpoint presentations can sometimes be a tortured, unpleasant experience for the audience, an experience that is often called "death by powerpoint" and other unflattering terms. Our ability to use powerpoint's potential in ways that actually improve presentations lags behind the adoption of the technology. The technology has leaped forward, yet human communication skills do not differ much from what they have always been.

The general assumption is that a presenter should intuitively know how to use PowerPoint and similar forms of presentation software. The creators of these software applications have strived to make the software easy to use, so creating good slides for a presentation should be a snap. Unfortunately, the truth is that ease of use does not translate into effective presentations. In fact, some presentation experts have suggested that the software's ease of use has created a contradictory situation. Many educators may overestimate the quality of their presentations by confusing the ease of creation with the quality of the final product. The thoughtless and untrained application of default powerpoint settings may be an important part of the powerpoint paradox: amazing technology resulting in weak presentations.

A Presentation Success Story

Imagine for a moment how better powerpoint presentations might positively impact student learning by considering a fictional case study. Let's pretend that Dr. Nuprof is a new assistant professor of History at a state university. She finished graduate school last year, so her teaching skills are still developing. She regularly teaches general education history classes, such as American History and Western Civilization, in moderately sized classrooms of 25 to 50 students. The class is largely a lecture format, although occasionally other educational strategies are used to promote critical thinking about controversial issues.

Dr. Nuprof's spent a lot of time during her first semester developing powerpoint presentations for her classes. Her reasoning was the powerpoint slides are a focal point of the student classroom experience, so it made sense to put a strong effort into developing a good slide deck to support her lectures. The development effort included making the presentations well-organized and full of the main key terms that were most likely to be on an exam. Most of the slides had a title and listed key terms with the corresponding definitions. Some of the slides came prepared from the textbook publisher. These prepared slides included vibrant colors and decorative graphics which seemed to be attractive and appealing to students. Dr. Nuprof believed that using the publisher's slides would be a smart choice because these slides are designed by professionals and are convenient to use. In particular, the convenience of a prepared slide deck was important to Dr. Nuprof because she felt overwhelmed by the need to develop content for her courses, several of which she had not taught before. Overall, she was pleased with her slides. Powerpoint presentations are expected in modern college classes and she had successfully met this expectation.

Dr. Nuprof began the semester with high confidence in her teaching abilities and her pedagogical approach. Her classroom presentations went over the bullet points on the slides in a dutiful manner. At first, it seemed as if everything was going according to plan. Over the course of the semester though it became apparent that something wasn't working right. Her students showed signs of disengagement, such as day dreaming and phone-fiddling. The students seem to come alive for a moment when a new slide was introduced. This was followed by quickly copying down the text on the slide. After this, the students fell back into disengagement and apathy. The cycle would repeat when a new slide was introduced. It was a frustrating experience to work with such uninvolved students.

The overall picture was not great either, with student performance being low on exams and Dr. Nuprof receiving lukewarm feedback on her student evaluations. Attendance seemed weak, with some students opting to download the powerpoint file from the learning management system rather than attend class. It seemed that Dr. Nuprof had checked all of the right boxes for a good teaching approach, but something vital was still missing. Her classes were not terrible, but they also could not be considered a great success.

Like every good teacher, Dr. Nuprof set out to improve upon her teaching practices for the next semester. She read expert advice about powerpoint presentations and did a thorough evaluation of the role of powerpoint in her courses. These ideas guided changes to boost the effectiveness of multimedia presentations in her courses. She began by throwing out the content-heavy PowerPoint slides that were provided by the textbook publisher. These were replaced with her own slide decks that had a story-like structure to the overall presentation (see Chapter 6). The useless colors and unnecessary decorations from the prepared slide decks were eliminated in order to focus student attention on the relevant ideas and information (see Chapter 11). The classroom time was changed to set aside time for active learning exercises as a break from pure lecturing (see Chapters 5, 10, and 12). Many slides that only contained bullet point information were replaced with the more effective assertion-evidence slide format that combines statements and supporting images (Chapter 9). Images with relevant educational content, such as pictures of important historical events, were used to increase student interest and deliver information more efficiently (see Chapters 5 and 9). The segments of pure lecturing were alternated with relevant stories from the topic and illustrative video clips to keep students emotionally involved and sustain their attention throughout the class period (see Chapter 10). In some sections, she tried posing questions to students on slides, with a student response system (sometimes called "clickers") for collecting student answers. This was a deliberate effort to employ a more active learning strategy (see Chapter 12). She addresses the low attendance problem by discussing note-taking strategies with the students, regarding how slide deck files were intended to provide an important resource for students' note-taking efforts instead of simply making class time unnecessary (see Chapter 13). In one section, she stopped posting the powerpoint slides to the learning management system, so the easily available slides could not contribute to the low attendance problem.

Dr. Nuprof's students responded positively to these changes. The degree of student involvement throughout the class period seemed better. The students felt that the class was more challenging that simply copying down text from a slide, but this challenge was positive and welcomed by the students. The class was now more interesting and thought-provoking to the students. More students were asking questions, which improved the interactions between teacher and student. Class time had been changed from a one-way transfer of information to a two-way dialog between the students and the professor. As a result, Dr. Nuprof's classroom experience was transformed from a dull slog through a mountain of educational content towards a more rewarding give-and-take intellectual exchange, for both the students and Dr. Nuprof. For the semester, the grades were up slightly and Dr. Nuprof's student evaluations also improved.

Looking back, Dr. Nuprof realized that an effective powerpoint presentation requires much more than simply filling out the bullets on a slide with some key terms or providing commentary on a slide deck provided by the textbook publisher. Her previous approach treated powerpoint like it was an electronic chalk board for showing words to students. The heavy emphasis on key terms and definitions was not engaging and did little to promote significant learning processes. She realized that this information-focused approach is too shallow. Effective instruction is more than feeding information to students on pretty slides. The real goal is to consider the larger educational strategy and purpose of each topic, then thoughtfully design the presentation and class activities in ways that promote student learning. This approach needs to consider the student as a whole person: emotions, perception, attention, cognition, and behavior. All of these dimensions must come together in a deliberate manner to make a presentation a meaningful learning tool.

This fictitious example is, admittedly, rather optimistic. The important point though is that powerpoint presentations can be much more than a lifeless information delivery machine. Bullet point lists are a starting point, but lists are not really sufficient to fully engage student learning. Ideally, the right pedagogical design and approach in powerpoint could help both the instructors and the students achieve the mission of better learning through balancing information delivery, student engagement, and questions that foster deeper forms of learning. There is much potential in powerpoint that currently goes unrealized or escapes critical examination. The right application is all that's needed to unlock it.

Let's Get Started

The dilemma posed by the visual media style of modern presentations is this: How should teachers use presentation technologies to improve education? No simple answer exists. Most educators have significant familiarity with Microsoft's PowerPoint or a similar program like Apple's Keynote. The average educator regularly makes basic presentations based upon powerpoint templates, such as slides with bullet point list designs and built-in color schemes. Unfortunately, the presentation design skills of most educators probably do not progress much beyond the most basic levels of powerpoint use. Most teachers have not received significant-enough advanced training that would enable them to do more than make a basic presentation. Consequently, most educators can make a decent basic powerpoint presentation, but probably not one that truly stimulates significant student learning. Simply replacing the chalkboard with a colorful slide is not going to accomplish much for helping students learn.

A need exists for thoughtfully designed and implemented classroom instruction that focuses on the learner rather than on the technology. Fortunately, over 400 published articles in professional journals examine questions concerning how powerpoint could work for improving education. These articles span a wide range of academic disciplines, such as education, business, psychology, and nursing. Most of these studies are based on empirical evidence, such as student surveys, teacher experiences, and experimental studies. Some laboratory-based studies have also been done by psychologists, typically ones who specialize in education or cognition. In total, the information acquired in these studies provides a wealth of interesting and useful evidence for improving the instructional effectiveness of powerpoint. The present book was written to translate academic research findings into practical suggestions about powerpoint that educators can use.

The higher aim of making powerpoint into a better educational tool is somewhat elusive, yet this effort is a worthwhile investment. While involving a greater degree of effort than simply filling out the next bullet point, carefully considering the advantages and disadvantages of modern presentation software will hopefully lead to effective presentations that avoid the dreaded "death by powerpoint" experience. Deliberate design can elevate a basic, dull presentation into exceptional teaching that results in a superior learning experience.

POWERPOINTLESSNESS

Exploring the Dark Side of Multimedia Presentations

PowerPoint could be the most powerful tool on your computer. *But it's not.* It's actually a dismal failure. Almost every PowerPoint presentation sucks rotten eggs. And much of the fault lies with Microsoft. (Godin, 2001)

Many critics have blasted powerpoint presentations. The following list catalogs the negative catch phrases that have been used describe powerpoint. These have been intentionally formatted into a powerpoint-style bullet point list for maximum irony.

- Powerpoint is evil (Tufte, 2003)
- Is powerpoint the devil? (Keller, 2003)
- Powerpoint makes us stupid/dumb. (Bumiller, 2010; Frommer, 2012; Simons, 2004; Thompson, 2003)

- Powerpoint is the Viagra of the spoken word. (van Jole, 2000)
- Powerpointlessness (McKenzie, 2000)
- Powerpoint hell (Vickers, 1999)
- Ban it now! Friends don't let friends use powerpoint. (Stewart, 2001)
- Powerpoint poisoning (S. Adams, 2000)
- Digital slideshows are the scourge of higher education (Schuman, 2014)
- Powerpoint pissoff (Soltan, 2015)
- Computer slide shows: A trap for bad teaching (Klemm, 2007)
- Powerpoint is like having a loaded AK-47 on the table (Peter Norvig, as quoted in Gunn and Raskin Gullickson, 2005)

We can even categorize these soundbite critiques into a special death-themed category:

- Death by powerpoint (Garber, 2001)
- Death to powerpoint (Parks, 2012)
- Death by bullet points (Heavens, 2004)

These examples clearly show that many people hate powerpoint presentations. The main concern is that powerpoint technology is making presentations worse, not better. Everyone who has suffered through a bad powerpoint-based presentation can certainly understand this strong, negative reaction. Similarly, some uneasiness persists about the use of powerpoint technology in the classroom (Keller, 2003; I. Parker, 2001).

Edward Tufte—A Powerful Powerpoint Critic

Let's consider the potential problems of powerpoint presentations. Edward Tufte is the most prominent critic of powerpoint presentations (Tufte, 2003, 2006). His critiques carry considerable influence because he is an internationally-recognized expert in the use of graphs, figures, and tables for the visualization and understanding of scientific data (Tufte, 1990, 1997, 2001). Tufte's view is that powerpoint seriously compromises the ability of the audience to comprehend complex information. In this summative paragraph, he writes:

> PowerPoint's convenience for some presenters is costly to the content and the audience. These costs arise from the cognitive style characteristics of the standard default [PowerPoint] presentation: foreshortening of evidence and thought, low spatial resolution, an intensely hierarchical single-path structure as a model for organizing every type of content, breaking up narratives and data into slides and minimal fragments, rapid temporal sequencing of thin information rather than focused spatial analysis, conspicuous chartjunk and [PowerPoint] Phluff, branding of slides with logotypes, a preoccupation with format, not content, and a smirky commercialism that turns information into a sales pitch and presenters into marketeers. (Tufte, 2006, p. 4)

Tufte's opinion is that the powerpoint medium itself, not the individual giving the presentation, is the source of the problem. We will consider his main critical points one by one.

"Foreshortening of evidence and thought, low spatial resolution"

An important concern is that presenters must greatly simplify their technical information in order to fit it into the limitations of powerpoint. This problem stems from the practical constraints imposed by the slide medium. The size of the text used in a presentation must be large in order to make that text visible to the audience. The unavoidable consequence of large type is that only a few words can be placed on a slide. In addition, colorful graphics, corporate logos, and/or special layouts often take up valuable slide space, thus further decreasing the space available for the presenter's information. These limitations encourage the use of short phrases over complete sentences, leading to Tufte's comment about "foreshortening" of thought. Any supporting graphics, such as graphs and diagrams, must also be very simple and direct, causing a loss of their complexity and details. Altogether, Tufte's view is that the limitations of powerpoint require presenters to greatly reduce the complexity of their information in order to make the message fit on a slide. This reduction culminates in a dumbing-down of the content for the audience. Only the highlights can be covered in a powerpoint presentation, which necessitates leaving out details that might be important. Comparing the limitations of powerpoint to printed formats, Tufte finds the latter as being able to carry a much higher information density.

Tufte is certainly correct that less information can be placed on a slide than on a printed document. However, the counterpoint to Tufte's critique is that we should not expect presentations to convey the same degree of information as the printed word

(Doumont, 2005). Too many details in a presentation will simply overwhelm an audience. When used correctly, the limitations of a powerpoint slide can be an asset by forcing the presenter to focus on only the most important information. Unimportant details should be deliberately excluded from the presentation in order to avoid distractions or overloading the audience. By limiting the information, the presenter quite literally points the main ideas out to the audience by directing their attention to the main message. The unavoidable drawback of these limits is that details might become lost or overlooked, although this may not always be a significant problem.

Fortunately, teachers and college professors have more ways of delivering content to their students than a mere powerpoint slide deck. The information presented during a class period is, to some degree, an introduction to the topic. Instructors typically supplement the information from a slide deck with information from other sources such as textbook content, supplemental readings, demonstrations, videos, and assignments. Thus, the classroom presentation can concentrate on the highly important information and the other sources can fill in the details.

"An intensely hierarchical single-path structure as a model for organizing every type of content"

Tufte's second major concern focuses on the organization of slide presentations, which is both sequential (slide after slide, in a predefined order) and hierarchical (headings with bullet points and subpoints). Unlike information presented on a traditional chalkboard, slide decks must be made before the presentation.

The instructor then follows this predetermined order, usually without deviations, during the presentation. The prepared slide deck ultimately controls their flow, thereby making instructors become excessively rigid and lacking in spontaneity.

In education, several critics have voiced concerns that slide presentations may encourage teachers to march through the course content with little interaction from the students (Frommer, 2012; Kjeldsen, 2006; Klemm, 2007). Teachable moments that might come from student questions can be lost if these questions go into directions that deviate from the order of the slide deck. A related problem is that the rigid structure may create a classroom environment that encourages the audience to be obediently quiet and listen instead of interrupting the presentation's predestined flow. This may promote an authoritarian relationship between teachers and students. A third possible problem is that powerpoint's strictly linear organization might suggest a simple linear relationship between topics (A then B then C) when, in reality, the true relationships between topics might be much more complicated (Kinchin, Chadha, and Kokotailo, 2008). The emphasis on serial order could lead to an erroneous or oversimplified understanding of how the various components of a topic relate to each other.

The possibility that the structure of powerpoint presentations stifles student participation may be a common view, but it might not have much research support. Knoblauch (2012) and colleagues conducted studies of live powerpoint presentations and carefully analyzed the social interactions. His conclusion is that "... audiences are not passive recipients of presentations but are actively oriented to both the technology as well as the presenter..." (p. 126).

Knoblauch observed that professional powerpoint presentations are a communication genre that specifically encourages audience interactions at predetermined points in a professional presentation, such as question and answer periods at the end of a presentation. He also found that audience participation was facilitated because both the presenter and audience can refer to the text or graphics shown on the slides when discussing the topic. The slide presentation can become a common point of interaction for the audience and the presenter, and this makes the presence of powerpoint visual aids actually increase audience participation. Knoblauch concludes his analysis by stating, "In summary, we can quite clearly see that powerpoint does not obstruct interaction between audience and presenter" (p. 133).

This rigidity problem, if it truly is an issue, can be addressed by an adept teacher. Knoblauch's analysis suggests that the social structure of the classroom, and not technology, drives student-teacher interactions. A class meeting period does not necessarily need to be a continuous powerpoint presentation from start to finish. Teachers can build specific periods or activities into their class time that encourage student-teacher interactions. The slide deck organization might be a helpful skeleton for organizing classroom activities, but it does not need to be the dominant force for determining social interactions.

"A preoccupation with format, not content"

A third concern raised by Tufte is that slide presentations may promote style over substantive information. Flashy graphics, logos, themes, colors, and animations may distract from communicating important information to the audience. At their worst, decorative features may be deliberately used by some presenters to give the illusion of a meaningful presentation. For example, the military sometimes gives powerpoint presentations to news reporters with the intent of not revealing very much information, a practice derisively called "hypnotizing chickens" (Bumiller, 2010).

The use of unnecessary special effects in powerpoint presentations has decreased somewhat since Tufte voiced his concerns. Much of Tufte's criticism over content-free presentations was centered upon a Microsoft PowerPoint feature called the AutoContent Wizard. This feature automated the development of presentations to some degree by suggesting formats for presenters to build their presentations upon. The AutoContent Wizard was heavily criticized (I. Parker, 2001; van Jole, 2000) and was not very popular with users (Knoblauch, 2012), so in 2007 Microsoft discontinued the AutoContent Wizard. Current users of PowerPoint consequently need to take a stronger hand in developing their own presentation content. Doing so may satisfy the "content-free" criticism that Tufte once aimed at PowerPoint software. Another positive development for presentation content is that current expectations for presentations are shifting away from the use of unnecessary flashy features. For example, early guides on using Microsoft's PowerPoint often suggested using built-in clip art of mostly decorative images that was supplied with the software. The best known clip art example was the group of "screen beans" characters: faceless stick figures portrayed in a range of business settings. In contrast, presentation experts currently encourage users to deliberately avoid the use of generic clip art and built-in themes to achieve a more professional-looking presentation.

Although the AutoContent Wizard is gone, some concern still lingers about powerpoint presentations relying too much on appearance and not enough on content. However, this criticism may be somewhat misplaced. Content is important, of course, but an effective presentation cannot be entirely content. To a significant degree, presentations are also about conveying emotion to an audience by, for example, displaying the presenter's enthusiasm for the topic (Duarte, 2010). A presentation that lacks an emotional connection with the audience will come across as being dry and overly abstract. The presenter is confronted with a choice between emphasizing content, which might seem dull, versus emphasizing emotionally-grabbing visual displays that could lack useful information. Thus, the counterpoint to Tufte's concern about an overemphasis on style is that the emotional qualities of a presentation are an important part of a successful presentation.

Is Powerpoint Making Us Dumb?

A more general concern is that modern technology is causing a decline in our cognitive abilities. This possibility should be deeply troubling to educators because it is completely contrary to the goals of education. The potential for negative cognitive effects has been proposed by numerous critics. Tufte, as we have seen, is concerned that powerpoint fosters a "cognitive style" that is characterized by light content and nonessential design features. Frommer's (2012) book *How PowerPoint Makes You Stupid* suggests that powerpoint fosters "faulty causality, sloppy logic, decontextualized data, and seductive showmanship." Several experts from the fields of business and the military also feel that powerpoint has weakened decision-making processes by encouraging presenters to omit important details (Bumiller, 2010; Hammes, 2009; Shaw, Brown, and Bromiley, 1998).

A number of educators have also raised alarms about the potentially-damaging effects of powerpoint on student learning (Creed, 1997; Hlynka and Mason, 1998; Kjeldsen, 2006; Klemm, 2007; Mason and Hlynka, 1998). A common criticism is that powerpoint is a teacher-centered technology rather than a student-centered learning experience. It has been suggested that powerpoint encourages teachers to give boring lectures that deliver information without fostering much critical thinking. In other words, powerpoint technology promotes the view of teaching as a passive transfer of information from teacher to student. It might not be the instructor's intent to lecture in this fashion, but slide technology might encourage this kind of teaching anyway. This problem might be a particularly significant issue for difficult topics that students tend to struggle with. It might be easier for the instructor to muscle through a difficult class period by marching through the slides rather than attempting to engage students in the complexities of a difficult topic.

New technology in education is often met with both enthusiasm and negative reactions. Educational critics often raise concerns about technology causing a decline in cognitive abilities. In the 1960s, many educators viewed television as an instructional medium that would revolutionize education, but others saw television as a "vast wasteland"(Minow, 1961). In the 1970s, math educators debated the use of calculators in math instruction (Ellington, 2003). The concern was that student overreliance on calculators would lead to a weakening of basic math skills. Studies of calculator usage have since found no detrimental effect on basic math skills (for a review, see Ellington, 2003). Most recently, critics have suggested that modern technologies, such as text messaging, Twitter, and web searches, are degrading our mental skills (Carr, 2010; M. Jackson, 2008). The concern is that people are replacing the sustained concentration of serious reading and critical analysis with a blizzard of small information snippets, and that these many small fragments of information are ultimately detrimental to focused attention and serious critical thought. Even the general concern about cognitive damage is frequently expressed in sound-bite form: "Is Google making us stupid?" (Carr, 2008).

Altogether, the concern about how powerpoint might negatively impact our cognitive abilities can be viewed in a cultural context of a vague uneasiness and apprehension of new technology. Innovations produce new ways of working and thinking that may feel unfamiliar and, therefore, are treated with some suspicion. Many powerpoint critiques express this feeling of vague apprehension. The critics aren't sure exactly what the negative effects of slide presentations might be, but they are convinced that these effects must be harmful somehow. Our approach to such negative views of new technology should be cautious. Valid criticisms must be examined, but we must also be careful to avoid being technology Luddites. Technology certainly can change the way that we think, possibly for the worse. Modern technology has an equally great ability to enhance and improve cognition in new ways.

Is Powerpoint Editing Our Teaching?

Some educational observers have raised the possibility that powerpoint could have unintended, insidious effects that might not be immediately obvious to the teacher. Marshall McLuhan, a media studies expert, famously used the phrase "The medium is the message" to express the idea that media can carry an indirect social message to the audience (McLuhan, 1964). In brief, McLuhan's argument is that every medium has an overt message that is accompanied by a more covert message about how people in the audience are supposed to act, think, or feel. This covert message might influence people in subtle ways. For example, perhaps slide presentations implicitly suggest a particular social relationship between the teacher and the student. The teacher is the expert authority whose word must not be questioned (at least not too much). The students, in contrast, are the followers who must assume a passive role, possibly without much awareness of this role. Curiously, the subtle communication effects about standards and social conventions may also influence teachers as much as students.

Concerns about these subtle media effects have led some commentators to suggest that powerpoint and other technologies can "edit our thoughts" (I. Parker, 2001; Turkle, 2004). This use of the term "edit" does not mean a literal change in our brain. Rather, the idea is that powerpoint standards that shape the basic features of a presentation may also have unintentional influences on the way that we present information to students (C. Adams, 2006; Stoner, 2007). The software guides teachers in subtle ways to encourage certain presentation styles, such as lecturing and the passive transfer of information to students. Over time, the use of presentation templates and other software guidance may even influence the thinking and the teaching approach of the educator. These implicit nudges effects that guide powerpoint presentations might also influence student expectations and behaviors.

Cognitive psychologists use the term "functional fixedness" to describe situations in which our past experience with using a tool may prevent or inhibit the tool user from thinking of new and creative uses for that object. Like blinders on a horse, the conventional use of a tool limits the possibilities we can conceive, so tool use can inhibit creativity. The powerpoint version of functional fixedness is the ubiquity of slides that follow default formats. Older versions of Microsoft's PowerPoint application started with a default blank slide that consisted of a heading— "Click to add title"—and a similar field for bullet points. For another example, Microsoft's PowerPoint give design suggestions when photos are inserted into a slide. Older versions of PowerPoint software kept images in a preformatted box, whereas the latest software versions give design suggestions that are less restricted. These defaults and guided activities form an "invitation" to make slides in a conventional manner (e.g., a title and bullet point lists; C. Adams, 2006). These features may help new software users get started as simply as possible, but it may, in the long run, send a subtle message that the best slide for a presentation should follow the bullet-point list layout (C. Adams, 2006). Once new users begin making slides with titles and three bullet points, the use of the default format gradually becomes a habit that influences how all presentations are made. In time, this habit influences the presenter's thinking by encouraging the view that all topics and instruction must be addressed the same way: how do I present this concept with a title and three bullet points?

The general concern is that powerpoint defaults could lead to habits of mind and, ultimately, teaching approaches that lack creativity and stifle best practices. This subtle influence is hard to measure directly. Indirect evidence for these unintentional guiding influences comes from the personal experiences of teachers when they describe how powerpoint has influenced their approach to teaching. The following example illustrates how this powerpoint functional fixedness might affect teaching

> 'I actually removed a book from my syllabus last year because I couldn't figure out how to powerpoint it. It's a lovely book . . . but it's very discursive; the charm of it is the throwaways.' . . . He couldn't get the book into bullet points; every time he put something down, he realized that it wasn't quite right. Eventually he abandoned the attempt. (I. Parker, 2001, p. 87)

Note the use of the term "powerpoint it." This phrase suggests the belief that all educational content must be converted into a form that fits powerpoint standards, such as bullet point lists (C. Adams, 2006; Keller, 2003). A similar example comes from another teacher who reports that when "sitting down to prepare a PowerPoint, I can't help but to think in bullets" (C. Adams, 2009, p. 5).

The common view here is that the powerpoint medium gradually exerts a weak yet significant influence over teachers through a functional fixedness encouraged by the software's default settings. At this point, it is worth remembering that Microsoft's PowerPoint application was originally developed as a business sales tool rather than an educational product (Gaskins, 2007). Therefore, the default templates and layouts of presentation software may be better suited to a business sales pitch than a classroom activity intended to foster critical thinking. If this is true, perhaps the guiding forces of powerpoint defaults might make our classes more closely resemble sales pitches or advertisements than engaging instructional experiences for our students.

In response to this critique, we need to understand that limitations are inherent in any kind of communication medium. It is somewhat unrealistic to fault slide presentation software for giving suggestions and imposing some constraints on the presenter. The more reasonable view is that no communication medium is completely free from limitations and influence upon the user. Musician and artist David Byrne expresses the issues about powerpoint guidance and constraints like this:

> There's a lot of criticism of powerpoint for encouraging users to do things in a particular way and discouraging them from other things, such as putting more than seven bullet points on a slide, he acknowledged ... Powerpoint restricts users no more than any other communication platform, he asserted, including a pencil: "When you pick up a pencil you know what you're getting—you don't think, 'I wish this could write in a million colors.'" (Powell, 2005)

The methods that teachers use can have subtle influences, and these influences, in turn, could have a negative impact on student learning. However, this situation is not entirely hopeless. No teacher is a complete slave to technology. Rather than faulting the limitations of powerpoint, we should focus on analyzing, understanding, and accepting these limitations. When necessary, teachers must actively work to find innovative ways to overcome the limitations of the software in order to achieve their instructional goals. The subtle influences of slide technology can be avoided by an awareness of the limitations accompanied by a well-thought out plan for using slides as an instructional tool. The best practice, therefore, is to use powerpoint in a deliberate and skillful way rather than uncritically following the defaults that the software might suggest (Vallance and Towndrow, 2007).

A More Optimistic View

In closing, we can see that powerpoint technology has its share of flaws. These difficult issues contribute to the powerpoint paradox: Amazing technology being used to give awful presentations. However, it seems that these concerns about the negative qualities of powerpoint presentations may be overstated. Some of the critiques seem to be mere opinions based on witnessing a few (or possibly more than a few) bad presentations. It is difficult to scientifically investigate criticisms like a possible "foreshortening" of thought caused by powerpoint presentations.

Many criticisms focus largely on powerpoint technology, but in many cases the real blame for bad presentations should be focused on the presenter, not the technology (Shwom and Keller, 2003). Bad presentations existed long before modern presentation technology was invented. It is unrealistic to expect that a special technology would magically transform bad presentations given by weak presenters into dynamic talks given by charismatic rock stars. In this sense, much of the criticism about powerpoint seems misdirected.

The root cause of many of bad presentations is simple: Most people dread giving presentations and do not give presentations on a routine basis. In addition, most presenters have received little training in either the use of powerpoint or the art of giving presentations. These inexperienced presenters tend to lean heavily upon powerpoint technology as if it were a crutch or handrail to get through the difficult and unpleasant task of giving a presentation. Considering these circumstances, we should not be surprised when the occasional presentation by these presenters is dull and uninteresting. In brief, the real problem with many modern presentations is often a simple lack of communication skills (Doumont, 2005; Shwom and Keller, 2003). It's a human failure rather than a technology failure. We therefore must be somewhat wary of critics who blame the technology rather than more accurately faulting the presenter who created the presentation.

Contrary to the critics, it can be argued that powerpoint is a great asset for people who struggle with presentations. The software imposes a structure on the presenter's message that could help the presenter organize their thoughts. The slides also give the audience something to look at during the presentation, thereby giving the audience a more valuable experience than they might have received from a strictly verbal presentation. The overall result is that a bad presentation with slides could in some situations be better than a bad presentation without slides.

Slide-based presentations do not need to be a totalitarian or lifeless teaching endeavor. Furthermore, slide presentations are not restricted to merely transferring information to students. When properly done, slide-based presentations can be a supportive and engaging aid to classroom instruction.

Educational Effectiveness and Student Perceptions

> The general theme of the interviews, journal, and surveys is "I like it, but...", which reflects the mostly positive responses to multimedia in large classrooms, but also notes less than complete satisfaction. (Pippert and Moore, 1999)

The computer-based instructional aids that replaced chalkboards and overhead projectors effected a paradigm shift in education. This cultural change was welcomed by many, but it was also troubling for some people (Keller, 2003; Knoblauch, 2012; I. Parker, 2001). A few educators and communication experts, however, had a distinctly negative view of powerpoint presentations. For example, "PowerPoint Invades the Classroom," an article published in the New York Times, focused on the increasing use of PowerPoint in K-12 settings (Guernsey, 2001).

The title's use of the word "invade" sets an ominous, negative tone. Some teachers had concerns about negative effects like intellectual "narrowing" and the PowerPoint AutoContent Wizard. In contrast, other teachers thought that PowerPoint might have positive educational benefits.

Although some of powerpoint's critics have been quite vocal, their criticism is often based on thin evidence. Even Tufte, the information literacy expert, does not provide much evidence to back up his assertion that powerpoint is "evil." Tufte's strongest evidence was a case study of how powerpoint may have led to poor engineering decisions that eventually contributed to the destruction of the space shuttle Columbia and the death of several astronauts. Tufte's view is that the disastrous shuttle decision occurred because important safety information was omitted from a powerpoint presentation. Important safety details would not have been missed in a more thorough written report. His other quantitative evidence is based upon a review of charts from twenty-eight books and publications. This analysis concluded that, compared to printed sources, powerpoint statistical graphics are "the thinnest of all" in regards to the information provided to the audience (Tufte, 2006, p. 5). Ironically, it has been argued that Tufte's evidence against powerpoint is itself rather thin (Doumont, 2005).

Because there have been numerous scientific studies of powerpoint and how it influences learning in the classroom, it is possible to take an evidence-based view of powerpoint and its potential usefulness in teaching environments. We will carefully examine the evidence from these scientific studies to determine if powerpoint presentations are helpful or harmful to student learning. This focus on scientific findings is more substantive and objective than the often unscientific approach that forms the basis of opinion pieces.

This review will address these two questions:

1. *Effectiveness*: Do students learn more with powerpoint?
2. *Perception*: How do students feel about powerpoint presentations?

Efficacy Studies: Does Powerpoint Help Students Learn?

Beginning in the mid-1990s, the question of powerpoint's educational effectiveness was the focus of numerous studies. Their motivating idea was the possibility that powerpoint presentations might be more engaging than chalkboards or overhead transparencies, and thereby have greater educational value. The general view was that the colors, styles, layouts, and animations in a typical powerpoint presentation would be more likely to engage student attention and emotions compared to older forms of instructional technology. This increased engagement would translate into better information retention and more learning. This idea has been described as an arousal view of educational media (Levasseur and Sawyer, 2006). In other words, powerpoint presentation effects would breathe some emotional life into otherwise dry academic topics and thereby improve learning through increasing student interest. Older technologies, in contrast, were viewed as being less dynamic or less interesting to the students, and would therefore have less impact on student learning. Some early studies supported the arousal view, with colorful powerpoint presentations being both highly rated by students as well as improving topic comprehension (Morrison and Vogel, 1998).

Educational psychologists use the term "media comparison studies" to address the question of how well students learn from different types of media. This research typically examines whether students would learn better from a more advanced, newer educational medium (such as powerpoint) compared to a less advanced, older medium (such as chalkboards) The research design of these effectiveness studies often divides students into two groups, with one group (experimental) receiving powerpoint-based instruction and the second group (control) receiving some other form of instruction. This alternate instruction may take the form of visual aids via the chalkboard or overhead projector, but in some studies, the control group had no visual aids at all during their lectures. At the end of the study, the experimental (powerpoint) and control (no powerpoint) groups are compared on a student achievement measure, such as test grades. The anticipated outcome is that students who received instruction via powerpoint presentations will learn more than students who did not, presumably due to the greater engagement, attention, and sensory arousal provided by the powerpoint presentations.

Although the basic media comparison study is straightforward, it is somewhat challenging to summarize the overall findings from these studies due to a wide range of minor variations in how the studies were conducted. The various studies sometimes used different software (e.g., Aldus Persuasion), student age groups, and control groups. In some studies, the powerpoint content was nearly the same as an overhead transparency, but in other studies the powerpoint presentations included video clips and animations, which made the powerpoint presentation a much stronger multimedia experience. In other studies, the participants were given both powerpoint presentations and handouts to accompany the lectures. Despite these differences, the common factor is that these studies attempted to compare powerpoint-based classroom presentations to other forms of instructional technology (or no technology). This key comparison forms the basis for determining the potential for enhanced teaching with powerpoint.

Since the early 1990s, at least fifty-eight media comparison studies on powerpoint have been conducted (see Appendix A), with some publications reporting multiple studies (e.g., Szabo and Hastings, 2000, provides three studies). Most of these studies were identified through searches of academic databases (Google Scholar, EBSCO, ProQuest) for articles published by the end of 2016. Two comprehensive review articles published in 2006 were also useful for identifying early publications (Levasseur and Sawyer, 2006; E. J. Shapiro et al., 2006). The references of the articles identified through these search methods were further scrutinized for additional papers that might have escaped the keyword search process. A strong effort was made to be as comprehensive as possible, but it is important to acknowledge that the round-up of studies was challenging because the scholarship of teaching and learning on powerpoint is spread across a wide range of academic disciplines. The first criterion for inclusion was the use of PowerPoint or PowerPoint-like multimedia technology to deliver the educational content during class time. A second criterion was that the studies needed to have an experimental design or a quasi-experimental design (most common) that compared students who received powerpoint-based instruction to a group that was not exposed to powerpoint. These comparison groups received a different form of supplemental media (usually chalkboards or transparencies) or possibly no supplemental media at all (lectures without any form of supporting technology). This effectiveness review did not include studies with nonexperimental designs, such as studies based upon correlational analyses or survey methods.

The general finding from these media comparison studies is consistent: Students who receive powerpoint-based instruction do about the same on student achievement outcomes as students who receive traditional, lower-tech forms of instruction (see Appendix A). Most of the media comparison studies (65.5%; n = 38) produced no evidence for improvements in student learning when the students were taught with powerpoint visual aids. Somewhat surprisingly, improved learning outcomes only occurred in 20.7% (n = 12) of the studies. The overall evidence from this research suggests that powerpoint instruction yields no educational benefit in most situations or maybe a slight benefit in some situations. This conclusion is supported by two comprehensive review studies, one of which found no overall evidence of increased teaching effectiveness (Levasseur and Sawyer, 2006) and the other finding only a slight improvement with powerpoint (E. J. Shapiro et al., 2006).

The conclusion that powerpoint lacks strong educational benefits is rather disappointing. It seems that a lot of work, energy, and money went into developing powerpoint presentations, yet this was largely a wasted effort because student learning did not improve. In spite of this seeming failure, these findings still provide some useful evidence for educators. Recall that the key idea behind these studies was the arousal viewpoint that the presence of color and other dramatic powerpoint features would capture student attention and emotions, and the increased engagement from these effects would enhance learning. The evidence, however, shows that the arousal theory is a failure. The anticipated engagement benefit of a powerpoint presentation actually produces little-to-no difference in educational outcomes. This outcome is important to keep in mind for educators who design their own powerpoint presentations. Powerpoint features that are meant to grab attention or arouse emotion may not necessarily have any benefit for learning. Teachers may intuitively feel that dramatic powerpoint presentation features like vivid colors would increase learning, but the evidence clearly doesn't support this view. It could also be argued from this evidence that powerpoint technology is not absolutely necessary to achieve meaningful student learning and engagement.

On a positive note, the effectiveness studies show that powerpoint does not seem to be hurting students. Only a few media comparison studies (13.8%, n = 8; Appendix A) find detrimental effects from powerpoint-based instruction. From this, we can conclude that the powerpoint "invasion" into the classroom does not seem to harm student learning. The grave concerns about cognitive damage raised by powerpoint critics (see Chapter 2) seem to be unfounded.

The results from these studies clearly indicate that powerpoint use does not produce superior learning outcomes when compared to older forms of teaching technology. Let's try to dig a bit deeper into these results. Given the potential for powerpoint to capture students' attention and present information in an organized and compelling way, why have so many studies failed to show that powerpoint has consistent, positive effects on student learning? This is a perplexing question for many education researchers. In retrospect, there are several reasons why media studies that compare powerpoint-based lectures to more traditional approaches have not established the educational superiority of powerpoint.

One common problem is that many of these studies have weak research designs that limit the researchers' ability to make strong conclusions. The practical limitations of classroom settings make it difficult or even impossible to randomly assign students to the experimental and the control group, thereby limiting researchers to quasi-experimental or correlational research designs that can make it difficult to establish unambiguous conclusions. Another research weakness in education is that the outcomes, like exam scores, might be insensitive. It is a challenge to increase the exam score average for an entire class by even a small amount. This insensitivity might make it difficult to measure small improvements in learning that might be attributed to powerpoint presentations.

The details of how the experimental and control conditions differed in educational content may be another possible reason for the failure to find improvements in powerpoint-based instruction. Most of these studies compared powerpoint-based class presentations to other classes that received the same instructional content delivered by chalkboards or overhead transparencies. Using identical content in both conditions was done to control for extraneous variables that might interfere with interpreting the outcome of the experiment. In retrospect, it seems likely that this effort to make the groups equal in regard to educational content made the experimental and control conditions so similar to each other that any potential benefits from the powerpoint presentations were completely eliminated. A related problem is that many studies do not fully describe how powerpoint was used to present information in the experimental condition. It is often unspecified whether the instructors merely used bullet point lists, or also included supporting graphics or multimedia such as animations and videos. This lack of information about the educational content of the powerpoint slides raises the possibility that maybe the content examined was simply ineffective regardless of medium.

These questions about educational content raise a sobering possibility: Perhaps many instructors simply copied lecture material from the chalkboard and the overhead projector into the newer powerpoint medium. Recreating a possibly-ineffective lecture format into a new instructional medium is not very likely to have a positive impact on learning. Despite its potential for engaging the audience, powerpoint instruction still favors a passive, lecture-style teaching approach, and this might explain why it often produces no measurable improvement in student learning outcomes.

These studies emphasize the comparison of lecture-based instruction done with or without powerpoint technology. This emphasis reflects the goal of media comparison studies, which is to see if one media is superior to another for instructional purposes. This comparison effort was fueled by the passion for new technology in the field of education over the last 20 years, but it's arguable that placing so much emphasis on comparing various instructional technologies is misguided. Unfortunately, there seems to be no research interest in comparing high tech learning approaches centered upon powerpoint multimedia instruction to low tech, nonlecture forms of instruction. Perhaps this is an area of research that would be useful to pursue in future studies.

The preceding interpretations of why powerpoint doesn't dramatically improve student learning are somewhat minor research details. Educational experts who specialize in technology and learning have raised another possibility that goes deeper into the heart of effective instruction. Maybe technology like powerpoint simply doesn't change the fundamental nature of learning very much, so ultimately, the technology is not very important. The pedagogy, in contrast, is the real driver of student learning. This is the somewhat controversial conclusion of some media comparison studies skeptics. Richard Clark performed a broad review of various technologies used for education in an effort to assess their educational effectiveness (R. E. Clark, 1983, 1991). His main conclusion was that many instructional technologies that were originally thought to be revolutionary— radio, television, personal computers, and the Internet—seemed, in retrospect, to produce no measurable improvement in student learning. In Clark's view, the teaching method (such as lecturing, collaborative groups, and discussions) is responsible for real changes in student learning, not the technology. It should be noted that while Clark's opinion was written before powerpoint became available in classrooms, he seems to have accurately anticipated the outcomes of the powerpoint effectiveness studies based on his examinations of previous technological advances. A clear bottom-line conclusion from the efficacy studies is that powerpoint does not provide a significant improvement in learning gains beyond older technologies like the blackboard and the overhead projector. The potentially-increased arousal or motivation from using powerpoint slides doesn't seem to improve the effectiveness of teaching. Accordingly, teachers should not expect that the use of powerpoint will dramatically improve student performance.

Student Perceptions: What Do Students Think About Powerpoint?

The second general approach for evaluating the effectiveness of powerpoint-based instruction focuses upon student perceptions of powerpoint. Modern students receive many hours of powerpoint-supported lectures throughout their educational career. This direct experience makes student feedback valuable for understanding what works or doesn't work about powerpoint presentations.

These student perception studies are relatively easy to perform and have been conducted in a wide range of settings and academic disciplines. The typical student perception study begins with students who are exposed to slide-based presentations during the semester. Sometimes, exposure to powerpoint-based lecture materials is alternated over the semester with traditional media such as chalkboards and overhead projectors. The students are surveyed at the end of the course to measure their impressions about powerpoint-based instruction. The students in these surveys compare their powerpoint experience to other instructional media, which they may have experienced in other classes. The students rate their perceptions of powerpoint-based instruction from "Strongly disagree" to "Strongly agree" on a numeric scale. Survey questions rated higher than neutral show a preference for the use of powerpoint. Many survey studies also include open-ended questions to collect more information from the respondents.

At least eighty-two published studies use surveys to ask students about their perceptions of powerpoint-based instruction (Appendix B). These studies were identified through a process that was similar to the review of the experimental studies: Keyword searches on databases followed by the identification of additional studies from careful evaluation of references in published papers. These papers were published in 2016 or earlier, with the earliest studies being in the mid-1990s. The inclusion criterion was the use of nonexperimental survey methods of student attitudes that asked students to report their feelings and thoughts about powerpoint-based instruction. These surveys varied in their questions, but all of them asked students about their general satisfaction level with the use of powerpoint for instructional purposes. The results from each study were broadly classified as evidence for positive, neutral, or negative attitudes towards powerpoint based on the majority of survey responses. Most surveys also had questions about other features, like the advantages and disadvantages of powerpoint. A qualitative analysis was performed to catalog the common student likes and dislikes about specific features. This analysis involved some degree of subjective interpretation given the variability of survey questions across these studies.

The key finding: Students clearly like powerpoint. Students have an overall positive attitude towards powerpoint presentations in the majority of student attitude studies, 76.8% (n = 63). The typical finding in these studies is that about 60% to 90% of the surveyed students indicate a preference for powerpoint-based lecture materials over chalkboards, transparencies, or no visual aids. In contrast, fewer studies report an overall neutral/mixed (13.4%; n = 11) or negative (9.8%; n = 8) student attitudes towards powerpoint.

The understanding of these survey results must be viewed in the context that the data is self-reported by students. We can gain a clear view of students' experiences with powerpoint instruction through self-reports. This is very important because we want students to have a positive experience in the classroom. However, self-reported views tend to be highly subjective opinions. The general finding that students like powerpoint doesn't necessarily mean that this kind of instruction is effective, engaging, or stimulating deep thoughts. There is a disturbing possibility that students might like powerpoint for the wrong reasons, such as using powerpoint to put less effort into their coursework. The finding that students like powerpoint is certainly encouraging, but it is not sufficient, by itself, to establish that powerpoint is a worthwhile technology for the classroom.

What are the specific features of powerpoint that students like? There is a wide range of reasons, many of which are pragmatic in nature. The following lists summarize what students like and dislike about powerpoint-based classroom presentations. These conclusions are listed in the order of preference from the most frequently occurring to the least frequent. For brevity, specific citations for each finding have been omitted.

1. *Interest*: Students report that powerpoint presentations are more entertaining and enjoyable than presentations that do not use powerpoint.
2. *Organization*: Students feel that powerpoint presentations are organized better than traditional chalkboard-based lectures. Powerpoint presentations may have a flow or logical order that is easy for students to follow.

3. *Understanding and Memory*: Students think that powerpoint presentations promote comprehension. However, this may be only a perception that does not necessarily correspond closely to reality (see below).
4. *Note-taking*: Students report that powerpoint helps them to focus on the key points of a presentation, which is especially important for note-taking activities. Note-taking may also be aided when instructors provide a printed handout or a digital powerpoint file before class.
5. *Instructor Qualities*: Students have favorable impressions of instructors who use powerpoint. These favorable ratings include being more organized, better prepared for class, more credible, and more professional compared to teachers who do not use powerpoint. Students are also more likely to indicate on course evaluations that they would take another class from a professor who uses powerpoint.
6. *Exam Preparation*: Students like reviewing powerpoint files or handouts provided by the instructor as they prepare for exams.
7. *Efficiency*: Students feel that powerpoint can be used to cover more information during a class period.
8. *Visual Aids*: Students approve of using visual aids, such as graphs and figures, to support learning.
9. *Technology Advantages*: The visibility of powerpoint presentations is better than chalkboards and overheads. The presentation delivery with powerpoint is also more professional and efficient because instructors do not have to rummage through transparencies or turn their back to the class while they write on the chalkboard.

10. *Memory*: Some students feel that their memory is better with powerpoint, although it is worth noting that this may just be a student perception.

There are a few other positive characteristics. Some students prefer the combined use of auditory (spoken) and visual (powerpoint) information. Student who miss class presentations appreciate having the powerpoint slides available online so they can access the material that was missed, though not all instructors engage in this practice. Some students feel that powerpoint helps to promote class discussions. Finally, powerpoint may facilitate the proper spelling of technical terms, which is particularly important for students who have learned English as a second language.

Overall, these benefits show that students have numerous reasons, most of them practical in nature, for preferring powerpoint presentations over traditional instructional media. Even though powerpoint may not significantly raise student grades, many students believe that it is still a worthwhile technology for supporting instruction. These strong student preferences provide a compelling reason for instructors to use powerpoint, particularly if there is no strong evidence that doing so is detrimental to student learning.

We must note that the results from student perception studies can be a bit misleading when students are asked to assess their own learning and memory. A few studies have directly compared student perceptions of their own learning to their actual learning performance. These studies show that students' belief that powerpoint improves learning is not necessarily accompanied by an improvement in exam scores (Apperson, Laws, and Scepansky,

2006; Selimoglu, Arsoy, and Yasemin, 2009; Susskind, 2008). In other words, students may feel like their learning is improved when they are taught with powerpoint, but the actual exam results may not show any improvement. The student view that more is learned with powerpoint instruction is likely to be an overly optimistic opinion.

The student survey research also provides a valuable source of information about what students *dislike* about powerpoint presentations. The following list has commonly-reported complaints or weaknesses about powerpoint from the sources in Appendix B. These negative features are listed from the most frequent to the least frequent. For perspective, keep in mind that these powerpoint problems tend to be less frequently reported than the positive responses.

1. *Powerpoint Overload*: Powerpoint enables instructors to deliver too much information or deliver information at a pace that is too fast for the students. In contrast, notes and diagrams delivered via chalkboard have a slower, more natural pace that may be closer to a student's natural comprehension and note-taking ability. In particular, students in math or science courses sometimes report that they prefer chalkboard-based presentations (El Khoury and Mattar, 2012). It may be easier to follow a sequence of mathematical operations when these are diagrammed step-by-step on a chalkboard compared to being flashed on a screen all at once in powerpoint (Feldkamp, 2008).
2. *Decreased Social Interaction*: Some students feel that powerpoint often leads to less interaction between students

and less interaction between the students and the instructor. Powerpoint presentations are sometimes described as being distancing, depersonalized, and less spontaneous.

3. *Boring*: Traditional lectures given via powerpoint can still be dull. This problem is not necessarily due to technology, however, because traditional lectures without powerpoint also have a reputation for being boring. This finding is consistent with the earlier speculation that technology alone cannot rescue a boring presentation.

4. *Technical Problems*: Technical difficulties can lead to dead moments in the classroom when the instructor must focus on fixing technology breakdowns instead of on teaching. It's understandable that students dislike these awkward technical failures that waste valuable class time.

5. *Distraction and Note-taking*: Some students report difficulty in simultaneously using the visual information from powerpoint along with the auditory information spoken by the teacher. Students may wonder which is more important, the verbal information from the teacher or the visual information from the slide?

6. *Using Powerpoint as a Teleprompter*: A common complaint, in both professional settings and education, is that the presenter simply reads the contents of the slide to the audience. The most obvious solution is that the presenter should not read from the slides word-for-word. However, doing so could create the problem mentioned in problem number 5 above. That is, that the audience may not know what to focus on if the slide content and the auditory commentary differ. It may be difficult for

presenters to achieve an effective balance between content and commentary that keeps the audience interested yet able to follow along.

7. *Insufficient Detail*: Some students complain that powerpoint slides do not have enough details. Curiously, too many details can lead to powerpoint overload (see issue #1), yet too few details also frustrates some students. The finding that too much or too little information are both problems shows how it can be difficult to find the optimal amount of information in a presentation.

8. *Attendance Problems*: Most students report that they would attend class even if the powerpoint file is available to them online in a course management system. However, some students may be more likely to skip class if they can easily obtain the slide deck without attending class, although this group represents a minority of respondents.

9. *Visibility Problems*: Powerpoint presentations have better visibility, in general, than traditional teaching media, but visibility problems can still occur. Students sometimes report difficulty in viewing poorly-constructed slides that are made with small font sizes or odd color choices. Darkened rooms may make the projected images on the screen more prominent, but the darkness also has the downside of making it more difficult for students to take notes or follow along in a textbook. Dark rooms may also make students sleepy. In contrast, using white or lightly colored backgrounds on the screen may sometimes make students seated in the front row feel that the presentation was blinding.

The good news about these drawbacks is that many of these problems can be addressed and eliminated. For example, powerpoint overload can be cured by paring down the amount of information in a presentation. Dullness and decreases in social interaction can be addressed by adding discussion exercises or question/answer periods into the instructional plan. Technical problems can be avoided with practice and proper preparation. With careful design and planning, the competent teacher can avoid most of these problems. Some of them, however, may have no easy answer that satisfies everyone, which is a situation not uncommon in educational settings.

Conclusions from the Scientific Studies

Scientific studies have not confirmed the alarms raised by powerpoint critics, which is good news. However, numerous studies that compare students taught by powerpoint versus more traditional media have not convincingly demonstrated a strong learning benefit. Student opinions, in contrast, are quite positive about the use of powerpoint, with students having a number of practical reasons for preferring powerpoint over older instructional aids. As a whole, the evidence suggests that powerpoint has a distinct place in the classroom. The beneficial characteristics of powerpoint that the students like outweigh the (as yet undemonstrated) potential for cognitive damage that was proposed by powerpoint critics.

Some hard-line critics might insist at this point that there is no need to continue using powerpoint because the media comparison studies have failed to establish the educational effectiveness of this technology. The counterpoint is that reasons still exist for using powerpoint, even if an improved learning outcome is not likely to be achieved. In particular, teachers should give emphasis to how students feel about powerpoint, which is largely positive and could, in turn, produce more positive student expectations and attitudes toward learning. Students also view teachers who use powerpoint as being more organized and credible. For all of these reasons, contemporary students have come to expect that their instructors will use powerpoint (M. J. Jackson et al., 2011). Teachers who do not use powerpoint may receive student demands to begin using powerpoint (Driessnack, 2005) and may suffer from lower student evaluations (Hill et al., 2012; Koeber, 2005; Schrodt and Witt, 2006; however, see also Daniels et al., 2008; Kunkel, 2004; Lowerison et al., 2006). Instructors who are ambivalent about using powerpoint should consider the students' enthusiastic viewpoint when deciding whether or not to use powerpoint technology.

The lack of evidence for powerpoint instructional effectiveness is perhaps a sign that the standard practices for using powerpoint are not working very well. Many of the common powerpoint uses seem like dry lectures that merely attempt to pass information along to students. As noted above, transferring lecture materials from chalkboards to a newer medium like powerpoint is unlikely to overcome the inherent dullness of passive learning approaches. The teaching strategies instructors employ most often in powerpoint presentations likely are simply ineffective. Using powerpoint well involves more than simply filling out a few bullet points on a slide.

Rather than despairing about this situation, we should view it as a challenge. Educators must attempt much more than the standard approach if we hope to achieve educational greatness with powerpoint technology. The main goal of this book is to address the question of how we can remake powerpoint presentations into effective learning tools. The guiding spirit is to determine how teachers should use this medium to augment their teaching and thereby improve student learning.

Avoiding Death by PowerPoint

It is striking that properties typical of powerpoint are mainly mentioned as annoyances. (Blokzijl and Naeff, 2004, p. 76)

As we have learned, the phrase "death by powerpoint" is widely used to describe the experience of bad powerpoint presentations. When death by powerpoint occurs, the presenter is often unaware of how their powerpoint presentations are experienced by the audience. The teacher may have good intentions, information, and ideas, yet the presentation still fails miserably. Presentation practices that seem reasonable to the teacher may be experienced as dull and possibly even insulting to the students.

An important first step toward making better classroom presentations is to examine the bad practices that produce the death by powerpoint experience. Put simply, a good presentation requires the absence of bad presentation practices. Some of these problems may strike the reader as being rookie mistakes, which is not inaccurate. However, these basic mistakes are common enough that we need to address them. Becoming aware of these basic problems will hopefully help educators avoid making these mistakes themselves. This is a good beginning point for the journey towards better classroom presentations.

Presentation Killer #1: Using Powerpoint as a Teleprompter

Dave Paradi is a business communications expert who conducts an annual survey about annoying powerpoint presentation practices. The statement "The speaker read slides to us" was rated the most annoying presentation problem in 2017, with 67.8% of the respondents agreeing with this statement (Paradi, 2017). This issue has been the number one problem in Paradi's survey for many years. The problem is that the presenter is basically using the powerpoint presentation like a teleprompter, reading the entire speech from the slides to the audience. Reactions to this kind of presentation are usually quite negative. In education, there are also reports of teachers who simply read the powerpoint slide text to their students (Gurrie and Fair, 2008; O'Quigley, 2011; Young, 2004). Educators are clearly not immune to the teleprompter problem.

Several reasons explain why reading the slides to an audience is a poor presentation technique. The audience can read the text faster than the speaker can speak it out loud, which leads to the audience waiting for the presenter to catch up with them. In addition, multimedia theories of learning suggest that it is redundant to have the same words presented to both vision and hearing. This double-dose of sensory information may pose a cognitive load problem (Yue, Bjork, and Bjork, 2013). A third problem is that reading large text passages from a projection screen focuses the speaker's attention in the wrong place. The teleprompter approach makes the speaker face the screen to read the text rather than facing the audience.

The solution to the teleprompter problem is to reduce the amount of text that is displayed to the audience. If notes are needed, they should be hidden from the audience on note cards or the PowerPoint "notes" view that is not visible to the students. Another strategy is to thoroughly practice the presentation before going in front of an audience. Well-practiced presenters can give their presentations from memory. Going without notes gives the presentation a spontaneous, fresh kind of feeling, as though the speaker is interacting naturally with the audience.

Presentation Killer #2: Too Much Text

The second most common problem in Paradi's annual survey is using too much text in a powerpoint presentation (Paradi, 2017). The problem is characterized by slides that have multiple complete sentences or possibly even paragraphs crammed on to a single slide. In teaching, this problem sometimes occurs when teachers use powerpoint files prepared by the textbook publisher. These prepared powerpoint presentations sometimes contain significant amounts of text that were copied verbatim from the textbook.

Several reasons explain why too much text is problematic. From a design perspective, we must keep in mind that the students who receive a presentation can only handle a low information density (see Chapters 10 and 11). This cognitive limitation means that key terms and brief outlines are the most effective for learning. In contrast, long sentences and paragraphs become problematic due to the increased amount of information. Large quantities of text just don't fit into the low-density requirements of powerpoint presentations.

The problem of too much text often relates to the first problem of reading text directly from a slide. Using powerpoint as a teleprompter requires a lot of text on the slides because the slides must contain the entire speech. Thus, problem #1 (reading from the slide) and problem #2 (too much text) tend to occur together. In addition, using a lot of text requires a small font size to make all of the text fit on to the slide. This problem leads us to yet another common problem: low visibility.

Presentation Killer #3: Poor Visibility

The third and fourth place annoying practices on Paradi's surveys are visibility problems created by small text (#3) and overly complex graphics (#4). In these situations, the presenter refers the audience to information on the slide, but the audience can barely see it. Maybe the students in the front row can see it with some effort. The students in the back, however, might not see the important information at all. The information on a powerpoint slide is simply not helpful if the audience cannot see it.

Sometimes, the visibility problem is caused by the amount of text required when using powerpoint as a teleprompter (Problem

#1) or a written report. Because these situations require a lot of text, the presenter consequently uses small fonts in order to create more room for text. Most visibility problems actually result from using powerpoint in an inappropriate manner to convey excessive amounts of information (see Chapters 10 and 11 about the problems of overload).

Another source of visibility problems stems from the classroom presentation environment being significantly different from the office computer screen. Text and images that look fine on the teacher's office computer screen might seem tiny when viewed from a distance in a large classroom. Likewise, color combinations and themes that look good in the office might look washed out or different in the classroom due to differences in the projected image and ambient lighting (see Chapter 7).

Teachers give a lot of presentations, and they may not have enough time to test each one before giving it to a class. Consequently, visibility failures are often noticed only when the presentation is being given to the students, and, if the teachers stay close to the screen, they may not notice these visibility failures at all. When a visibility failure occurs, a good practice is for the instructor to make a note of this problem in order to address it before giving the presentation again. One means of doing so is using the "insert comment" feature on a problematic PowerPoint slide (Figure 4.1). This note provides a useful reminder of a problem that can be fixed when preparing the file for the next class.

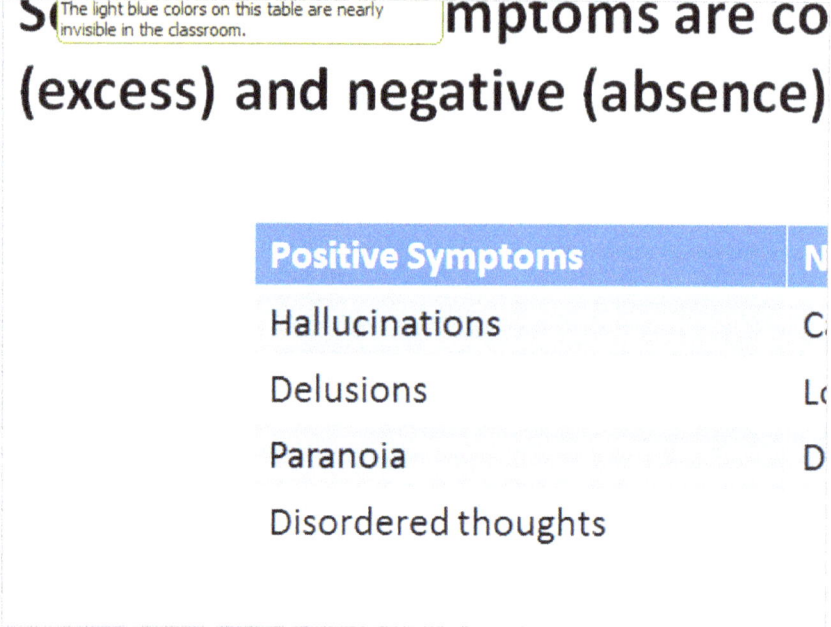

Figure 4.1: Documenting a visibility problem that needs to be addressed

Another consideration about the presentation venue is to consider how the position of text and images on the projection screen might affect visibility in the classroom. You can easily see all parts of your computer screen when you are sitting behind the computer display in your office. This equal visibility across the screen may not, however, carry over into the classroom. The poor visibility of the bottom part of the screen may be particularly problematic for people who sit in the back of the classroom because their view may be blocked by other classmates or objects such as chairs or laptop screens. For example, the students seated at the back of the classroom shown in Figure 4.2 must stand up to see any information that is presented at the bottom of the slide.

Figure 4.2: A student-centered blocked view of the projection screen from the back of the classroom.

A useful visibility guideline is to horizontally divide the screen into three equally-sized parts. The top third of the screen is the most visible, and the bottom third is the least visible in the classroom. Evidence from the study of web page designs also suggests that most attention is directed to the top of a display (Nielsen, 2006). Therefore, if you want to make a statement to your students, put it at the top of the slide. In contrast, the bottom of the display receives less attention.

Presentation Killer #4: Style Over Substance

The visual teaching aids that existed before powerpoint were pretty tame. The degree of movement was minimal, such as the teacher's hand moving across the chalkboard. Powerpoint changed presentations by offering a much richer range of sensory possibilities, particularly visual features such as flying bullet points, fancy slide designs, dynamic slide transitions, clip art, stock photography, 3-D graphs, and a broad assortment of colors. Designers use these features with the good intentions of making their powerpoint presentations more dynamic and interesting.

Teachers in particular often face the task of presenting dry academic information to audiences of unmotivated, disinterested students. Teachers often hope that adding vibrant graphics or zooming bullet points to a presentation will stimulate student attention. The special effects may seem like a quick solution to adding interest to an otherwise dull presentation. The problem with special animations and fanciful graphics is they fail to meet the long-term goal of maintaining audience interest (see Chapters 5 and 10). These special effects may receive some student interest at first, but the interest only lasts a brief moment. After that, these special effects can become a distracting or even fatiguing experience for the students, especially if they occur again and again over the classroom period. Teachers need to resist the urge to fix boring presentations by adding unnecessary special effects. The real solution for the problem of dull topics needs to focus on improving the educational content or the story line of the presentation.

The gratuitous use of unnecessary animations and graphics has become the hallmark of amateurish presentations. Examples of this bad practice often appear in student presentations. Students sometimes attempt to pump-up their presentations and make them more special by adding special effects of various kinds.

Again, the problem is that this approach can backfire and produce the unintended feeling that the presentation lacks substance.

The good news is that designers can easily fix the special effects problem simply by eliminating all of the extra features that lack educational content. This elimination can include animated bullet points, flashy slide transitions, unnecessary stock art or photography, and overly fanciful slide layouts and decorations. Learning restraint and tasteful design may take some intentional effort, but this effort is worthwhile.

Presentation Killer #5: Technology Problems

No significant concern about technology failures occurred when chalkboards were the height of teaching technology. Today's presentation technology is much more fragile, which can lead to presentation disasters caused by technical failures. Students and teachers find it frustrating when valuable class time is spent fixing technology problems instead of teaching (Young, 2004).

Sometimes technology problems are unavoidable and cannot be anticipated. For example, projector bulbs can blow out at surprising moments, leaving the instructor without a critical resource. Not much can be done about random failures in technology when these occur. In these situations, the short-term goal is to improvise your way through the class period, without a powerpoint presentation to show. The long-term goal is to fix the system after class is done.

A greater concern is when technology problems are caused by reasons that can be controlled by the teacher, such as a lack of adequate preparation. Teachers need to be certain that the projection technology in the classroom is compatible with the software in the office they used to develop the presentation. For example, presentations prepared on an Apple Macintosh computer might not be fully compatible with a PC-based system that uses Microsoft PowerPoint. The cables that connect a computer to a projector come in a range of connector styles (VGA, DVI, HDMI), which creates another potential source of incompatibility. It's easy to forget that the powerpoint file must be transferred from the office to the classroom somehow. Instructors must check links to web pages or videos on YouTube before class because sometimes these resources disappear. It is disappointing to work up to a critical moment in a lecture for a short video clip only to find that it has been removed from YouTube. Similarly, sometimes web pages or YouTube clips can take some time to load, which again creates dead space at an otherwise important moment.

Instructors need practice and training to become proficient with classroom technology, such as wireless presentation devices and student response systems. If you are new to a particular classroom technology, it might be worthwhile to take some time to learn how these systems work before attempting to use them with students during class time. Unfortunately, most teachers and professors receive very little training in the use of classroom technology. The responsibility of learning how these complex systems work often falls on the individual faculty member, who doesn't have much time to learn new technology. The result is that teachers often learn new technology by trial and error while they are in the midst of teaching.

Presentation Killer #6: Presenting in the Author Mode

Microsoft's PowerPoint program has two basic modes of operation. The default view that comes up when the program is launched is an authoring mode. This view displays all of the menus, buttons, and tools that a presenter might need to create a slide deck, as well as small views (thumbnails) of each individual slide. When it is time to present, the program can go into a full-screen mode called "slide show" that displays only the slides. The various authoring tools are hidden during the slide show because they are unnecessary and would just distract the audience from the presenter's message. The full-screen mode is the standard view for giving a presentation.

The difference between the authoring mode and the full-screen presentation mode may seem obvious to most PowerPoint users. However, some presenters prefer to give presentations in the authoring mode, with all of the buttons, tabs, and other development tools visible to the audience. Some powerpoint users are apparently uncomfortable with giving presentations in the slide show mode. However, giving presentations in the authoring mode is clearly a bad presentation practice because the buttons and other software features, not to mention the presence of the other slides in the queue, are a distraction to the audience. Giving a presentation in the authoring mode also reduces the size of the primary slide, which can amplify some of the visibility problems already mentioned.

The accomplished presenter needs to be well-practiced in the ways of PowerPoint navigation, even when the program is in full-screen mode. The most fundamental skill is being able to switch between the authoring mode and the slide-show mode. The software way, which is the method that most people seem to use, is to click on the "slide show" tab in PowerPoint and select either the "from beginning" or "from current slide" buttons. The hardware method of launching a slide show is to use the F5 function key to start a presentation from the beginning slide. Slide navigation in the full screen view can be accomplished through the arrow keys (right = forward) or the mouse button, as well as through buttons on a wireless remote.

Presentation Killer #7: Too Much Content

The problems described here may seem trivial, yet they are very common in presentations. Mastery of these basic issues will put your presentations ahead of many of your colleagues. The good news about these fundamental problems is that they can be relatively easy to address. Instructors can avoid many problems simply by not using problematic features or avoiding ineffective practices

Other "death by powerpoint" problems are more abstract and, therefore, more difficult to address. One such problem is too much information covered in a class period. Powerpoint makes it possible to click through a slide deck in a rapid-fire way and completely overwhelm students with too much content. A related danger with too much information is that important ideas can get buried in a sea of details. When students are overwhelmed, it may seem that all information is equally important, even though this is not usually the case.

The too much information problem occurs for several reasons. Presentations need to be information-light, but the goal of educators is that students need to learn as much as possible. These competing needs are not always easy to resolve. Furthermore, instructors have no clear-cut standard to follow for deciding how much information is the right amount for a class period. Too much information is undesirable, but too little content is not good either.

This ambiguous situation leaves it up to the instructor to judge the degree of content to be covered. There really is no substitute for experience as a guide for how much information is the right amount. Feedback is also important. After a classroom presentation, teachers should take a moment to assess how well the class period went. If there was too much or too little content, it is a good practice to note, possibly even in the slide deck (see Figure 4.1), that the degree of content for this class period needs to be adjusted up or down before giving the presentation again.

Another strategy for dealing with the degree of content question is to rely on external aids to deliver some of the content. Tufte (2006) and other business communication experts recommend the use of handouts for carrying the high-density information that might complement the main messages of an information-light presentation (see Chapters 10 and 11). The idea is that the main themes of the presentations are fleshed out with the details from the handout. Both mediums have their strengths, and these can work together in a complementary way.

Presentation Killer #8: Too Many Bullet Points

The standard powerpoint presentation relies heavily on slides that use bullet point list layouts. Bullet points may have a strong appeal to business people who emphasize a bottom-line, expeditious way of handling matters. It has become ubiquitous in modern society to distill complex topics into clean, itemized lists. However, the use of bullet points may encourage teachers to overemphasize lists and sequences. Some educators have criticized the overly structured, highly linear nature of information delivered in bullet points (C. Adams, 2006) Bullet points may also suggest an overly simplified view of a topic and thereby lead to passive note-taking and disengaged learning.

Life after Death for Powerpoint Presentations

Powerpoint software is easy to use, yet the presentations made with it often have some serious shortcomings. The good news, though, is that teachers and students are not doomed to the death by powerpoint experience. Many of the problems described here are really beginner mistakes that reflect a lack of training, effort, or experience. Teachers and other presenters can quickly raise the effectiveness of their presentations just by knowing about these common traps that many presenters fall into and taking some reasonable efforts to ensure that these problems do not ruin the classroom experience.

DESIGN FOR EMOTION I

Capturing and Maintaining Audience Interest

If a lecture is no more than a reiteration of the contents of a paper we might as well choose to stay home, do some reading, and avoid the ruinous expense. Learning is improved by the addition of some form of emotional component to the material and the presence of the distinguished or up-and-coming lecturer might provide some of that—should we be able to see them in the first place and interact with them afterwards. (Taylor, 2007)

When I was in graduate school, the process of writing scientific papers was seemingly endless. I spent many hours crafting the very finest sentences that I could muster. I thought that I was doing a terrific job, but my dissertation adviser disagreed. His complaint: my writing lacked a "story." He would mark my papers up and send them back to me, with the chief problem being a need for more "story." When pressed, my dissertation adviser could never quite articulate exactly what he meant by the need for a story, so the concept was rather elusive. At first, it seemed to me that stories were really quite unnecessary for scientific research. I believed all that my writing really needed to do was report the facts to the reader in a straightforward way. In retrospect, it's clear that my early efforts at scientific writing had decent sentence mechanics. The real problem was that the writing failed to establish to the reader why the research was important or interesting.

What I learned from this writing experience is that scientific papers need a carefully-constructed persuasive message about the importance of the study. The "story" that my adviser was asking for was not a literal "story" in the sense that there was a hero, a villain, and an epic struggle between good and evil. His use of the term "story" simply meant that the document had to (1) communicate the importance to the reader; (2) present a problem worthy of investigation; (3) follow a logical, orderly sequence; and (4) arrive at a reasonable resolution to the issue. It would also be accurate to say that the scientific "story" was a persuasive argument that presented ideas and information to the readers in a compelling way.

Many powerpoint presentations have the same problem as my early attempts at scientific writing. The facts and information are excellent, but the importance, interesting features, and emotionally-compelling reasons for the topic are not communicated well to the audience. Information-rich but emotionally-flat presentations are ones in which an audience struggles to stay focused or, even worse, stay awake. They may communicate some information, but they do not encourage the student to take this information to heart; alternatively, it may not sufficiently stimulate the student's mind. Much, perhaps even most, of a presentation's content is based upon nonverbal or emotional material (Duarte, 2010). To a significant degree, instructors should view presentations as a form of emotional communication rather than as the pure transmission of facts and information. The effective presentation is simply not a written report that that the teacher reads aloud.

It might be tempting for teachers to think that emotions and persuasion are unimportant, just like I once thought that scientific writing was just getting the facts on paper. However, an effective teacher must firmly establish an emotional connection with the students at the beginning of each class. The students must be persuaded that the information is of high importance. This emotional connection is really a prerequisite for student learning. Students are unlikely to get involved in a topic if they cannot be convinced from the start that it is interesting and important.

Another way to consider this situation is to examine the roles of the instructor and the textbook in a course. The textbook often contains all of the information that a student might need to master the key ideas of the course. We could, in theory, just assign the textbook to the students and give them a test at the end of the semester to see how well they have learned the content. In reality, however, this textbook-only approach just wouldn't work. Most people wouldn't read through a textbook on their own. It would just be too dull. The teacher is necessary to communicate passion and interest in the topic to the students, acting as a cheerleader to get students excited about the course content. The teacher provides emotional and social support for the students to help them achieve their highest potential. The teacher can also answer questions and clarify information, which a textbook cannot do by itself.

The Presentation as a Story

Storytelling is the oldest form of pedagogy. Many prehistoric cultures had oral storytelling traditions that preceded written language. Important historical events were remembered in these societies through oral traditions, such as *The Odyssey* by Homer. These stories were passed down from generation to generation to preserve a cultural memory. Fables and religious texts also frequently use stories for teaching moral principles. Expressing important moral teachings in story form is much more persuasive than simply outlining key points with commands like "spend money wisely" or "be responsible." Although an ancient art, modern storytelling is still successfully used for teaching. Many award-winning documentaries are simply stories that have embedded facts and information into the overall framework of the story.

Information presented in a narrative form works well because our brains are essentially wired to remember information in a story form. Human long-term memory for personally-experienced events is a kind of personal history, a story about our lives. The distinguished biologist Edward Wilson expressed it this way in an article that promoted the use of stories in science education:

> We all live by narrative, every day and every minute of our lives. Narrative is the human way of working through a chaotic and unforgiving world. ... [The brain] develops stories to filter

and make sense of the flood of information that we are exposed to everyday. (E. O. Wilson, 2002)

Although a common analogy is to compare brain functions to a computer, human cognition and memory does much more than simply process and store information. The human brain excels at connecting the information between data points through an associative process that ultimately ends in story-like memories. Evidence for the story-like nature of memory comes from cognitive psychology research on memory. It may seem like memory should be an exact duplicate of an event that has been experienced, somewhat like a video recording. The truth is not so simple. Human memory is more accurately understood as being reconstructive in nature. This means memory is partly the real information from the event that was experienced plus a plausible explanation that fits our expectations. These combine to produce a memory experience that is similar to reliving the original event from our lives. Our memory for personal events, which is called autobiographical memory, is experienced as being a story, with ourselves as the central character.

Neurobiological evidence for story-like functions in the brain comes from the study of the so-called 'split-brain' patients. These were a small number of people with severe epilepsy who were treated with a radical surgery that separated the two cerebral hemispheres. Michael Gazzaniga, the world's leading expert on these cases, found that the left hemisphere of these special patients seemed to have an "interpreter" function (Gazzaniga, 2000). The interpreter links together environmental events into plausible explanations—stories—of events or cause and effect relationships that are taking place.

The functioning of this interpreter also occurs in a memory disorder symptom called confabulation that is typically caused by brain damage or extreme alcoholism (Schnider, 2008). Confabulation occurs when the interpreter function in these people keeps on operating, despite the loss of memory, taking whatever information is available in the mind and making a story out of it. The result is fabricated stories, some of which might be quite fantastic and impossible, that are experienced by the patient as being real memories.

Altogether, this evidence suggests that important human memory functions are understood and stored in a story-like, narrative fashion. Accordingly, information that fits into these story-like brain functions will be readily processed by the brain. This is why stories are effective structures for presentations.

The Educational Presentation as a Story

A common approach to developing a presentation is to fire up the computer, launch powerpoint, and then start typing up the slides. It seems natural to begin with the technology. The problem with this approach is that starting with the technology leads to presentations that are more like technical events than engaging presentations (Ohler, 2005). A typical fault is that many powerpoint presentations lack an adequate beginning that engages the students. In our passion for our topic, the teacher who is designing a presentation may launch into the details of the content without adequately establishing to our audience why this topic is interesting, important, and potentially useful.

A better approach would be to begin the development of a presentation by considering the overall story for the presentation.

The presenter should begin by asking themselves questions about the purpose of the presentation. What is the important message that needs to be conveyed to the audience? Why should someone who doesn't know much about this field care about this topic? What about this topic is exciting to me, and how do I communicate this excitement to others? The important idea is to start by determining what the audience needs and then working to meet their needs. Duarte (2010, p. 4) eloquently expresses the situation like this: "The audience does not need to tune themselves to you—you need to tune your message to them." The presenter must put their own needs aside in order to focus on what the audience really wants or needs.

Once the audience needs are established, it is important to consider the overall structure and organization of the presentation. Good presentations are like stories with plot lines that follow a well-known structure (Duarte, 2010). The typical fiction story begins with a likeable hero. After the audience gets to know the hero, a challenge or dilemma occurs that throws the hero's life out of balance. Will the hero succeed in overcoming this challenge? The hero may face many obstacles during the middle section of the story. In the end, the challenge is overcome, hopefully with a happy ending for everyone who is involved.

An inspiring presentation successfully incorporates the main elements of a story structure. The beginning sets the stage for the importance of the lesson. In fiction, this beginning is sometimes referred to as the "call to adventure" (Ohler, 2005) or "call to action" (Duarte, 2010). We become personally invested as the characters face a significant challenge that they must address. It would be a stretch to call most classroom settings an adventure. However, the beginning of a good presentation is somewhat similar to a work of fiction in that it must convince the audience about the importance of the topic.

The instructor should address the question of "Why should I care?" at the beginning of the presentation. A significant barrier to engagement is student cynicism about the value of courses. At the college level, freshmen and sophomores commonly think that core courses are wasted time, something to "get out of the way" before the major courses are taken. At the K-12 levels, students often fail to appreciate the real-world relevance of topics. Math problems, for example, may seem to be esoteric exercises in abstraction or pointless puzzles. Teachers need enthusiasm and creativity to engage these difficult audiences. The teacher must start by being a persuasive salesperson. The goal is to draw the students into our world and show them the new intellectual possibilities, which is a task that is often difficult to accomplish.

It is a common trap for experts, such as teachers, to think that the importance of the course content must be obvious to everyone. The truth, however, is that our students lack the experience and specialized knowledge that we, the teachers, already have. It may not be apparent to students why math is important or why they should care about historical events that happened long ago. Teachers must meet the students at the level where they are currently at in order to engage them in the course content.

The teacher has many possible ways to engage student interest. One way is to connect academic topics to events from everyday life. A benefit of teaching psychology is that I get to draw upon examples of psychological phenomena that come from real people in the everyday world. Other fields can employ relevance to everyday life as an emotional hook, too. I once observed a colleague teach about the U.S. Constitution in an American Government class. It occurred to me that the constitutional debate about the power relationship between the states and the federal government is still quite relevant today. Many current political issues revolve around the question of whether the states or the federal government have the right to regulate firearms, abortions, drugs, immigration, and other controversial issues. This relevance to modern political struggles would be a natural opening for this topic. A savvy history professor could open with, "Who do you think should regulate _____, the states or the federal government?" After a brief discussion, the natural segue would be something like, "You know, the founders of this country struggled with this question, too." Once the relevance of this issue to modern life is established, students might be sufficiently intrigued to explore how this problem has been treated in the past.

A second approach for engaging student interest is to tap into curiosity about our complex world. Human beings have inborn curiosity. Some people also have a need for cognitive stimulation. An example opening line for this strategy is, "Have you ever wondered why _____?" When I teach about color vision, I often open class with this question: "As a child, did you ever wonder if other people internally experienced colors like you do? Perhaps what I experience as being the color green you might experience as being a different color." This question usually brings up some head nodding in agreement and brief discussions about how it is impossible to know exactly what other people are experiencing as colors. The opening question naturally leads to a discussion of how color vision works (common between people) as well as common color vision deficiencies (different between people). The conversation might eventually lead to how we can determine that some people are insensitive to certain colors through careful testing procedures. This may answer the opening question by demonstrating that not everyone may experience color in the same way.

A third story-like way to engage student interest is through biographies or the chronological unfolding of events. Sometimes, presentations can start with literal stories. The presentation can describe an important person's life, and then the contributions and ideas that this person had fit within the context of the personal story. Many documentaries take this approach.

A fourth idea for opening a class is to appeal to personal interests. Many college students are interested in career possibilities, such as how much money they could earn in certain occupations. Instructors can use this personal interest of students to stimulate their interest in the class topic. In Statistics, I tell my students that many statistical experts have salaries over $70,000 per year. This information often surprises students who tend to view data analysis as a boring waste of time. When I cover clinical topics in other courses, such as sensory deficits, neurological disorders, and psychological disorders, I sometimes mention how many professionals work in these fields and earn good incomes. Of course, most students will not pursue these clinical careers, and extrinsic rewards should not be the sole motivation for learning, but the mere mention of occupational possibilities is enough to demonstrate that a pressing need exists for this particular knowledge in the real world. These topics are not just esoteric or pointless academic exercises.

A fifth idea is to use foreshadowing to create intrigue about upcoming topics. In literature, foreshadowing occurs when narrators give subtle hints about the outcome of the story. These suggestions about the direction of the topic are engaging because people are interested in anticipating the outcome of future events. For presenters, a useful tool for starting a presentation is to give a brief outline of what the students can expect. A mental roadmap can give students a general feeling of the overall purpose and flow of the presentation.

Finally, a last possibility is to make a connection to previous topics. This connection can help students put the current content into a bigger context and make connections across class periods. For some topics, such as math, there is a definite progression of ideas as the course proceeds. I often take time at the beginning of each Statistics class to draw attention to how today's topic is related to and builds upon the topic that I covered during the last class period. This connection shows that today's ideas are not just random, isolated thoughts. Rather, the current topic is another step forward in a logical progression of ideas. All information needs to be understood in a context. A brief review of a relevant previous topic helps to establish the context for new ideas and thus orients student learning.

Emotional Food for the Educational Journey

After establishing emotional engagement, a good educational presentation will move on to the middle or body of the presentation. This is the time for covering the main concepts and facts, the essential parts of the lesson plan. In regard to student engagement, the problem in this phase of the class is that the emotional energy that started at the beginning of the class can slowly decline and become lost. A lecture that starts off on a high note and then slowly grinds down to dull facts will not be effective. Teachers need to be aware of this diminishing emotional energy as the class period proceeds and take appropriate measures to keep the classroom energy high until the end.

One strategy for maintaining the emotional energy of a class session is to follow the drier academic ideas with educational activities or multimedia resources that stimulate a higher level of student engagement. Instructors can follow a period of lecture information with a discussion activity or a hands-on demonstration. Another possibility is to illustrate a concept with a video example of the key idea. When I cover psychological disorders in the Introductory Psychology course, I follow a fact-example sequence. The sequence starts with a brief lecture about the symptoms and causes of each disorder. This emotionally-dry information is followed with short video clips (about three to five minutes long) of people who display symptoms of these disorders. This fact-example sequence accomplishes at least two desirable goals. One benefit is that the brief video gives students an emotional boost after listening to the dry lecture material. Watching real people do things is interesting and intriguing, so the example helps to maintain student interest. Another benefit is that I can ask students to identify the specific symptoms in the video clip, which turns the video into a more engaging active learning process.

Another emotional strategy that can help students through the middle part of a presentation is to introduce some humor at opportune moments (Berk, 2003). The students don't really expect much in the way of humor in the classroom, so even modest attempts to be funny can be helpful for emotional energy. The goal is to use safe, simple humor like harmless one-liner jokes and puns, which Berk (2003) describes as "low stakes humor." Good judgment must be used to avoid humor that has the potential to be offensive to students. Jokes that are racist or sexist, for example, might be a quick end to an academic career. Leave the provocative humor to the professional comedians in the comedy clubs. The classroom is not an appropriate place for pushing the socially acceptable limits of comedy.

Humor can be particularly effective if you can find a joke or cartoon that is highly relevant to the course content. A good cartoon in the middle of a powerpoint slide deck can do a double duty by simultaneously illustrating an important concept and giving the audience an emotional boost. These moments provide a means for the presenter to really reach the audience on both the intellectual and emotional levels. Don't just use any random joke or cartoon. Use one that will help to reinforce the idea that you are trying to teach.

Wrapping-Up a Class Period

Sometimes educational presentations just seem to end in the middle. For example, the teacher's lecture is going and going through the topic content. At the end of class, the teacher is surprised to notice that the class period is almost over. The class abruptly ends with a statement like, "We'll pick up here next time." It's almost like putting a bookmark in a novel to mark the stopping point and then picking up the book again at a later time. This sudden stop is less than ideal for class instruction. Endings that lack closure are unsatisfying to the audience and also represent a missed opportunity to make an educational impact.

The ending of a presentation is a good place to reiterate some key points from the overall presentation. The goal should be to bring the various content details together to give the students a holistic overview of the topic before the class ends. Efforts to bring closure to the topic may be helpful for long-term memory. Memory research has demonstrated that the last bit of information is recalled better than other information, which is a phenomenon called the "recency principle." Although this phenomenon is usually studied in the lab, it seems likely that the recency principle would also hold true for presentations (Duarte, 2010, p. 44). The ending is, therefore, an important last chance to leave students with a particularly memorable idea.

The very best presentations end on an uplifting, possibly inspirational note (Duarte, 2010). For an example, think of the greatest speeches in American history, such as Martin Luther King, Jr.'s "I have a dream" speech. An ideal outcome would be for students to leave the class with a sense of wonder, excitement, or curiosity that might be helpful for motivating their further studies. Although perhaps a bit grandiose for every class, finishing with such an inspirational quality when the right occasion arises is a good aim.

Too Much of a Good Thing: Avoid Overdoing Emotion

The average teacher can go a long way toward being more effective by starting with an interest-provoking introduction and adding some activities that stimulate emotion in the middle. Carefully consider, however, an opposite extreme. If presentations have too much emotion, these strong feelings can overwhelm the academic message and be detrimental to learning. Instructors face the real risk of having too much style and not enough substance when trying to add emotion to their presentations. This situation might be emotionally satisfying to the audience yet provide little benefit for their educational needs.

A fitting analogy is that the emotion in a presentation is like putting some seasoning on food. A small amount of salt or hot sauce makes food taste better. Likewise, students will appreciate having a bit of emotion and humor added to the educational material. It will spark some interest in the topic and facilitate learning. However, the chef should be careful not to get too carried away: too much salt or hot sauce can overwhelm the flavor. In a similar way, too much emotion in a classroom can be a distraction and be detrimental to learning.

The use of graphics to increase the emotional content of a powerpoint presentation is generally a positive feature. However, doing so could also cause problems if the emotional images overwhelm the presentation's message. Educational psychologists use the term "seductive details" to describe a similar phenomenon that can occur in textbooks or multimedia presentations (Mayer, 2009). Many textbooks attempt to be more appealing by including images to liven up the textbook content. The potential problem with seductive details is that some of these images are not important for learning the topic and do little or nothing to promote student understanding. In fact, these unnecessary emotional details may even be harmful to learning. For example, many Introductory

Psychology textbooks will have a picture of a sleeping person in the chapter that covers sleep as a state of consciousness. The purpose of the picture is to generate interest, but such a picture is hardly necessary because everyone has seen someone who is asleep at some point in their lives. The problem is that students might remember the picture of the sleeping person but forget the important information about sleep that was described in the text. It seems likely that the seductive detail effect can occur in powerpoint presentations, such as with graphics that add little or nothing to the presentation's content. The danger is that the audience may remember a good cartoon or a memorable picture but forget the important content of the presentation.

Interestingly, the results from seductive details research are somewhat inconsistent. Earlier studies suggest that the irrelevant emotions triggered by unnecessary information may harm learning, but more recent studies suggest potentially positive benefits (Mayer, Heiser, and Lonn, 2001; Park, Flowerday, and Brünken, 2015; Rey, 2012; Schneider, Nebel, and Rey, 2016). These mixed research findings suggest that the role of emotions in education can be somewhat tricky. Sometimes emotional content is helpful for learning, and sometimes it is not.

Design Goal: Emotional Needs as a Starting Point

Presentation experts agree that the starting point for creating a presentation should be to focus on the overall story at the beginning of the creative process. The emotional needs of the audience are often an afterthought in educational presentations because instructors usually place the emphasis on the factual content. The truth, however, is that the emotional needs of our students should be given a higher priority.

Powerpoint has features that can assist teachers in achieving these emotionally-centered goals. Students typically report that powerpoint-based images are more engaging and interesting than presentations that are purely verbal or are accompanied by the chalkboard. The graphics can add an emotional spark to the presentation. These features make powerpoint a persuasive medium (Guadagno et al., 2013), and perhaps instructors can use this persuasive nature to help disengaged students become more involved in the course.

DESIGN FOR EMOTION II

The Organization of Successful Presentations

Powerpoint is like being trapped in the style of early Egyptian flatland cartoons ... (Tufte 2006, p. 29)

At some point in your life, you may have experienced what I call the "random teacher." This person gives spontaneous lectures that seem to skip from point to point without much connection between the ideas. This teacher may have a nearly endless collection of stories that are loosely connected to the topic. While some students will be able to make the connections between the stories and important concepts, others are likely to get lost. Another problematic situation is teachers who start out with a planned structure for their presentations but can't seem to stay on topic. This teaching style is characterized by frequent digressions and detours that might be interesting, but the problem is that too much class time is spent off-topic. These unfortunate situations illustrate a need for order in effective teaching. Spontaneity is good, but it can be a potential problem if the class seems to get lost due to a lack of structure. Balancing order and flexibility is important for being an effective educator.

Powerpoint presentations can be both an aid and a hindrance to teaching goals due to the competing demands of order and spontaneity. Powerpoint imposes a structure and order upon a presentation that can be beneficial. Students approve of powerpoint's organizing effects for note-taking and the overall structure of a lecture (Susskind, 2005). On the other hand, some educators are concerned that powerpoint presentations can be too linear or excessively organized (Hlynka and Mason, 1998). A high degree of powerpoint structure may stifle student questions and discussion if the students feel that it is impossible for the class to deviate from the predetermined course of the slide deck. Powerpoint may also make controversial topics with ambiguous evidence seem to have an artificial sense of order. The linear nature of a powerpoint presentation may therefore be problematic for situations that require a more complex, intricate understanding of relationships (Kinchin et al., 2008). We will now examine the role of structure in a successful powerpoint presentation.

The Organization of Powerpoint Presentations

Conceiving an overall plan for an effective class session can be difficult. In this section, we will aim for a generic class structure that instructors can use for a wide range of topics to create an effective organization for a lecture. The proposed structure follows the basic elements of a storyline (see Chapter 5). Here, we will put the storyline concept into practice to see how it might be implemented.

I developed the following storyline structure through many years of experience in teaching Statistics. This is a challenging course to teach because many students dread topics that involve mathematics. The generic structure I describe here proved to be effective for Statistics, and it can be applied in a general sense to other courses.

Step 1: Setting the Stage

A common problem in lectures is that the teacher simply launches into to the main body of the topic without adequately preparing students (see Chapter 5). It is a mistake to begin a lecture with the facts and key terms that form the body of the lecture. The first part of a successful lecture needs to take a preparatory step by informing students about what the topic is and why it is important. We cannot assume that students bring the same level of interest and understanding to the topic that teachers already possess. Teachers must, therefore, carefully cultivate an interest or intellectual curiosity about the topic before the lecture moves into the main part with facts and information.

Teachers can start the process of building student interest before the lecture has even started. An easy yet very useful technique for promoting student interest is to begin with a dramatic title slide. This slide should contain a short title, a compelling graphic image that is relevant to the topic, and possibly a brief outline (just a few words) of the topics to be covered. The graphic image could be a picture or cartoon that triggers a bit of emotion. Another possibility for increasing intrigue is to make a 'promise' in the title slide followed by an ellipsis: "Your PowerPoint Slides are About to Get So Much Better. . .". It is a good practice to begin projecting this introductory slide about five minutes *before* the class starts (Kosslyn, 2007). At least a few students will have their interest drawn in by a dramatic image on the title slide. The best part about this approach is that it takes almost no effort on the part of the instructor to spark some interest.

When the class begins, many possible introductions might capture student interest at the beginning of the lecture. The common element of these openings is their intention to intrigue students and motivate them to learn more. Some introduction possibilities are introductory stories, emphasizing curiosity and relevance to everyday life, and appealing to personal interests (see Chapter 5). Even when student interest is not aroused, making the effort to engage students is still worthwhile. Students who are not emotionally moved by these engagement efforts likely will appreciate the instructor's attempt to draw their interest into the topic.

Step 2: Important Facts and Concepts

After establishing student engagement, the next step is to introduce the key facts, information, and concepts of the topic. Most teachers are strong in this informative aspect of the lecture, with the focus on communicating important information and ideas. The slides in this part of the lecture will emphasize information. These slides might contain key terms with definitions or a topic with associated subtopics. Some information-oriented slides will contain more pictorial content, such as charts, diagrams, or photos.

In Bloom's taxonomy, the goal at this stage of the lecture is described as knowledge and comprehension or, in more recent versions, remembering and understanding. These are the lowest levels of Bloom's taxonomy, which is appropriate for this stage of the lecture. The students must know something about the topic before efforts to engage higher-level learning can begin. The knowledge expressed in this part lays a foundation for subsequent higher-level learning processes.

Step 3: An Example

Communicating information to students is essential, but it is really just the start of the learning process. Students are quite capable of memorizing a key term with a definition yet may completely fail to recognize an example of this concept occurring in the real world. To address this possibility, the third stage is to illustrate the key terms or ideas by showing an example of how these might work or appear in everyday life. This step bridges a gap between the abstract key terms and more practical real-world phenomena.

In Bloom's taxonomy, this part of the presentation represents a focus on application and the ability to use the concepts in some real-life situation. Application is positioned in the middle of Bloom's taxonomy, between the lower-level memory and understanding and the higher-level mental abilities. By following the basic information from the concept to an application, an instructor is slowly building the cognitive abilities that relate to this idea. This application stage may also involve a more active learning process than simple comprehension or memorization.

The slides or other media shown during this part of the lecture need to emphasize examples rather than delivering more information. This need can be accomplished through the use of images, video clips, and/or instructional animations, but these examples must be relevant to the instructional content. Another way to provide an example is through a hands-on demonstration of some sort. Regardless of how they present the example, the instructor's role during this application is to guide the students through the example to show how the application should be done. This guidance is important because the students may not be ready in this stage to apply the concept completely on their own. They may still need an expert role model to point the way.

Students benefit from the change of focus or activities that occurs in the application phase because they cannot continually absorb more information without experiencing fatigue and decreased learning. Changing up the format of a lecture is an important component of effective lectures (Bligh, 2000). For example, switching from information delivery to watching a short video clip changes the dynamic of the lecture and helps to keep students engaged in the topic.

Step 4: The Challenge Activity

The challenge part is the point where students must begin to demonstrate mastery of the material, such as by working with the provided concepts on their own. Many kinds of possibilities exist for this step. Instructors could give the students a question that must be discussed in small groups, with the goal of reaching a consensus and reporting this result to the class. The discussion questions need to be somewhat ambiguous topics with evidence that can support two or more viewpoints of the issue. Trivial questions with straightforward, factual answers—Is the sky blue? —will result in little or no discussion. Teachers can choose from many other activity possibilities. For ideas, the teaching supplements that come with textbooks have instructor resources that might provide good exercises for this portion of the class period. Some disciplines, such as psychology, also have collections of activities published in book form.

The slides during this part of the lecture should not aim to present new information. Rather, the slides should guide or support the challenge activity. The powerpoint slides might, for example, pose questions or describe procedures for a small group discussion. The powerpoint slide can also serve the purpose of communicating a switch in classroom activities and thereby help to coordinate the challenge exercise.

This part of class is for the higher level cognitive skills of Bloom's taxonomy: application, analysis, synthesis, evaluation, and/or creation. The students have some freedom to run with the ideas of the day and use them in their own way, giving this this part of class a constructivist approach. Once again, the class period has changed focus from a more passive information delivery to a more active learning approach. These changes help to keep students engaged in the topic. Although the focus is on student activities, the instructor is still involved in the learning process. When the individual or group results are reported to the class, the instructor has a chance to weigh-in and provide feedback on student work.

Step 5: Conclusions

The last phase in a successful class is to wrap up the class with some kind of take-home message, such as a big-picture, holistic view of the topic. For controversial ideas, the instructor can emphasize using evidence to carefully evaluate two or more competing options, and then make an informed decision about which viewpoint seems to be the most accurate. The concluding phase of class could have a metacognitive emphasis, such as having students identify what they perceived to be the main ideas or difficult topics of the day's lesson. An example is the two-minute paper exercise, which allows students two minutes to write their overall reaction to what they learned during class. This type of assignment can help students consolidate information into long-term memory and also give the instructor feedback about what the students got out of the class session.

The slides during this part of class should emphasize holistic conclusions that summarize the class period. For this purpose, a powerpoint slide could contain a few complete sentences that effectively summarize the key points from the class period. The purpose for using complete sentences is to encourage complete thoughts.

Ending a class period with video clips, discussions, or demonstrations may fail. The reason for this problem is that the last slide in the slide deck will send a strong signal to students that the class is done. The students will interpret the last slide as an ending even if the instructor does not intend to send this message.

If the powerpoint presentation ends and the class finishes with a short video clip, the students will mentally check out during the video and begin preparing for their next class. Student interest will be lost once you've reached the last slide, so any new information or activities done after this point will be met with an indifferent attitude.

Overall, this framework for a successful class period can be applied to many course needs. It is a pedagogically sound strategy that begins with student engagement and then progressively builds up to higher levels of Bloom's taxonomy. We should note how powerpoint was not used from beginning to end to simply deliver ever-increasing amounts of information. The role of powerpoint can shift during the lecture: delivering information; presenting media that stimulates discussion; instructing students in performing an activity. In this sense, powerpoint can be an organizing backbone for course activities, not just a means for delivering information.

Potential Problems from Excessive Organization

A common concern raised by educators is that powerpoint imposes a rigid linearity on the instructor and the students. The software requires the slides to be arranged in a predetermined order, but classroom interactions between students and teachers may sometimes go in unexpected directions. The fixed order of a slide deck may make it difficult to accommodate topic deviations, and thereby detract from the spontaneity and organic flow of classroom interactions. A related problem is that the predetermined organization of a powerpoint presentation may stifle student-teacher interactions in a subtle way. Students might be reluctant to ask questions if preserving the order of the slide deck seems to be the teacher's highest priority.

We can begin addressing this potential problem of excessive linearity simply by being aware that powerpoint can encourage an overly-structured teaching style. Powerpoint does not necessarily mandate a linear sequence of ideas, but the nature of powerpoint might suggest or even promote this kind of teaching style. Teachers also need to be aware that students may have reservations about interrupting the predetermined slide sequence with questions. Being sensitive to the basic linear nature of powerpoint is an important starting point for addressing these shortcomings. We must be aware of the potential problems posed by the slide structure before we can seek solutions to overcome it.

A second step toward promoting student-teacher communication is to explicitly inform students that they have permission to ask questions, and that asking questions is encouraged. A good time to introduce this idea is on the first day of class. Teacher-student dialogue can be promoted during the first and second weeks of class by seeking student opinions. Teachers can demonstrate that they are sincere about teacher-student communication during class by positively reinforcing students who ask questions. These words and deeds early in the course will show students that your individual style is open to questions and observations.

Teachers will also find it useful to plan for discussion opportunities while preparing their slide decks. Some natural points in the class may occur in which student discussion is most likely or appropriate. The overall structure can cover the topic, yet the instructor can set aside a few key moments for students to ask questions or engage in a discussion-based activity. Natural points for questions might be transitions between topics, such as moving from the information-focused parts of a lecture to an application exercise or an activity. The application and challenge parts of the lecture (see above) might also be good times for student-teacher interactions. For example, instructors can follow video clips with a question and answer period. If the students have no questions themselves, the instructor can pose questions to the students about the video that might encourage application of the concepts or other higher-order thinking activities.

A tip for promoting discussions is that the best questions will be specific and focused rather than vague and open-ended. For example, let's say that following a discussion of the symptoms of schizophrenia, a class was shown a video with examples of the disorder. The instructor-posed question, "Which behavior illustrated the presence of hallucinations?" might be more likely to get an answer that promotes discussion compared to an unfocused question like, "Are there any questions?" If someone gives a partial answer, the instructor can promote further discussion by saying something like, "That was good. What other symptoms did you notice?" Doing so encourages other students to build upon partial answers in a collaborative manner.

Instructors can use the powerpoint slide itself to encourage classroom interaction. The slides can directly encourage questions and discussion by communicating to students that the class direction is changing to discussion. One possible approach is to use a blank slide to break away from the tendency to deliver more information and refocus attention on the teacher. Perhaps instructors might place structured questions on a slide about the things that students should be considering in order to promote discussion. Aim to keep these discussion-promoting questions short. A one-word questions like, "Symptoms?" might be more effective than using an entire sentence, such as, "Which symptoms does this person have?" In order to encourage discussion, these slides should not provide further information. Students should not be writing down more information when the real goal is engagement in a discussion activity.

Knoblauch (2012) reports that the contents of a powerpoint slide can often be a common point of discussion for presenters and the audience. In education, an informative graph or an intriguing image presented without text may be a good way to stimulate discussion. For example, Maxwell reports successfully using powerpoint in history classes to present primary sources such as photos rather than bullet point lists of information (Maxwell, 2007). He stimulates class discussion by showing dramatic images of historical events. One of his examples is the impact of hyperinflation in Germany before World War II. He illustrates this historical event through the use of photos that show people using paper money to light a stove or using money as waste paper. These moving images are much more likely to promote student interest and discussion than a dry bullet point item like "hyperinflation was a problem."

Some technology solutions may also help to provide more flexibility from the predetermined order of the slide deck. Most presenters know that the arrow keys on the keyboard will go forward or back in the slide presentation. Relatively few presenters, however, seem to know that presentation software programs often have a feature that allows the presenter to jump to any particular slide in the presentation. In PowerPoint 2016, a right mouse click on the presentation in slide-show mode will bring up a context menu with a "see all slides" command. This feature reveals thumbnail images of all the slides and allows the presenter to jump to any slide in the slide deck. The online version of PowerPoint has a similar "go to slide" option that can jump to a particular slide number. Yet another possibility is to enter the slide number into the keyboard, and then press 'enter' to jump to a particular slide. Instructors can also make the order of powerpoint slides more flexible by using hyperlinks that can jump to predetermined slides or web pages. A situation in which the nonlinearity of hyperlinks might be useful is for questions and answers at the end of a presentation. The presenter could insert hyperlinks in the final slide that go to key slides in the presentation, such as a graph with important results. If a question arises about this graph, the presenter can jump to the graph by simply clicking on the hyperlink in the conclusion slide. One drawback, however, is that the instructor must build these hyperlinks into the slide deck before class.

Other supplemental technologies can help powerpoint presentations be both more flexible and interactive. The oldest of these technologies is a chalkboard or whiteboard. They can offer a flexibility that nicely complements the inflexible structure of a slide deck. If a student asks a good question, the instructor can respond by writing key information on the board off to the side of the powerpoint projection. The instructor can provide this information in an improvisational way, adding text as the flow of discussion suggests. Smart boards and similar products represent a step up the technology ladder. These technologies enable the instructor to write notes such as text, arrows, circles, and other embellishments on top of a slide, making a slide more like a chalk board. PowerPoint also has some built in features for annotating slides in the slide-show mode with the pen tool or the highlighter tool. Another approach to increasing the flexibility of powerpoint presentations is to use student response technologies to allow students to express an opinion or convey their understanding of a topic (see Chapter 12 for a review). Altogether, these supplemental technologies can promote greater spontaneity and flexibility during the presentation.

Nonlinear Approaches to Presentations

Some educators address the possible linearity problem by using presentation technologies that are less structured and more nonlinear than Microsoft's PowerPoint application. Prezi is an online presentation technology that has received significant attention for being less rigid than a standard slide deck. The Prezi presentation begins with a large master slide—the infinite canvas—that works like a cognitive map of the overall presentation. The speaker can zoom into this canvas to reveal more details about a specific subtopic. The speaker can move through the subtopics in any desired order, which makes the flow of the presentation less confining than the linear order imposed by a conventional PowerPoint presentation. Microsoft is also working to give presenters a greater degree of flexibility for navigating through a slide deck with the "show all slides" command. These new technologies may help educators tailor their presentation needs on the fly to best fit where the flow of their presentation is going.

Several studies have been conducted to see if nonlinear presentation technologies like Prezi have educational advantages. Student perceptions of Prezi are generally positive (Brock and Brodahl, 2013; Conboy, Fletcher, Russell, and Wilson, 2012; Virtanen, Myllärniemi, and Wallander, 2013). However, studies of educational effectiveness that compare PowerPoint to Prezi do not find higher student performance with Prezi (Castelyn and Mottart, 2012; Castelyn, Mottart, and Valcke, 2013; Chou, Chang, and Lu, 2015). These negative results suggest that the linear nature of powerpoint presentations is perhaps not a major problem.

Kinchin and colleagues address the linearity of powerpoint by supplementing powerpoint presentations with handouts that have information organized in a nonlinear fashion (Kinchin, 2006a, 2006b; Kinchin and Cabot, 2007; Kinchin et al., 2008). These handouts have concept maps that present the same information as the powerpoint presentation, but the handout's organization of information better reflects the nonlinear complexities of the subject matter. These educators suggest that the combination of a linear powerpoint presentation with a nonlinear concept map on a handout is a powerful combination for promoting student learning. Using handouts in this fashion is a strategy worth considering for educators who might be concerned about the potential problems created by the linear structure of powerpoint presentations.

Balancing Structure and Student Interaction

Many teachers struggle to find an effective yet engaging way to convey their topic material to students. Powerpoint can help with this process by guiding instructors into forming an organized path through the topic. Students generally appreciate presentations with an orderly structure. In one study, only 17% of the surveyed students felt that the predetermined order of a powerpoint slide presentation was a significant problem (D. Burke and Apperley, 2003). However, while teachers must provide their students with a path to follow, learning is often not as straightforward as staying on a particular path. The students must, to some degree, find their own way as they learn. All learning is a bit constructivist in nature as students find their own understanding of the material. This need for each student to discover their own way sometimes makes learning a nonlinear process, one with diversions, dead-ends, and convoluted turns. The creative use of powerpoint navigation can be used to address these nonlinear teaching moments in a manner that is effective and exciting in the classroom.

DESIGN FOR SENSATION

The Need for Visibility

". . . of all the senses sight best helps us to know things, and reveals many distinctions." Aristotle

After the story line of the presentation has been established, instructors should next consider the visual aids that will support the presentation message. However, it is still premature to fire up the computer and start creating slides. The accomplished teacher must have a clear understanding of how the visual elements of powerpoint will communicate information to the audience. Far too many presentations fail because the sensory qualities of the slides just didn't work for the audience. Possible problems include small text, faint text, and odd color combinations that detract from the value of a slide presentation. Visual aids with poor visibility will obviously not work, yet many presenters fall down on this fundamental feature of their presentations.

We will now will focus on the basic sensory qualities of slides, such as contrast sensitivity, spatial frequency, and color. The emphasis will be on vision because powerpoint is primarily a visual communication medium. Examining the basic science of vision suggests best practices for slides that will be highly visible to the audience.

Contrast Sensitivity: The Most Basic Visual Function

Vision is fundamentally about detecting small differences in light intensity across the visual scene. Photons, which are the particles and waves that make up light, have the ability to strike objects and bounce off. This reflected light energy from our environment is spread unevenly, with some areas of the environment being darker (e.g., shadows) and others being lighter (e.g., full sun). This uneven distribution of light energy provides important information about our environment, such as the size of objects and depth information. The reflected light, which is called "luminance," eventually enters our eye and is converted into a nervous system signal in the retina at the back of the eye.

The visual function of being able to sense comparatively lesser or greater amounts of light throughout our environment is called "contrast sensitivity." The idea of contrast sensitivity is illustrated in the two following examples of powerpoint slides (Figure 7.1). The backgrounds in these slides vary in luminance, from darker (top) to lighter (bottom) areas. The text is a constant color of white (left) or black (right). Contrast sensitivity allows us to distinguish the text—the foreground—as being separate from the background. A high degree of difference is easy to read.

Figure 7.1: Contrast between text and background

The relationship of the text to the background in these examples makes an important point about contrast sensitivity. When the contrast is high—such as light text on a dark background or dark text on a light background—words will be very legible and easy to read. For this primary reason, books are typically printed as black text on white paper. Low contrast situations, such as light text on a light background or dark text on a dark background, are difficult to read.

Our first best practice conclusion for visibility is that presenters need slides with high contrast in order to promote visibility and easy reading. Low contrast is simply too difficult for the audience to see. Under low contrast situations, the text seems to disappear. Which is the best way to achieve high contrast? Figure 7.1 shows the two possible ways to accomplish high contrast: dark text on light backgrounds, or light text on dark backgrounds. The best approach depends on the presentation context, with the most critical factor being the degree of the ambient light in the classroom.

Some presentation experts, usually from the field of business, recommend light text on dark backgrounds for a professional look. This recommendation is particularly good for small classrooms. The dark background is easy on the eyes for people who are seated near the screen. However, a potential problem with using light text on dark backgrounds is that, contrary to intuition, projection systems do not project black onto the screen. It's problematic, therefore, to use black backgrounds in bright rooms with a high degree of ambient light. The light coming from various sources will strike the screen and make the dark parts of the slide appear much lighter. For example, a black background can become more like grey in a room with strong ambient lighting (Figure 7.2). The implication is that black or dark backgrounds will look best in dark rooms without much ambient light. The practical problem that this may pose is that, as already mentioned, darkened rooms may put students to sleep and cause difficulties for note-taking efforts. Students may also find it difficult to see the instructor in a dark room.

Figure 7.2: A black background that appears to be grey in a classroom with strong ambient lighting

The other high contrast possibility is to use black text on lightly colored or white backgrounds, just like most reading material. This approach seems to work better in rooms that have strong ambient lighting. For example, the classrooms that I teach in have large windows and overhead lighting near the screen that cannot be turned off. The black text on a white background seems to have higher contrast, and therefore greater visibility, in this lighting situation. Another advantage of this approach is that the classroom lights do not need to be turned off during the presentation, because the white light projected on the screen is much brighter than most of the ambient lighting.

A white slide with black letters under high ambient lighting conditions is shown in Figure 7.3. This photo was taken from the side of a classroom approximately twenty-two feet (6.7 meters) away from the projection screen. The screen is approximately twelve feet (3.7 meters) wide. Even though the slide is designed to be high contrast—black text on a white background—the intensity of ambient light from the windows and other sources significantly lowers the contrast. This effect makes the black font appear to be a washed out grey color and shows that it is best to aim for the highest possible contrast. Lower degrees of contrast would be even harder to discern under conditions with significant ambient lighting.

Figure 7.3: Black text appearing grey under strong lighting

A final point to consider about contrast sensitivity is the uniformity of the background. Backgrounds that are a solid color with a uniform text, like black or white, will have the same contrast sensitivity in all parts of the slides. Backgrounds with variations in color or photographic backgrounds will have uneven degrees of contrast in different parts of the slide. Consider the slides shown in Figure 7.4.

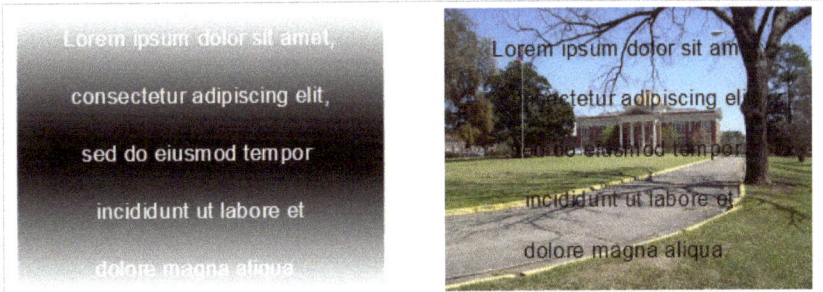

Figure 7.4: Contrast for backgrounds with varying light intensity

The left slide has high contrast only in the middle of the slide. Text placed at the top or bottom of the slide will be difficult to read. This kind of uneven contrast between the text and the background can be even more problematic in slides that have photographic backgrounds (Figure 7.4, right). Overlaying the the text on to a photo can be dramatic and is sometimes recommended by presentation experts. However, the uneven contrast may create visibility problems. For example, the text that is superimposed on the darker parts of the photo (such as the middle row of text) is simply not visible due to low contrast. This situation can be difficult for making legible text. Sometimes this problem is addressed by adding a text box with a solid color background, such as a white box for containing black text, to make sure that the text has high contrast for the audience. Most teachers lack the professional design expertise needed to make complicated photographic slides that are appealing yet highly readable, although the latest versions of Microsoft PowerPoint can provide helpful design suggestions for these tricky situations.

Photographic slide backgrounds can make slides more dramatic, but a better approach for visibility and high contrast is to simply keep the slide background a single solid color. Black text on a white background is probably the easiest and best approach for most classroom situations, although it can appear somewhat boring. It would also be best for teachers to keep their slide designs simple in order to emphasize the visibility of important content. Maximizing visibility is more important than making dramatic slides.

Spatial Frequency: The Resolution of the Eye

Most of our visual world is complex, just like the photo in the background of the second slide in Figure 7.4. A typical scene may contain millions of slight variations in light intensity. In contrast, the number of fine changes in luminance that the eye can capture is limited. The technical term for these small changes in lighting is "spatial frequency." The sensitivity to luminance changes in a given amount of a visual image is the degree of visual angle.

Figure 7.5 shows a very basic powerpoint slide and how this slide would be perceived by the eye of a student. The background (light) and the text (dark) reflect more or less light, respectively, from the slide. The differences in light intensity between these white and black areas are preserved as the light travels through the eye as small angles.

Design for Sensation | 107

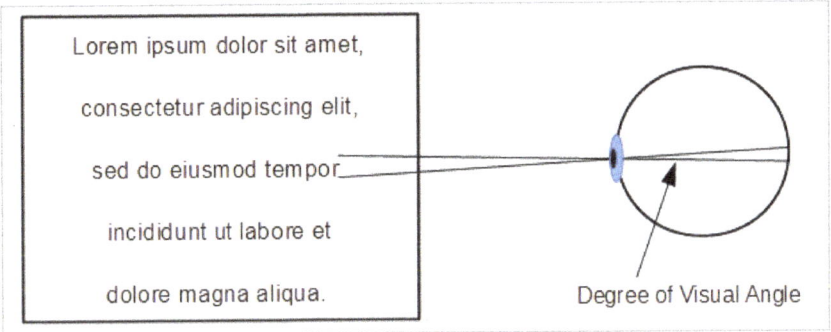

Figure 7.5: The degree of visual angle in the eye

An everyday example of this phenomenon that most people can relate to is the visual acuity testing done in optometry clinics. The standard test of visual acuity is to read black letters from a white chart. The classic Snellen test of visual acuity determines the smallest line of letters than can be seen at a distance of twenty feet (six meters). A diagnosis of 20/20 (6/6 in meters) means that the patient can see letters at twenty feet that the average person should also be able to view from twenty feet, which is a complicated way of saying someone has an average or normal visual acuity. Although the Snellen test is known to most people, modern optometrists and vision researchers use a more sophisticated measure of visual acuity called the degree of visual angle. As previously stated, the differences between the light and dark parts of the visual display form small angles as they travel through the lens of the eye. The degree of these angles can be used to measure the smallest differences in light intensity that people can reliably see.

The practical question about spatial frequency for presenters is how small these differences (the degree of visual angle) between light and dark can be, yet still be distinguishable by the audience. For example, how small can a presenter make the text on a powerpoint slide, yet still have text that is easy for the audience to read? If the text size falls below the spatial acuity ability of the audience, it will be nearly impossible to see, just like it is almost impossible to read the smallest lines on the eye chart at the optometrist's office. However, text that is too large may be overwhelming to people seated in the front row. Large text will also limit the amount of information that can be put on a slide, which could also be problematic.

It would be convenient if the answer to this question was something simple, like, "Always use a 32 point font or larger." Although many articles make such suggestions, a simple recommendation for a specific font size doesn't completely work. The degree of visual angle for people in the audience will depend partly on the size of the image shown on the screen, which is determined by both the font size and the screen size. A second less obvious factor that influences the degree of visual angle is the audience members' distance from the slide. If the image size stays the same, the degree of visual angle will become smaller and smaller as the audience members get farther and farther away from the screen. Once again, the analogy of visual acuity testing is helpful. As you get farther away from the chart, the degree of visual angle for the chart letters becomes progressively smaller to you, making it harder to see the letters. The basic point is that the degree of visual angle is a relative measure that will depend both upon the size of the image on the screen and the viewer's distance from the screen.

The relationship between screen size and distance for a hypothetical powerpoint slide is shown in the following Figure (5.6). The eyes of the nearby viewer (top) should have little or no difficulty reading this slide. The degree of visual angle is sufficiently large enough to enable easy reading. In contrast, the distant viewer seated at the back of the classroom (bottom), might have difficulty viewing this slide. The degree of visual angle is so small for this person that it might be nearly impossible to distinguish the letters. Both viewers are seeing the same screen with the same-sized images. The only difference is the distance from the screen to their eyes.

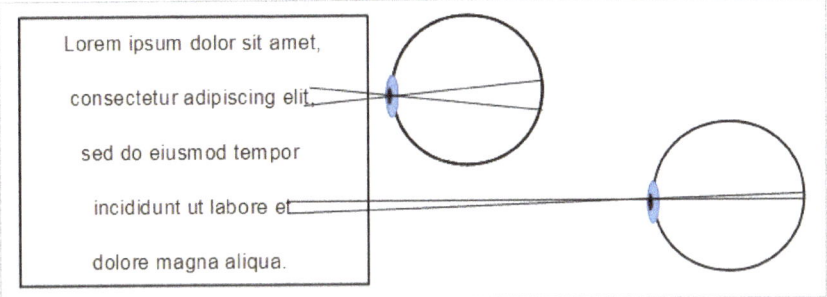

Figure 7.6: Visual angle as a function of distance from the display

Let's return to the practical question of how large our text and graphic features need to be in a presentation. Microsoft has put great care into making the default font sizes in PowerPoint large enough to work well for most situations. Starting with PowerPoint 2013, the default font size for bullet points is a 28-point font. This size has decent visibility in a standard college classroom. Figure 7.7 shows a 28-point font (the top bullet point) along with other font sizes. The screen is about twelve feet (3.7 meters) wide and the photo was taken approximately thirty-three feet (10.1 meters) from the screen. Most of the words in the 28 -point font line of this figure are between one to two degrees of visual angle. The size of the room is an important qualifying factor. In larger rooms, like auditoriums, 28-point font may not be large enough, particularly for students in the back of the room. For small rooms, a 28-point font size may be more than enough. In a room small enough, the presenter could even go smaller than 28-point, to 24 or 18-point, without sacrificing visibility.

Figure 7.7: Different font sizes presented in a typical classroom

Powerpoint users often just go with the software defaults when they create their slides but then sometimes get caught off guard when it comes time to actually deliver the presentation. The problem that can arise is that the appearance of font sizes on the computer screen in the teacher's office may significantly differ from the appearance in the classroom. The only way to know for sure that a font is a sufficient size is to test it in the classroom, particularly to see how it looks from the back of the room. Testing in the classroom is the best approach because it doesn't rely upon questionable rules about font sizes or complicated mathematical formulas. Once you know the font size that works for your classroom, you can make this size a standard for all of your future presentations.

A more technical way to consider this problem is to think of the visual acuity of an average viewer. If someone has an average 20/20 Snellen visual acuity, a five-letter word will take about a half degree of visual angle from left to right. This size might work for some students with good vision, but people with lower vision would likely struggle with words presented at this size. A general design recommendation is to aim for a larger size, such as words that are 1 to 2 degrees, in order to be more visible to people who have low visual acuity.

You can use an easy method to quickly determine the visual angle of the text in your slides. If you stick your arm straight ahead and hold up your thumb, the width of your thumb will cover about two degrees of visual angle (Figure 7.7). You can use the thumb measure as a quick test for your slides in the classroom. If the width of your outstretched thumb is about the same width as most of the words on the screen, then your words have about two degrees of visual angle and will be easily visible to most students. If the thumb measure seems unnatural, you could simply go by your subjective impressions about visibility from the back of the classroom: Is this easy to read, or not?

You can use other practical means to judge the size of the letters in a powerpoint presentation. One practical test is to print the powerpoint slides out on a standard sheet of paper and then place the sheets of paper on the floor. While standing over the sheets, ask yourself if you can read them easily. If the answer is no, the font size is too small and needs to be increased (Guetig, 2011). A second testing idea is to back up at least three feet from the computer monitor in your office and read the screen. Font sizes that are difficult to easily read from this distance are too small (Kosslyn, 2007). A third test possibility would be to reduce the size of the powerpoint application window on your office PC to be about five inches (13 centimeters) wide. This shrinkage of the application window will simulate the effects of seeing the screen from the back of the classroom and allow for a quick judgement about the visibility of particular font sizes.

Color: The Perception of Wavelength

A third fundamental visual function is color vision, which is the perception of different light wavelengths in the visible light spectrum. Color information is important for guiding behavior, such as assisting honey bees to find flowers or enabling people to respond to traffic signals. Color perception may have enabled early human ancestors to distinguish food like ripe berries from the surrounding vegetation, which is usually green. People and animals who could detect these color differences may have had an evolutionary advantage over others who had more limited sensitivity.

One of the major changes that occurred with powerpoint is that presenters were given a wide range of color possibilities. Most presentations use color to provide a positive aesthetic quality—pretty slides—and thereby add visual interest. Color may do more, though, than simply enhance the appearance of slides. Experimental evidence suggests that the presence of color can enhance memory for photographs, such as pictures of natural scenes like rock formations, fields, and forests (Homa and Viera, 1988; Wichmann, Sharpe, and Gegenfurtner, 2002). In support of this idea, an early study that compared black and white presentation visual aids to color aids found that the addition of color increased comprehension and retention (Morrison and Vogel, 1998).

Part of the reason why the presence of color might enhance memory is that color can make photographs more salient or prominent (Wichmann et al., 2002). A likely practical use of color in teaching, therefore, is to highlight important text or graphics. A "pop" of color can direct student attention to a particularly important part of the slide. This has also been called the signaling principle if teachers use color highlighting as a cue for pointing out important information (Mayer, 2009). This color highlighting will only work if the color is distinctive and stands out on the slide. When there are many colors, highlighted words or colored arrows may not be effective because the highlighted color will simply be lost in the kaleidoscope of colors on the slide.

It is important to consider the potential emotions that colors can trigger (for a review, see Elliot and Maier, 2014). The color red is particularly noteworthy for being associated with strong emotions, like aggression, failure, losses, or danger. These strong reactions suggest that red is a color that should be used with caution because it may elicit emotional responses that are counterproductive to teaching. Other colors may also have emotional qualities, although these are not typically a strong as red. Pink is stereotypically associated with femininity, whereas blue is stereotypically associated with masculinity. Blue, green, and other cool colors are believed to have calming and generally positive emotional effects. Some of these color-emotion associations may be based upon culture-specific values. For example, green is associated with money in the U.S.A because American currency is green, but this association is not necessarily true in other countries. The emotional values associated with certain colors suggest that the colors used in a presentation may have emotional effects upon audiences, and these effects might indirectly influence student learning. The audience might not be overtly aware of the influence, yet the emotions induced by color may have a measurable effect upon their behavior (Hanke, 1998). However, not much systematic color research on emotions has been done with powerpoint presentations.

The use of color also has potential downsides. Certain color combinations can have conflicting or clashing effects when presented together. For text, presenting color opposites next to each other can make reading difficult and produce unsettling emotional qualities. For example, red text on a green background can produce a feeling of vibration or fuzziness (Figure 7.8, left). Blue text on a black background is also problematic because it makes the letters fuzzy and indistinct (Figure 7.8, right). Other poor color combinations include brown/green and blue/purple (Hanke, 1998)

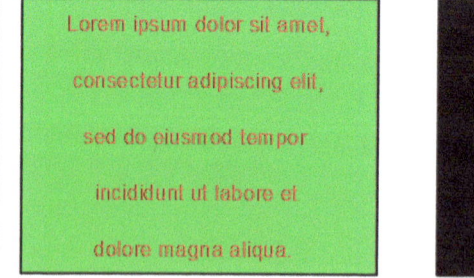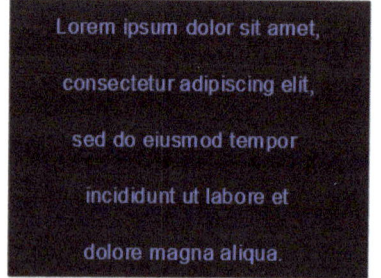

Figure 7.8: Visibility problems created by odd color combinations

Visual Impairments

Teachers must consider the possibility that some students will have visual impairments that require special accommodations. It would be mistaken to assume that all students will have normal visual acuity or contrast sensitivity. Slide designs must aim to be accessible to individuals with low vision in order to be inclusive for all students.

Recall that visual acuity depends upon the relationship between the size of the object and the viewer's distance from the object (see Figure 7.6). This relationship suggests a simple solution for students with low visual acuity: These individuals should be encouraged to sit at the front of the classroom. Being as close as possible to the screen will increase the retinal image size and degrees of visual angle. This small change in behavior is an easy way to accommodate students with visual acuity impairments.

Most teachers work with students who are young and have good visual sensitivity. However, we cannot take visual sensitivity for granted when the students are middle-aged or older. People over forty typically have presbyopia, a condition that produces difficulty in changing focus from near to far objects. This normal aging process may make it more difficult to focus on text and fine details. Older adults can also experience a wide range of additional visual insensitivities that may be caused by diseases or age-related changes in the visual system. Large fonts with high contrast will be best for these mature audiences.

Regarding color, a significant proportion of people are insensitive to red and green wavelengths. Although this insensitivity is commonly called "color blindness," this description is somewhat inaccurate because most of these individuals can see some color wavelengths, such as blue and yellow. About 8% of male and 0.4% of female Caucasians are estimated to have red-green color insensitivities, with lower prevalence rates for people of other races (Birch, 2012). The relatively common occurrence of this color insensitivity suggests that presenters should aim to minimize or eliminate the use of red and green colors from their presentations.

Design Goal: Aim for Visibility

Though it often happens, we should not take vision for granted. The real solution to such issues as tiny fonts, poor contrast, and odd color combinations in powerpoint presentations is to keep the visual sensitivities of the students in mind when creating a powerpoint slide deck. Aim for making the important visual features prominent to increase the visibility by using relatively large fonts (24 to 28 points minimum for most classroom situations) and high contrast (black/white or dark/light color combinations). Be mindful that differences in luminance, the size of the images on the projection screen, and the students' distance from the screen effects what the students will experience in the classroom. Testing is necessary to make sure that your presentations are just as highly visible in the classroom as in your office.

DESIGN FOR PERCEPTION I

How the Brain Interprets Powerpoint Images

Professionals everywhere need to know about the incredible inefficiency of text-based information and the incredible effects of images. Then they need to do two things:

1. Burn their current PowerPoint presentations
2. Make new ones. (Medina, 2008, p. 239)

For the teacher or presenter, the visibility of a powerpoint slide is only the starting point for communication. After the eye, visual information undergoes extensive analytical processing in the brain to make our visual experience possible. Approximately 20% of our cerebral cortex is solely dedicated to processing visual information, with an additional 20% to 40% of the brain also having some degree of relationship to vision (Felleman and

Van Essen, 1991; King, 2013). In fact, people who have extensive damage to the visual areas of the brain are described as being "cortically blind." These unfortunate people have rudimentary visual functions, such as being able to tell light from dark, but they cannot recognize objects or do simple tasks like telling how many fingers the doctor may be holding up.

Teachers need to consider how the perceptual abilities of students enable them to process and analyze modern presentation graphics. A basic knowledge of perceptual functions can allow the presenter to take advantage of these functions and create graphics that will inform the audience in an effortless way. The goal is to use perception to promote understanding and thereby aid the learning process. If successful, the students will experience the presentation as being intuitive. However, presenters can only achieve this goal of easy understanding via perception by giving careful consideration to the design of their graphic aids.

Gestalt Psychology: The Perception of Patterns

A fundamental function of visual perception is the ability to recognize important objects in our environment. For example, a person in a classroom will recognize that they are surrounded by meaningful objects like chairs, tables, windows, and computers. This object recognition is called "form perception." Think for a moment about what the world would be like without form perception. It would be like living in a world without visual meaning. This kind of condition, which is called visual agnosia, sometimes occurs in people who have experienced strokes or other forms of brain damage. These individuals can draw objects or copy diagrams, which shows that they are not blind, yet they cannot identify the objects that they see.

One of the earliest and most influential approaches to understanding form perception was proposed by German psychologists in the early twentieth century. This movement was called Gestalt psychology, with the word German word "gestalt" translating into "form" or "shape" in English. A famous quotation from Kurt Koffka to describe the concept of gestalt was, "The whole is different from the sum of its parts" ("Gestalt psychology," 2016). This means that the human mind makes connections between the parts of a system to arrive at a relationship or understanding that is different from merely perceiving the individual components. For example, when we look at a chair, we perceive it as a cohesive, single chair object and not as several separate objects (legs, seat, back) that just happen to be connected to each other.

The Gestalt psychologists described several perceptual principles, or laws, that described how information was grouped into meaningful patterns. The Gestalt psychologists believed these rules were useful for much more than basic visual perception. For example, some of the Gestalt psychologists studied creativity. They felt that creative solutions occurred when people developed new perceptions of relationships between the components of a problem. Some of the Gestalt psychologists also proposed that Gestalt principles were important for education in that a teacher's role was to promote understanding by helping students perceive relationships between concepts (Wertheimer, 1959). The idea is that meaningful learning occurs when students mentally "see" relationships that are new to them and form a new perception of previously unrelated pieces of information.

The Gestalt laws can be used to help students make the proper associations between ideas and help to promote understanding. A good example to begin with is the Gestalt law of figure-ground, which states that visual information from a scene is segregated into a prominent, important point (the figure) which is distinct from the rest of the scene (the ground; Todorovic, 2008). The ground or background tends to be less important than the figure and, accordingly, receives less attention or processing. For powerpoint slides, this perceptual phenomenon suggests that each slide should have a main prominent feature that contains the essential information that the teacher is trying to convey. The remaining elements of the slide, such as background colors or patterns that surround the figure, will not have much impact on the audience.

The segregation of visual information into a figure-ground relationship suggests that having too many features on a slide might overwhelm and visually confuse the audience. When a slide is complex, it becomes more difficult for the audience to segregate the information into a main point (figure) and background. The multiple slide elements compete with each other to become the figure. The real need in this situation is to edit the number of slide features downward to the most basic, essential features. This reduction in features will help the important figure part to stand out. Although this idea of simple design seems straightforward, it is sometimes difficult to accomplish in practice.

Many other Gestalt grouping principles have been proposed (for a review, see Todorovic, 2008), with some being especially relevant to the design of slide graphics. The Gestalt law of proximity is that components that are physically near each other will be perceptually grouped together (Figure 8.1, upper left). This example shows four identical circles. If these circles were evenly spaced, the overall pattern would be perceived as one group or unit. By spacing some circles closer together, two groups seem to form (left and right).

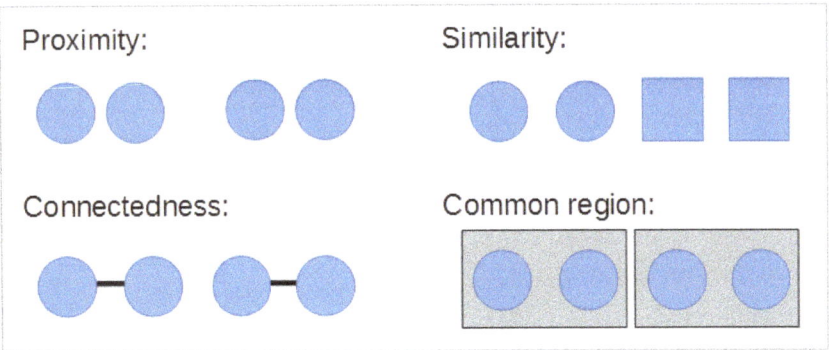

Figure 8.1: The gestalt laws of form perception

For presentations, the proximity principle means that the items which are physically close to each other on a powerpoint slide will be perceived as part of the same group. If we want to label a graph, for example, we should put the label next to the appropriate place on the graph. The Gestalt law of proximity would cause the audience to intuitively perceive that the label and the graph feature go together. In contrast, a label that is located far from the graph might seem odd and disconnected from its target object. In some situations, the proximity principle suggests that having appropriate text labels that are located near a visual feature that they belong to might be more effective than a text header placed at the top of the slide. The proximity principle may also be valuable for the layout of the slide elements. The parts that belong together should be placed in close proximity to each other to make it appear that they belong together.

Another way that the proximity principle can be used is to make creative use of the empty space between items. This empty space can serve as a boundary that creates two separate groups. Consider the following example as a bulleted list:

- Lorem ipsum dolor sit amet
- consectetur adipiscing elit

- sed do eiusmod tempor
- incididunt ut labore et

This example clearly seems like two groups. The white space between the upper and lower bullet points creates a separation that makes the proximity different between the upper and lower bullet points, thereby grouping them into two separate groups. Judicious use of spacing on powerpoint slides could thereby take advantage of the proximity principle to guide the audience to perceive certain elements as being together, which in turn could reduce the need for explanatory text on the slide and simplify the slide's appearance.

The Gestalt law of similarity states that items with similar shapes, colors, and other characteristics form perceptual groups (Figure 8.1, upper right). The law of similarity can also be used to create groups of text that share a similar characteristic, like font families, styles, colors, or sizes. For the overall design, a suggestion based upon similarity is that the headings in a document should all be the same type and size. This will distinguish them from subheadings, all of which should, again, be similar in type and size. Each category throughout the document will seem to be a consistent and organized part of its family because the appearance is similar.

The law of connectedness makes items that are attached by a connector appear to be part of the same group (Figure 8.1, lower left). The practical use of this principle in a slide is to have labels that link to a particular spot on a diagram by an arrow or line. The presence of this line between the label and the diagram part will make these features into a perceptual group. These connectors are also useful for diagrams that involve flow charts or organizational charts. The relationship between units can be expressed by the presence or absence of connecting lines.

The law of common region states that elements that are contained within a common boundary will seem to be part of the same group (Figure 8.1, lower right). Teachers can use this grouping principle to make groups from numerous elements. All you need to do is draw a circle or square around the elements to make the groups. This grouping effect naturally communicates to the audience the various groupings that might be present in the display and, again, may allow the presenter to simplify the slide appearance by reducing the need for explanatory text.

Several Gestalt laws of perception are applied to a powerpoint slide in Figure 8.2 to illustrate how these grouping principles might be used. This slide, which is from a lecture on intelligence, is designed to show that people with cognitive disabilities make up approximately 2% of the overall population. The slide has a clean figure-ground organization because the graph of IQ scores stands out prominently from the white background. There are no decorations or other graphics that might compete or interfere with the figure-ground segregation. I used the Gestalt law of common region to group together the segments of the graph that represent the bottom 2% of IQ scores by drawing a box around this area of the IQ score distribution. Using a bracket graphic (left brace or right brace) could also be an effective grouping graphic for this purpose. I positioned the label "lowest 2%" very closely to the green box that represents the bottom 2% of the curve, so students will associate this label with the box group due to the Gestalt law of proximity. I could also have made this association by connecting the "lowest 2%" label to the box with a line or arrow, thereby taking advantage of the law of connectedness.

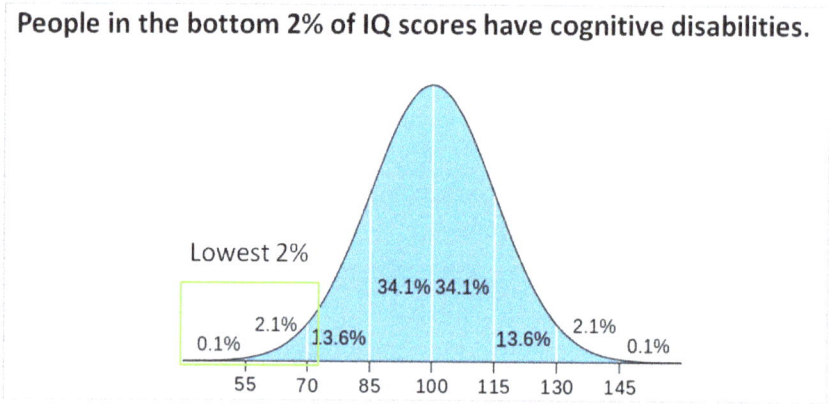

Figure 8.2: The application of Gestalt laws to a powerpoint slide

Such deliberate application of Gestalt grouping principles can usefully convey important information about relationships in a way that seems effortless and intuitive to the audience.

A second example of using Gestalt grouping principles to make understanding intuitive and effortless is shown in Figure 8.3. This figure shows three forms of long-term memory with examples, and also shows these three forms relate to each other. The types are grouped into unconscious (implicit; orange outline) and conscious (declarative or explicit; blue outline) memories by using different color coding for each type. The two forms of declarative memory are grouped by positioning them close together (the Gestalt law of proximity) and using the same color lines for the related forms (the Gestalt law of similarity). In contrast, the procedural (or implicit) memory category seems different because it is positioned farther from the others and has a different color. In all of the specific examples, a box around the text and the associated icon helps to group these together via the Gestalt law of common region. Using the visual system's ability to group information in this matter will make the different ideas and their relationships to each other seem natural and obvious to the students. Designing such intuitive educational images does take some careful planning and intentional decisions about applying the grouping laws in a manner that is conducive to learning.

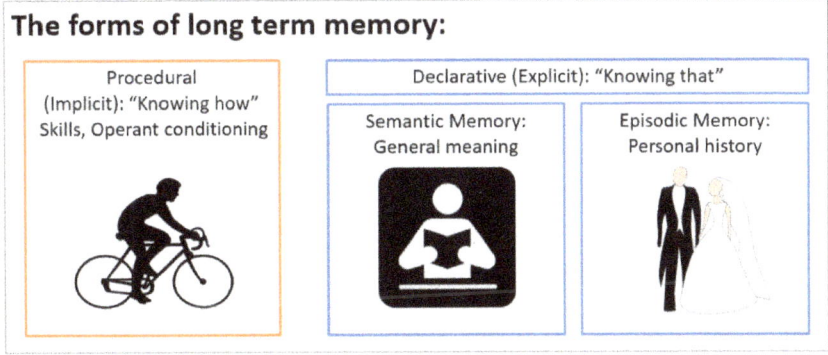

Figure 8.3: Using the Gestalt laws of perception to facilitate understanding of conceptual relationships. The iconic images are from pixabay.com and have open licenses for reproduction.

Animation and Motion Perception

A second perceptual function is the ability to understand and appreciate movement in our environment. Motion perception begins with cells in the retina that are specialized for detecting motion. The processing of motion information continues all the way to the higher order areas of cerebral cortex, where some brain areas—called V5 or MT—specialize in the understanding of motion. The ability to perceive motion contributes greatly to our ability to survive in a dynamic environment. We are able to accurately judge the speed of oncoming cars and use this information to judge when it is safe to cross the street. Motion perception is a way of noticing and understanding the changes that occur in an ever-changing environment.

In education, the use of animated presentations has been investigated as a way of promoting learning by using our built-in ability to perceive motion. The "motion paths" feature in PowerPoint allows users to take objects, like squares or circles, and make them move in certain paths that are defined by the presentation author. This form of animation has potential instructional value by guiding students through a complicated process in a step by step manner. Instructors can also use animations to gradually build complexity in diagrams by adding features in a progressive fashion. This gradual building of information assists comprehension by decreasing the possibility of cognitive overload (Kosslyn, 2007). Another instructional use of animation is to promote the understanding of three-dimensional structures through the use of movement. For example, instructors can promote a deeper understanding of anatomy by displaying a three-dimensional model of brain anatomy through an animation that rotates brain images on the screen.

Is animation an effective teaching tool? A review of studies that use animated multimedia for teaching reveals mixed results: some studies suggest improved learning with animation, whereas other studies show no improvement (Fisk, 2008). A closer inspection of the research results suggests why animation is not always a successful instructional tool. Animated instructional materials seem to work best when the animations are closely aligned with the instructional goals (Rieber, 1996). An effective use of instructional animation is to show how relationships between the parts in a complex system change over time. For example, Treleven and colleagues developed a set of instructional animations for teaching operations management (Treleven, Penlesky, Callarman, Watts, and Bragg, 2012, 2014). They divided these instructional animations into two categories: quantitative technique examples and concepts. The technique examples included topics such as the computation of project time, project completion dates, safety stock/reorder points, and materials requirements planning. Examples of concept animations included group technology, project network diagrams, quality cost theory graphs, and Six Sigma quality graphs. The student opinion was that these complex instructional animations were valuable for learning. This example is a noteworthy illustration because it shows that animation can be beneficial for illustrating highly specific instructional concepts.

Contrary to the above, some animations seem to have little to no educational benefit (Fisk, 2008). A good example comes from a study that used an animated, Einstein-like character called "Dr. Phyz" to narrate an educational animation on the ways the electric motors work (Mayer, Dow, and Mayer, 2003). A control group of students saw the same educational animation but without the animated Dr. Phyz character. The results from this study showed no learning differences between the groups, indicating that the presence of the animated Dr. Phyz character did not promote student learning. Studies like this show that motion, by itself, is not enough to produce better learning outcomes. The reason for this failure is that animations like the Dr. Phyz character are basically content-free. Only animated motions that are be closely tied to the educational content will produce real learning gains.

The term "animation" in PowerPoint presentations does not refer to the educational animations described above. Instead, PowerPoint animation usually refers to specific software features that are meant to add a dramatic quality to the presentation. Animation is commonly used for bullet point effects, such as bullet points that zoom into the screen or appear when the presenter clicks on the mouse. Some animation effects can even be used to create movement in the background of the slide, such as graphics of moving gears. Other examples of movement in powerpoint include slide transitions, such as dissolve and fade effects that are triggered when the presenter advances the presentation to a new slide. Unfortunately, these content-free forms of animation probably will not produce a positive educational impact on students, just like the Dr. Phyz example. The reason is simple: There is no educational content to be gained from a zooming bullet point.

A powerpoint animation feature that has been the topic of some debate is the use of animation to make bullet points appear one-by-one at the appropriate time in the speaker's delivery, and thereby keep the speaker in control of the pace of slide information. This animation feature is variously referred to as presenting bullet points "on-click" or the gradual build technique. The advocates for this technique cite several advantages. Cognitive psychology evidence suggests this form of animation could be beneficial because it prevents students from being overwhelmed with too much information at once (Kosslyn, 2007). The on-click delivery of slide information can more closely match the speaker's verbal delivery, which prevents students from getting ahead of the speaker. Also, student survey studies suggest a preference for slides that gradually build-up bullet points over slides that introduce all of the points at once (Apperson et al., 2006; Blokzijl and Naeff, 2004; Kask, 2004).

There are also some strong reasons for not using on-click animations to control the appearance of bullet points. Experiments conducted by Mahar and colleagues found that animated bullet point lists that gradually build had harmful effects on student learning (Mahar, Yaylacicegi, and Janicki, 2009a, 2009b). Some presentation experts also oppose the practice of using animation to control the appearance of bullet points. Tufte describes this practice as "the dreaded slow reveal" after which "the audience flees" (Tufte, 2006, p. 6). Another presentation expert feels that the gradual building of bullet points is "tiresome" and "painful" (Alley, 2013, pp. 146, 152).

Overall, it seems that using animation to control the appearance of bullet point list items cannot be recommended, particularly because this practice may have detrimental effects on learning (Mahar et al., 2009a, 2009b). The reason for using a gradual build-up of bullet points or complex information is to prevent giving the students so much information at one time as to overwhelm their cognitive capacities. Perhaps the real problem, though, is that the slide simply holds too much information to begin with. In these situations, the use of animation to reduce cognitive overload doesn't really address the root of the problem. Dividing the excessive content of one complicated slide into multiple slides seems preferable to trying to remedy this situation with animations that gradually build the slide content.

Using motion perception in practical ways can help students understand complex relationships that change over time or the three-dimensional qualities of objects; for instance, seeing a complex system in motion can help students better understand how the parts might work together. However, animations need to convey useful information. Empty animations are more of a distraction than a benefit.

Perceiving Quantity through Graphs

Visual perception enables people to estimate size and quantity. This ability is evident in young children, even before the children can count. For example, toddlers and young children are quick to point out which cookie is the largest, as any parent knows. Experimental psychologists have even found that people are able to do simple counting from just a brief glimpse of information (Mandler and Shebo, 1982).

Statisticians have long appreciated this built-in perceptual ability to judge quantities and relationships. Data that is expressed in visual form like a graph can be much easier and more intuitive to comprehend than data that is listed as numbers in tables. Therefore, complex data sets are often expressed in graphs or other visual representations to promote communication and understanding (Tufte, 1990, 1997, 2001).

Many people feel that making graphs is simple. Perhaps they feel this way because they have been making graphs since third or fourth grade and they regularly see graphs in the news.

Another reason why people view graphs as being simple is that the visual system makes the interpretation of graphs feel effortless. However, this common view that "graphs are simple" is somewhat inaccurate, especially in regard to the creation of good graphs. Although statistical graphics are based on data, the effective use of graphs also depends strongly upon good design and visual perception. Unfortunately, it is easy to create graphs that confuse or even mislead people. Most people overestimate their abilities to make good graphs, so a few pointers are in order for making the most of statistical graphics.

A good starting point to consider is the powerpoint medium. Most of your audience will simply not be able to see fine details in your graph. Therefore, the graphs in powerpoint presentations will need to have large, bold elements such as big columns, large text, and saturated colors. Fine details will not work well because the audience simply will not be able to see it. There is a trade-off between complexity and visibility. As the complexity increases, the visibility of the graphics will decrease, as will the value of the graphics for promoting understanding. This need for simple, bold graphs poses no problem for small data sets or basic relationships. The problem arises when data sets are large and complex. It can be difficult to make good powerpoint graphs from complex data, as noted by Tufte's scathing review of powerpoint (2006).

The teacher who needs to convey complex data in a graph has some difficult choices to make. The teacher can simplify statistical graphics to fit into powerpoint, but this approach risks an oversimplification of the statistical evidence. A second possibility is to use complex statistical graphics in the powerpoint presentation, recognizing that this is done at the risk of overwhelming the comprehension abilities of the audience. A third possibility, which Tufte (2006) recommends, is to put complex statistical graphics into a paper handout for the audience. Paper-based graphics have a higher resolution than powerpoint, which will help the audience understand small details or complex situations. Additionally, instructors can include supplemental or explanatory details on the paper handout without overcomplicating the information on the powerpoint slides.

Once instructors address the resolution problem, they must still make a number of crucial design choices. Many graphs can be faulted for problems with the axes. For most bar or line graphs, it is best to use a Y axis (vertical) that is slightly shorter than the X axis (horizontal) because the length of vertical lines tends to be overestimated (Kosslyn, 1985). Another common Y axis problem is the scaling. The best approach is to start the scale at zero and go up. In practice, many graphs start with scales that are well above zero, which causes viewers to overestimate the magnitude of change or difference between categories. Yet another axis problem occurs when the graph maker fails to put labels on the axis. For powerpoint, doing so may not pose much of a problem during the presentation because the presenter can verbally tell the audience about the scales, although it is still advisable to label the graph's axes for the sake of clarity. The axis labels need to be present in order to make the graph work in a stand-alone document. The presence of labels on graphs might also be helpful for students who are taking notes about the slide.

Powerpoint features can also tempt users into making poor design choices about their graphs. A potential problem is turning two-dimensional bar graphs or pie charts into three-dimensional graphics (Mackiewicz, 2007b). The addition of a three-dimensional effect is meant to add visual interest to the graph and make it more appealing to the audience. The problem, however, is that the three-dimensional qualities of the bars or pie chart slices may create distortions that interfere with the understanding of the relationships represented by the statistical graphics. The recommendation for powerpoint graphs is to resist the temptation to turn two-dimensional statistical graphs into three-dimensional graphs (Mackiewicz, 2007b). Instructors can achieve visual interest in the graph by using cool colors (e.g., blue, green) that contrast with the background of the slide (e.g., white) rather than using unnecessary three-dimensional effects (Mackiewicz, 2007b). The recommendation to avoid unnecessary three-dimensional special effects, notably, is not universally shared by all graph perception experts. Some evidence suggests that the addition of three-dimensional effects has a minimal influence on graph comprehension (Kosslyn, 2007; Shah and Hoeffner, 2002; Zacks, Levy, Tversky, and Schiano, 1998).

One of Tufte's concerns about graphs is the general tendency for presenters to feel that charts are intrinsically boring, which creates a motivation to improve the chart in some way to make it more interesting or appealing to the audience. Some presenters add unnecessary graphics to improve the visual interest of the charts and "jazz it up." Tufte famously coined the term "chartjunk" (Tufte, 2001, p. 107) to describe this phenomenon of adding unnecessary artwork or pointless graph features, including unnecessary three-dimensional effects. His view is that chartjunk can harm the content of a statistical graphic by making readers draw the wrong conclusions or miss the main point of a relationship. Instructors do not need to embellish the basic features of a chart just to add interest. The emotion should come from the presenter rather than gratuitous, unnecessary graphics.

Design Goal: Use Perception to Make Ideas Intuitive

Vision is an information-rich sense for human beings. The visual perception centers of the brain automatically and effortlessly process visual information. From the workings of these brain centers, we can simply intuit relationships and quantities. These abilities are amazing, but they are largely taken for granted. Teachers should instead attempt to use these visual perception strengths to make ideas more intuitive to students. Teachers can use Gestalt principles to indicate relationships, instructional animations to help students visualize complex changes that occur over time, and graphs that convey quantitative information in an accessible manner.

Human beings are largely unaware of how they process perceptual information. Therefore, such effective use of instructional graphics requires some deliberate design effort and creativity on the part of the presenter. By doing so, our instructional aids become more intuitive. Indeed, the goal for teachers using powerpoint presentations is to use graphical examples that can almost teach by themselves without any assistance from the instructor.

DESIGN FOR PERCEPTION II

Assertion-Evidence Slides and Educational Images

> Bullets allow us to skip the thinking step, genially tricking ourselves into supposing that we have planned when, in fact, we've only listed some good things to do. (Shaw, Brown, and Bromiley, 1998, p. 42)

Anyone who regularly sees powerpoint presentations can tell you that slides with bullet point lists are the heart and soul of most presentations. Studies of the slide formats used in powerpoint presentations confirm the heavy emphasis on bullet points. One study of slides from 117 presentations found that approximately two-thirds of the slides in the body of the presentation contained a bullet point list (Garner, Alley, Gaudelli, and Zappe, 2009). A similar analysis of fifty-eight presentations showed that 60.5% of the slides included bullet point lists (Pötzsch, 2007 as cited in Knoblauch, 2012).

The bullet point list is clearly the standard slide layout for modern presentations, a kind of cultural convention. The word "point" in "powerpoint" even suggests an association with the bullet point list.

The bullet point list format may have some significant drawbacks even though it is a standard used in millions of presentations. An early criticism of the bullet point list was made by Gordon Shaw and other managers at the 3M Corporation (Shaw et al., 1998). They suspected that their business plans "failed to reflect deep thought or to inspire commitment" (p. 42) due to the excessive use of bullet point lists. An internal review of hundreds of 3M business plans suggested problems that originated with the bullet point list format. Bullet point items often tend to be vague goals such as "increase sales" rather than specific ideas. They also found that bulleted lists often lack clarity about relationships and omitted important assumptions. Shaw and colleagues concluded that bullet point formats tend to oversimplify business plans and thereby compromise deep thought. These concerns are similar to criticisms raised by other powerpoint critics (e.g., Frommer, 2012; Tufte, 2006).

We will now closely examine the bullet point list slide layout and consider some alternatives that might be more effective for educators. The teaching goal should be to use fewer bullet point lists and, when these are used, to employ them in a judicious manner. We will also examine alternative slide formats that may help educators escape the fragmentation of thought that may occur when complex ideas are converted into tiny bullet points.

Making Better Bullet Point Slides

Let's begin the discussion of slide formats by considering the problems that bullet points can introduce. With a sense of irony, here are common problems with bullet point list slides presented in a bullet point list format:

- Short, vague phrases
- Too much text
- Poor visibility
- Too many bullet points
- Reduced space for graphics

Given all of these problems, you can see why some presentation experts have suggested completely dropping bullet point lists.

Various rules have been proposed for making bullet point lists more effective. A common suggestion is 6x6 or 7x7 rules, in which the first number refers to the maximum number of bullet points per slide and the second number refers to the maximum number of words per bullet point. Other word limit recommendations include using no more than three words in each bullet point (Altman, 2012) or that the entire slide should have no more than six words (Godin, 2001). The problem with such recommendations is that these rules seem to lack a strong empirical justification (Blokzijl and Andeweg, 2005). No clear reason explains why a slide must be limited to seven bullet points that have seven words each, a fact which makes the recommended limits rather arbitrary. These rules seem to generally suggest that having a small amount of concise text tends to be more effective than having many items with lots of text (Yue et al., 2013; however, see also Blokzijl and Andeweg, 2005).

Altogether, the evidence and recommendations from presentation experts encourage presenters to reduce the usage of bullet point lists. A limit of four bullet points is a good recommendation based on the limitations of visual short-term memory (Kosslyn, 2007). In addition, limiting the length of each bullet item to no more than three words will be much more effective than using long passages (Altman, 2012). Keeping each bullet point item short will also make the bullet points a true list rather than some kind of hybrid list/narrative format. These recommendations are in general agreement with multimedia learning theories stipulating that excessive on-screen text is detrimental to learning. Keeping bullet point lists short, in both number of bullets and length of bullets, will eliminate a common source of information overload in powerpoint presentations.

The Assertion-Evidence Slide Format

Michael Alley is an engineer and communications expert who has worked towards reimagining the basic layout of the powerpoint slide. His work was inspired by early efforts from the field of engineering (R. Perry, 1978) and from working with graduate students at Virginia Tech and Penn State. His view is that presentations that are based upon standard powerpoint conventions like bullet point lists are often ineffective. His conclusion is that a better slide layout is needed.

Alley's redesigned slide layout is called the assertion-evidence format, or sometimes the "headline style" slide. This slide design horizontally splits the powerpoint slide into two major parts, the upper and lower part of the slide. The assertion part of the slide at the top uses a complete sentence that directly states the key idea of the slide. The assertion text should be a "short sentence headline, left-justified, and no more than two lines" (Alley, 2013, p. 129). The assertion can be a hypothesis, a research finding, or a direct statement. In contrast, the lower part of the slide is for evidence: "a supporting image, such as a photograph, drawing, or graph." (p. 129). The purpose of the image is to reinforce the idea from the assertion part of the slide. An important feature for the evidence part is to keep the evidence visual in nature, such as graphs and images. Bullet point lists of evidence are discouraged.

Figure 9.1 is an example of a slide with a standard bullet point list slide layout and how this slide might be redone in the assertion-evidence format. A slide with a standard topic-subtopic layout from an Introductory Psychology course appears on the left. It contains the usual powerpoint slide features: a short phrase heading (topic), points, and subpoints (subtopics). A slide similar to this example is probably used by hundreds of psychology teachers in Introductory Psychology courses.

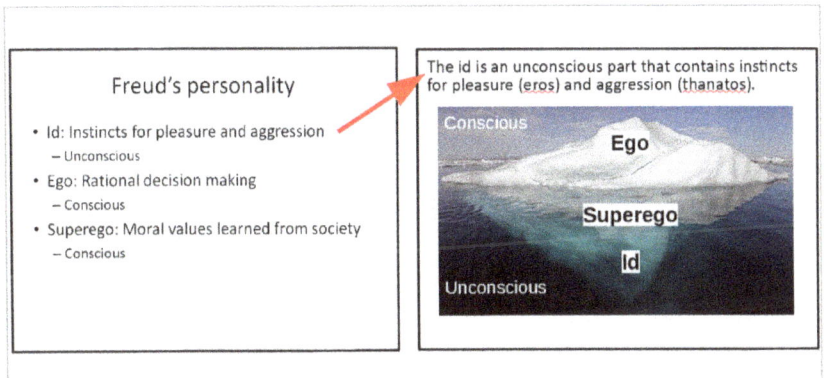

Figure 9.1: Comparison of the topic-subtopic and the assertion-evidence slide formats. The iceberg image was contributed to Wikimedia by user AWeith, who released the image under a Creative Commons license. It is reproduced from commons.wikimedia.org.

Let's begin our critique of the standard slide layout by starting with the title. The problem is that this title is not very informative. The students were probably told at the beginning of the presentation that this presentation would be about Sigmund

Freud's ideas about personality, so the instructor has no reason to repeat this information again in the slide heading. Also, students may misinterpret the slide's title to refer to Freud's own personality and not his theory of the structure of personality in general. The instructor can safely delete this title without removing any important content from the presentation. The body of the slide is also problematic. It comprises a total of six bullet points, which is probably too many. The descriptions of the key terms are short and fragmentary rather than being complete ideas.

The right side of Figure 9.1 shows how the top bullet point and subpoint have been turned into an assertion-evidence slide. The first bullet point was made into an assertion statement (top) that communicates the main idea of the slide in a complete sentence. This statement communicates the more complete thought that the bullet points were based upon. To make room for this assertion sentence, we had to move the title field up and stretch it horizontally, as well as reducing the size of the font. The increased title space provided some freedom to add new information about the id from the subpoint. The evidence part of the slide (bottom) is an iceberg image based on Freud's analogy that the personality structure is like an iceberg. Immediately, we can see that this slide is highly attractive and visually interesting compared to the basic bullet point layout, even though the slide formatting is a very simple black text on white. Students may be intrigued by this image—Why is there an iceberg on this slide?—and this intrigue may help to increase student engagement. With this slide, the instructor can discuss the basic characteristics of the id, and then segue nicely into Freud's analogy to illustrate how the id relates to consciousness. (In brief, the above-water parts of the iceberg are analogous to the small and limited conscious mind, but the larger and more powerful below-water parts of the iceberg are like the unconscious mind.) Note how the iceberg graphic will support and complement the assertion made at the top of the slide. The iceberg image, with labels in the appropriate places, will help the instructor explain this famous analogy to the students. The labels on this slide have been formatted for high contrast (white text on dark backgrounds and vice versa) to facilitate reading. The image gives the instructor something interesting and memorable to discuss with the students.

Altogether, the assertion-evidence slide is much more information rich than the bullet point formatted slide, with more details about one bullet point item. This new information is not overwhelming though, at least partly because some of the information is presented as an image rather than text. The assertion-evidence slide is less likely to overload students because it contains less text than the bullet point formatted slide: fifteen words vs. twenty-one words, respectively.

We also need to consider the information omitted from the assertion-evidence slide. We removed the title from the slide with the bullet point layout because it was unimportant, redundant, and ambiguous. We can eliminate the subpoints of how each part of the personality relates to consciousness by working this information into the assertion sentences. This change makes it more cohesive. Finally, fancy colors and slide design graphics were eliminated to decrease potential distractions. The instructional graphic generates sufficient visual interest. The lack of extraneous information from unnecessary colors and decorations makes the students be more focused and avoids a short-term memory burden.

The assertion-evidence slide in Figure 9.1 also left out the bullet point information about the other personality parts (ego and superego). The information from the second and third bullet points of the standard slide can become headlines for two new slides with the assertion-evidence layout. The coverage of one point per slide will help keep the class focused on the part under discussion (the id in this example) and thus keep the pace of the lecture on track. Students have no opportunity to be distracted by getting ahead of the teacher. In this example, the students will not be writing down information about the ego (main bullet point #2) and superego (point #3) while the teacher is still discussing the id (point #1). Presenting one idea on a slide in this manner will help to avoid information overload.

A second example of an assertion-evidence formatted slide appears in Figure 9.2. In this example, the key idea—an increasing autism diagnosis rate—is clearly stated for the students at the top of the slide. This assertion is supported by a graph based on data from the Centers for Disease Control. The graphic helps the speaker make an important point about the degree of change. The use of a colored arrow directs attention towards the most critical part of the graph. The upward direction of the arrow accentuates the increase and makes understanding the graph more intuitive for the audience. Another positive feature is that the graphic is more visually appealing and interesting than bullet points. It might even be interesting enough to become a common point of discussion between the speaker and the audience. Finally, note how the slide formatting is very plain in order to focus everyone's attention on the message.

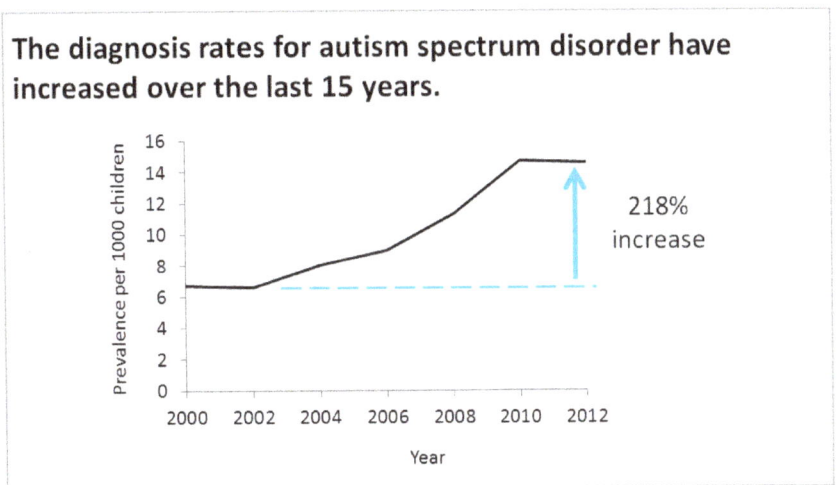

Figure 9.2: A second example of a slide with the assertion-evidence format

Alley gives the following guidelines for the assertion part of the assertion-evidence slide layout (Alley, 2013, pp. 131–132). Note the emphasis on readability.

1. Keep the headline to no more than two lines.
2. Left justify the headline for easier reading
3. Capitalize the headline as you would a sentence.
4. If the headline goes more than one line, break the first line such that phrases stay together for easier reading.
5. For formatting, the recommendation is for a 28-point, sans serif font (e.g., Arial, Calibri, or Helvetica) in bold.

The sentence structure of the assertion-evidence slide is also important to maximize audience comprehension. Presenters need to aim for a concise, direct, and clear writing style for the headline statements. Active voice sentences, in which the subject of the sentence performs an action, are preferred over passive voice sentences.

For the evidence part of the assertion-evidence slide, Alley recommends visual features such as ". . . photographs, drawings, diagrams, graphs, films, equations, or short tables" (Alley, 2013, p. 131). In contrast, the use of text, including bullet point lists, should be avoided or minimized. Using images in this space will have a greater impact on the audience than presenting more words. This evidence area also gives teachers the opportunity to pair visual images with text statements and achieve the synergistic benefits of multimedia learning. Although the use of text in the evidence area is generally discouraged, strategically placed key words in this part of the slide can be helpful guides that highlight important features. For example, complex diagrams may need labels that serve as orienting cues for the important elements of the visual evidence.

It's worth noting that the assertion-evidence layout was developed to specifically meet the needs of science and engineering instruction. The evidence used in these STEM disciplines has a mostly visual basis. In contrast, faculty members who teach English and foreign language courses have informed me that text rather than images would be the subject matter for the evidence part of their slides. It seems likely that the assertion-evidence format could be successfully adapted to language-focused courses. In these situations, the assertion statement would, for example, convey a writing principle to the students. The evidence part of the slide would be examples of sentences that illustrate the principle from the assertion statement. The instructor would use these example sentences from the evidence part of the slide to support the discussion of the writing principle. It might be a good practice in these situations to provide students with a brief period of time to silently read through the example sentences in order to reduce the possibility of cognitive overload. This suggested use of assertion-evidence in the humanities would need further research to determine if it is an effective approach.

The assertion-evidence format has numerous advantages. One benefit for the speaker is increased focus. The process of summarizing the main idea of the slide in the assertion forces the speaker to fully develop the key components of the message. A second benefit is that the assertion-evidence style allows the presenter to make a clearer statement about the thesis of the slide. The audience benefits from the assertion because important assumptions and relationships can be expressed more clearly in a single sentence than several bullet point list items.

Although writing an assertion as a full sentence might seem rather wordy, the assertion-evidence slide layout tends to have less text overall than slides with the standard bullet point list. An assertion-evidence slide has more space for visual images compared to a standard slide that has a title, bullet points, and a graphic area. Making the images larger improves the visibility of the graphics and increases the overall emotional impact that the slide might have on the audience. These changes improve the effectiveness of both the text and the image information.

A variation on the assertion-evidence format that may be especially useful for teaching is the evidence-assertion sequence (Alley, 2013). The first slide in the evidence-assertion sequence poses a question, in headline format, along with visual evidence. The visual evidence might be a graph, table, or other graphic display of information. The instructor asks the students to answer the question posed in the slide headline by using the visual evidence provided in the slide. This question leads to a dialogue between the instructor and students about the idea that the graph might demonstrate. The second slide in the sequence contains the answer, in the headline format again, along with the same visual evidence, thereby providing closure to the question posed in the first slide of the sequence. This clever approach increases active learning and student engagement.

Given the strengths of the assertion-evidence slide format, slides using this format should result in better learning and higher test scores than slides containing standard bullet point lists. Positive evidence supports their educational effectiveness. A pioneering study evaluated the educational impact of assertion-evidence slides by comparing these to standard powerpoint slides in an undergraduate Geology class (Alley, Schreiber, and Muffo, 2005). The students who received the assertion-evidence style slides performed better on select multiple-choice final exam questions (82% correct) compared to students from previous semesters who received the standard powerpoint format (71% correct). In addition, student attitudes towards the assertion-evidence slide format were positive, with the assertion-evidence style slides being preferred by a greater than seven to one ratio. Subsequent studies by Alley and colleagues replicated these findings of better exam performance with the assertion-evidence formatted slides (Alley, Schreiber, Ramsdell, and Muffo, 2006; Diesel, Alley, Schreiber, and Borrego, 2006; Garner and Alley, 2013; Wolfe, Alley, and Sheridan, 2006).

A number of reasons explain why the assertion-evidence slide layout is superior to the typical bullet point list layout. The assertion-evidence layout represents the epitome of multimedia learning by combining a statement (text) with a supporting and informative visual image. Using headlines that contain complete thoughts may also be beneficial. A sentence headline can clearly communicate and organize key ideas better than a short phrase title, which is an example of the signaling principle of multimedia learning (C. Atkinson and Mayer, 2004). Headlines may also help because the key idea of the slide is not mixed together with bullet list items of varying importance in the body of the slide (Alley et al., 2006). The assertion-evidence layout guidelines also recommend reducing the overall amount of text on the slide (consistent with the modality principle of multimedia learning) and eliminating unnecessary slide features (consistent with the coherence principle), both of which are beneficial practices.

Finally, the assertion-evidence structure, in its essence, reflects scientific thinking. The assertion sentence is similar to a hypothesis. The evidence part of the slide resembles the results of an experiment. These two elements combine in a meaningful way to make each assertion-evidence slide a miniature example of the scientific method (ideas and supporting evidence). In this manner, the assertion-evidence format might engage deeper thinking processes than the usual bullet point list slide layout.

The assertion-evidence format has a great deal of promise for educators. Unfortunately, the educational effectiveness of the assertion-evidence slide format has received little attention outside of the field of engineering. We clearly need more research evidence to fully establish the educational effectiveness of the assertion-evidence slide format, especially in disciplines other than the natural sciences and engineering.

Assertion Titles with Bullet Point Lists

An important inspiration for the assertion-evidence format was the observation that standard slide titles with large fonts (e.g., 44-point) are very short, which leads to uninformative, brief titles (Alley, 2013). In contrast, assertion statements are based on complete ideas rather than sentence fragments. This general assertion-evidence idea, that the titles should be complete thoughts, may be useful for slide layouts that use bullet point lists. Consider the following example in Figure 9.3 which has a sentence structure that is left unfinished. The bullet items effectively complete the thought started in the assertion. In this way, the combination of assertion and completing bullet points makes the slide into a series of three coherent ideas. Another variation on this idea is that the sentence in the assertion could be a question with a blank in place of a key term, and the bullet point items could be the potential solutions. This would make the slide into a multiple-choice question, which could benefit assessing student comprehension.

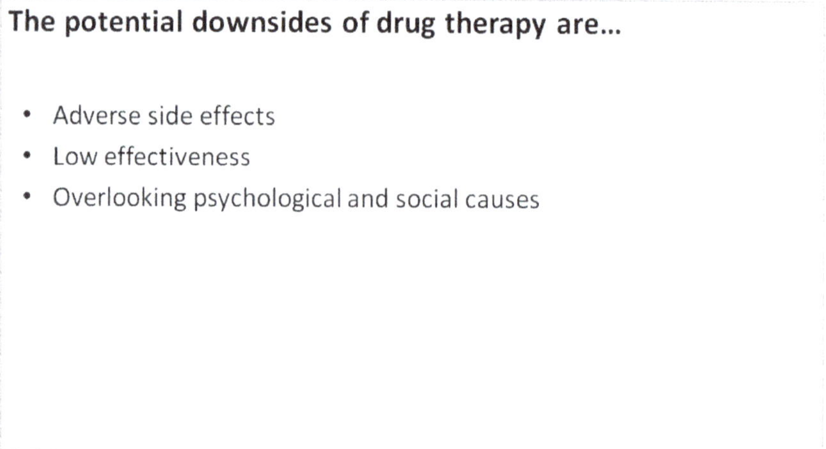

The potential downsides of drug therapy are...

- Adverse side effects
- Low effectiveness
- Overlooking psychological and social causes

Figure 9.3: A hybrid style of an assertion title with a bullet point list.

Alley (2013) recommends against the use of bullet points in the evidence part of the assertion-evidence format. The present example suggests, however, that using an assertion statement with a bullet point list might be a significant improvement over the standard bullet point slide layout. No research to date specifically compares the educational value of assertion titles with bullet point lists to the shorter standard titles used in most presentations.

Eliminating Text with the Graphic-Only Slide

A general guiding principle for making good powerpoint presentations is that too much text on a slide typically has negative effects on the audience. In general, less text is better. This raises an interesting possibility: How far could we go in eliminating text? Would it be worthwhile to completely eliminate all of the text and just use instructional images?

Research on multimedia learning has investigated the role of on-screen text in educational materials and provides some informative answers. A consistent finding from research studies is that on-screen text that duplicates the information provided by narration leads to lower scores on tests that involve higher-order thinking skills. These findings form the basis of the redundancy principle: "People learn more deeply from graphics and narration than from graphics, narration, and printed text" (Mayer, 2009; see also Sweller et al., 1998). Another form of redundancy can occur in situations that have two forms of word-based information, such as narration plus written words, presented at the same time without instructional graphics (Moreno and Mayer, 2002).

The problem posed by redundancy—the same words presented by both narration and visual text—bears a striking resemblance to a typical powerpoint presentation. In many powerpoint presentations, the speaker provides the audience with the same words through vision (on-screen) and hearing (spoken) at the same time. Therefore, the standard powerpoint presentation closely resembles the redundancy situation studied in the lab. Applying the redundancy principle to powerpoint presentations suggests that the best format might be to use powerpoint primarily for showing instructional graphics. Text should be used sparingly, possibly as cues for important points, or not at all. In other words, a good instructional slide could focus entirely on instructional images (no text) with the explanatory words coming entirely from the teacher's voice.

The idea of using slides that emphasize instructional graphics also has support from presentation experts who recommend using full-screen graphics and as little text as possible. The presentation design books *Presentation Zen* (Reynolds, 2008) and *Slide:ology* (Duarte, 2008) contain many examples of presentation slides that are predominantly images with little-to-no text. These large images support the speaker's main points but do not overwhelm the audience with unnecessary on-screen text. Alley calls the full-screen graphic slide the "TED slide structure" after the popular educational video series. It is characterized by "few words (if any) and powerful images that often fill the screen" (Alley, 2013, p. 184). This format might be particularly useful when scientific experts communicate their research findings to the general public.

Only a few studies have scientifically tested the educational effectiveness of emphasizing images over words in slide content.

One study examined the educational effects of slides that had short sentences integrated with evocative images (Johnson & Christensen, 2011). The study compared students who received the "simplified-visually rich" (p. 294) slides to students who received a standard bullet point format. Student interest was increased for the simplified-visually rich format slides, but their performance on examinations was the same as students in a condition that received the standard bullet point list format. Another study compared a group of students who received a standard powerpoint presentation (bullet point lists) to students who received powerpoint slide graphics that varied in the degree of relevance to the topic (Tangen et al., 2011). Students who received the presentations with images had higher interest in the topic than students in the text condition, suggesting that students prefer images over bullet points. Not surprisingly, student performance was lowest in the conditions with the least relevant graphical images. These studies show that images are an effective way of increasing student interest in a topic, but, again, the images must be highly relevant to the educational content in order to promote learning. Images that are evocative yet irrelevant may be ineffective or possibly even harmful due to producing distractions or seductive detail effects.

One research study has investigated the educational outcomes of replacing bullet point lists entirely with relevant instructional graphics. Holstead compared course sections taught with the standard powerpoint slide formats (i.e., bullet point lists and instructional graphics) to other sections of the course taught with slides containing only instructional graphics (i.e., no bullet point lists; Holstead, 2015). The student performance on exams was the same for the first two exams, but the graphics-only sections did better than the standard powerpoint sections on the final exam. Student feedback in the graphics-only course was more positive than the standard powerpoint condition in regards to "general intellectual development, instructor-student relationship, importance and relevance, and overall perceptions of the course" (p. 345). In addition, students in the graphics-only sections found the course to be easier and reported paying more attention due to the slide format. The instructor also felt that the flow and pacing of the lecture were improved with the graphics-only slides. There were, for example, no requests to go back to the previous slide because someone was struggling to write down all the text. These results show that the elimination of bullet point lists seemed to produce a neutral to weakly beneficial effect on exam scores, and a positive benefit on student perceptions of the lectures. Intriguingly, student performance was not harmed by the complete elimination of bullet point lists.

The findings of the Holstead study are consistent with laboratory findings on multimedia learning. The student feedback that the course was "easier" without bullet point lists may indicate that they experienced less of a short-term memory cognitive load. Students might find it easier to pay attention to the instructor's voice when they face no bullet point list to copy down. In addition, the absence of a bullet point list in Holstead's (2015) study may have promoted active learning. The increased student need for active engagement with the teacher may have occurred, in part, because the students were not provided with online access to the powerpoint file or some other form of instructor notes. The student note-taking effort was entirely dependent upon listening closely to the instructor and developing a personal understanding of the key points for note-taking.

The use of images may also have beneficial effects for promoting student-teacher interactions. Class discussion can be improved when the slides emphasize instructional images or assertion-evidence slides with large images (Kahn, 2007; Maxwell, 2007). These increased student-teacher interactions might occur because the image projected on the screen can become a common point of discussion between the presenter and the audience (Knoblauch, 2012). This evidence suggests that instructional images might be more effective than bullet point list items for promoting classroom discussion. Possible explanations for this might be increased emotion from images or possibly because the students are not preoccupied with writing down all of the text in their notes. Further research will be necessary to explore these possibilities.

Surveys of student opinions about powerpoint features also suggest a preference for less text (Apperson et al., 2006). The best teaching styles in one study were associated with using a wide range of features in their powerpoint slide decks, including photos, charts, graphics, sound, and animation (Brock and Joglekar, 2011). Their recommendation for teachers was to use slides that are light in text (three bullet points or twenty words per slide) and to add visual elements to text slides (Brock and Joglekar, 2011).

In summary, the research findings suggest interesting possibilities for the role of instructional graphics. Slides that focus on educational images rather than bullet points stimulate a higher degree of student interest. Again, these images must be highly relevant instructional graphics that support the verbal message from the instructor. The effects of these image-focused slides on student achievement, however, must be cautiously interpreted as neutral to slightly beneficial. Still, these preliminary findings are encouraging possibilities that go beyond a bullet point list layout. Perhaps these image-focused slides would be a good option to use after bullet point lists, especially in the middle of a class when student interest and attention may be waning.

Breaking Free from Bullet Points

The typical bullet point list layouts of powerpoint slides have guided millions of slide presentations. Although the bullet point format is a widely used standard, the evidence suggests that the slides produced with this layout are weak and ineffective presentation aids. These presentations may have a slick, professional look with the bullet points and accompanying decorations, but at their heart bullet points often lack the intellectual substance that the presenter and audience desperately need. Alley urges presenters to go beyond the common use of bullet point lists and other standard powerpoint approaches. His view is nicely captured in this short phrase about the default values of powerpoint, such as bullet point lists: "We can do better." (Gilbert, 2015). Like Alley suggests, teachers should aim to do better by avoiding the overuse of bullet point lists, a practice that seems to be a common cause of presentation mediocrity.

From this review, we can generally conclude that relevant instructional images, such as diagrams, charts, and pictures, that support the instructional message may have a stronger educational benefit than a multitude of bullet points lists. There are several advantages. Instructional images can convey a higher degree of information to an audience than written text without causing a cognitive overload problem. Informative images can complement and support the spoken word in many different ways, and thereby provide an educational benefit that goes beyond words. The use of images also promotes more student engagement than a bullet point list format.

A good starting point for improvement is to decrease the text and number of bullet points on slides, aiming for a maximum of four bullet points per slide and keeping the text of these bullet points limited to short phrases. After this initial effort, the next step is to convert bullet point list items into separate slides in an assertion-evidence format or a graphic-only format. Perhaps it would be enough to simply sprinkle a few graphics-only slides between existing bullet point slides. Switching to assertion-evidence formatted slides can be difficult at first, but this extra effort is well worth the time and energy. Students will experience this method of teaching as being effortless and even fun compared to the usual endless lists that they typically receive.

DESIGN FOR ATTENTION

Focusing on the Information That Matters

"A good teacher, like a good entertainer, first must hold his audience's attention, then he can teach his lesson." John Henrik Clarke

Basic sensory and perception processes are important first steps. However, a third fundamental process must also take place before learning can occur. This third process is attention. Teachers are intuitively aware of the importance of attention. It is well known that students who are off task, like daydreaming, are learning little or nothing. Additionally, cognitive psychology research has consistently demonstrated that failing to pay attention to information, whether when initially learning it or when attempting to solidify it in memory, results in poor recall. In other words, sometimes we fail to remember information not because we forgot it, but because we never paid enough attention to it in the first place.

The following widely-cited quote on attention is from William James, who was one of the first American psychologists:

> [Attention] is the taking possession by the mind, in clear and vivid form, of one out of what seem several simultaneously possible objects or trains of thought. Focalization, concentration, of consciousness are of its essence. It implies withdrawal from some things in order to deal effectively with others.... (W. James, 1890)

The quote expresses how attention requires ignoring some sensory information in order to dedicate more processing power to the most important matter at hand. In spite of this early insight, attention was not scientifically studied for many decades because psychologists thought that attention was too vague and slippery to be the subject of scientific study. Fortunately, the last several decades have seen an increased interest in scientific research on attention. The phenomenon of attention is much better understood now, even though it still remains a somewhat elusive subject.

An important discovery made by modern attention research is that attention is not just a single, unitary process. What we broadly call "attention" in everyday life is actually made of several separate processes that complement each other. We can break attention down into an earlier process (orienting) and later processes (selective, sustained). Examining each of these processes and considering practical ways teachers might use these different aspects of attention will help facilitate teaching and learning.

The Orienting Reflex: Grabbing Attention

Attention begins by noticing the things and events that are happening around us. We are almost magnetically drawn to sensory changes produced by moving objects and loud noises. These dynamic sensory changes alert us to something interesting that is occurring in our environment. Certain brain regions are specifically wired to direct our attention to whatever might be changing in our environment. This early and basic form of attention is called the orienting reflex. A good example of the orienting reflex is how the flashing lights, bold colors, and loud sirens of an ambulance can grab our attention. These dramatic features alert us to an important situation.

A downside to having an orienting reflex is that people can be easily distracted by any sudden sensory change. A classroom example of the orienting reflex occurs when students arrive late to class. It seems like the eyeballs of the classroom are automatically drawn to look at the latecomer, taking attention away from the teacher. The same problem occurs during studying when distractions like television, phones, and ambient noise capture attention and leave fewer mental resources available for doing coursework. There are growing concerns that people are not very capable of managing the continuous interruptions produced by modern technology (Gazzaley and Rosen, 2016; M. Jackson, 2008). Minimizing distractions, whenever possible, is a good strategy for educators to follow because distractions can be an enemy of the learning process.

The experienced teacher is aware of the orienting reflex and uses it to their advantage to promote learning. Have you ever taken a course from a professor who drones on and on in a boring monotone voice? The stereotypical boring professor might also have little motion, and stay fixed in one place behind the lecture podium. It's unnatural for people to maintain their focus on an unchanging, never-moving object. Students can pay attention to an unchanging presentation delivery for a brief time, but it becomes progressively harder and harder to maintain the focus, which leads to daydreaming, phone fiddling, and other distractions. The solution is for the teacher to use some sensory changes in the delivery to engage the orienting reflex. Varying the volume and tone of voice makes the verbal dimension of the presentation more dramatic and easier to listen to. For vision, it helps for the teacher to get away from the podium and move about the room. The orientation reflex will cause students to follow the variations in your voice and track your movements around the room. These small variations will trigger the orienting reflex and make your presentation more engaging.

Powerpoint presentations can direct attention via the orienting reflex in a number of ways. One of the most basic ways is the slide transition. Switching to a new slide can alert students to a change and draw attention. Likewise, highlighting an important part of a slide in a dramatic color that is different from the rest of the slide draws student attention to the highlighted area. Colored circles or arrows that stand out can highlight an important part of a figure or graph. Laser pointers can also usefully provide both color and motion to point out an important feature in the presentation.

It has been suggested that today's students, who have been raised with visual stimulation from many sources, will respond positively to having lots of visual stimulation in their education. If this is true, perhaps it would be advantageous to put as many special effects as possible into a powerpoint presentation. Examples would include dramatic slide transitions, flying bullet points, and other animation effects. The potential problem with this idea, of course, is overdoing it. People tend to shut down or direct their attention away if there is too much stimulation. Excessive motion and other sensory stimulation can also make a presentation look amateurish and unprofessional. The best approach is to use motion and auditory changes in moderation because too little stimulation is undesirable, but too much stimulation is also undesirable. This suggestion matches with the Yerkes-Dodson law from psychology: Increasing arousal improves performance up to a point, but further increases in arousal may actually produce declines in performance (Yerkes and Dodson, 1908). Attention is a valuable resource, so instructors must take care to not overwhelm the students with content-free sensory stimulation.

Selective Attention: Zooming In for a Closer Look

The orienting reflex starts the attention process by alerting us to the most interesting things that are occurring around us. The next step directs our focus more specifically. Selective attention occurs when the brain narrows sensory input down to concentrate on the information that is most important. Selective attention works through subtraction. Most of the incoming sensory information is actively ignored so that one particularly important matter can be examined in great detail, as William James described in his famous passage. This limitation reflects a judicious trade-off in processing. The brain can only think deeply about a single thing at any given moment, so unimportant information must be discarded.

A number of analogies have been used to describe the focused and limited nature of selective attention. A popular analogy is to liken selective attention to a filter. Most of the sensory information gets trapped in the filter and receives little to no processing. A small amount of important information is selected to pass through the filter and on to consciousness for deeper processing. Another common analogy for selective attention is to liken attention to a spotlight in a theater. Imagine a play being performed on a large theater stage. When a spotlight shines on the main character, we see this character and the nearby parts of the stage in great detail. The highlighted features are prominent and stand-out from the rest of the stage. In contrast, the darker areas of the stage that are outside of the spotlight recede. Activities in the areas outside of the spotlight may go completely unnoticed. The spotlight serves to focus and thereby enhance our attention on one point of the stage, but this increased focus comes at the expense of ignoring events that are occurring on the other parts of the stage. Both analogies feature the essential aspect of the limiting nature of attention. People possess a very narrow capacity to deeply process sensory information. Deep thought is limited to about one topic at any given moment.

Selective attention describes what most educators are thinking about when they ask a class to "pay attention." In classroom settings, we would hope that the teacher and educationally relevant activities would be the focal point of attention. Students must filter out less important information in order to properly focus on the lesson. Interestingly, the phrase "paying attention" implies that attention is like money. Attention, just like money, is a limited resource. Like money, attention must be spent wisely.

The limited capacity of selective attention suggests that an audience has a limited ability to process the amount of information on a powerpoint slide. We've seen that the most common student complaint about powerpoint presentations is that too much information is presented. This problem occurs because the limitations of selective attention can make it easy to overwhelm the audience with too much information. The obvious solution to this problem is to reduce or limit the amount of information on the slides. The more effective approach for slides that have numerous bullet points, including multiple levels of organization, would be to split the information over several slides with only a few bullet points on each slide. In addition, it is generally recommended that each bullet point item should be kept short, such as one-to-three words in length, rather than being lengthy sentences (Altman, 2012).

Powerpoint presentations can also overwhelm selective attention if the pace of information delivery is too fast. Powerpoint makes it easy for the teacher to simply click through the slide deck without giving students enough time to comprehend the information, leading to information overload. The solution to this situation is to be mindful of how much information students can learn from a powerpoint presentation. Teachers must watch carefully to see how students are reacting to the pace of the presentation and be prepared to slow down if needed.

The Problem of Divided Attention

A key feature of selective attention is the limited capacity. This limitation may create problems when students try to attend to two or more events at the same time. This situation is called "divided attention" and can lead to decreased learning. A common classroom example occurs when students attempt to take notes and respond to cell phone text messages at the same time. This splitting of attention between two tasks leads to lower performance on both tasks, but doing poorly on the note-taking task is our primary concern.

Although it's called divided attention, this term is a little bit misleading because selective attention cannot be truly divided. Divided attention really involves rapidly switching back and forth between two different tasks that require attention resources. For example, a student who attempts to take notes and keep up with phone text messages at that same time is not really doing both activities simultaneously. Instead, they are really switching back and forth very quickly between tasks. When they focus their mind on the cell phone, they filter out all other information, including the lecture or class activities, so their learning drops from little to none at all. Since attention is a limited resource, limiting distractions of all sorts beneficially minimizes the potential problem of divided attention.

Several aspects of educational presentations might involve divided attention problems. One divided attention situation occurs when the spoken part of the lecture is accompanied by a visual slide presentation. This situation gives the students two competing sources of information: auditory and visual. Which one does the student attend to and learn from? Having multiple elements together on a slide may also possibly create a divided attention problem. This division of attention would be particularly likely when a powerpoint slide gets loaded with more and more elements that compete with each other for how students should allocate their attention. A third problem is that students may focus their attention on slide features that are emotionally vivid—pretty pictures—yet light in instructional content. A fourth possible problem is that note-taking creates a divided attention situation. Students are not attending to the current verbal information when they are composing a sentence in their notes. Only after the student finishes composing the sentence does their attention become free for redirection back to the lecture message.

Given this limited nature of attention, the teaching mission is best served by eliminating as many competing elements as possible in order to help students focus on the most essential components of the presentation. This idea is supported by multimedia learning research findings that providing unnecessary information can decrease student learning (Mayer, 2009; see also Chapter 11). A good starting point is to eliminate or minimize classroom distractions frequently recognized as potential problems, such as loud noises, student conversations, and electronic distractions like cell phones. These distractions may interfere with instruction due to both the orienting reflex and divided attention problems. Next, a clean presentation design that eliminates or minimizes unnecessary features—extraneous colors, logos, and cutesy pictures—will also help direct attention towards the important parts of the presentation. Digital technologies like powerpoint sometimes make it too easy to keep adding features. The best teachers, however, know when to apply restraint to keep inessential embellishments from obscuring the main message. Finally, teachers need to consider how the slide presentation complements the spoken word and avoid situations in which the visual and auditory components might be pitted against one another for the students' attention.

An old saying used by designers is that "less is more." This saying is not intended to encourage boring or featureless designs. Rather, the essence of "less is more" is that removing unimportant features can help to direct attention towards the instructional components that really matter, and thereby improve the overall learning experience. "Less" suggests a kind of editing process that enhances the main goal—paying attention to essential course content—by carefully cutting out unimportant features. Eliminating unnecessary information might help students by improving their focus on the most important information.

Sustained Attention: Keeping Students Engaged Over the Course Period

A third component of attention that psychological researchers have uncovered is called sustained attention. This component is the ability to hold and maintain attention over extended periods of time. An example of sustained attention is the task faced by a hunter in the woods. The hunter must stay still and be vigilant while waiting for game animals, sometimes for hours at a stretch. The hunter must focus on watching for game animals so that nothing will be missed. Unfortunately, maintaining attention over long periods of time can be difficult to do. Boredom creeps into the task, and the mind wanders away from its intended purpose.

In the classroom, teachers have long known that it can be difficult to engage student attention over a seemingly long class period. A commonly-cited statistic is that student attention drops off after about twenty to thirty minutes of lecturing. The evidence behind this statistic comes primarily from studies of educational television programming in the 1960s, which was a hot research topic at that time. For example, one study found a considerable drop in the number of students paying attention to educational television shows over the course of thirty minutes (Bridges, 1960). In a similar fashion, 84% of surveyed college juniors reported that "...20-30 minutes was the maximum amount of time during which they could tolerate uninterrupted lecturing and note-taking during a lecture period." (MacManaway, 1970, p. 322). Other research has suggested that the drop-off in attention occurs in as little as ten minutes (Hartley & Davies, 1978; Medina, 2008), although the quickness of this decline is somewhat uncertain (K. Wilson & Korn, 2007). A fast drop-off in attention is plausibly due, at least in part, to the sophisticated multimedia exposure of today's students. On YouTube, the most popular videos from 2014 had an average length of four minutes and twenty seconds ("The best video length for different videos on YouTube"). Class lectures that go on for over an hour may seem quite dull compared to the latest viral video clips.

In some respects, the exact time point when students begin to lose interest in a lecture doesn't matter. Teachers can safely assume that the drop-off in student attention occurs fairly quickly and declines progressively throughout the course of the lecture. The sustained attention problem brings up two important questions about lecturing during classes. First, is lecturing a valid teaching approach given this dramatic drop-off in attention? It seems like lectures could be completely futile if attention declines so rapidly. Second, what can teachers do to counteract this lost attention?

In the influential book *What's the Use of Lectures?*, Donald Bligh suggests that lecturing is still an appropriate teaching method even though student attention may drop off dramatically during the course of a lecture (Bligh, 2000). The lecture approach particularly excels at the transmission of information, so lecturing is worthwhile to educators for this purpose. Bligh proposes that the key to successful lectures is to plan for a decline in attention by alternating lecturing with other teaching approaches. The students need periodic lecture breaks that switch away from lecturing to other teaching-related activities. These other approaches tend to engage emotions and interest, and thereby keep the students emotionally involved. After these break points, lecturing can resume for a short while and then be followed by another educational strategy switch to maintain student interest. The successful teacher is, in some ways, like a juggler who must constantly switch between various educational approaches during the class period in order to maintain student interest.

A similar recommendation is made by John Medina, who is a neurobiologist and the author of *Brain Rules* (2008). Medina's successful lecture organization is centered upon the limited ability of students to sustain attention through a lecture (p. 89—92). The class period starts with an overview that outlines the topic for the day. After this introduction, class time is divided into 10-minute modules based upon evidence that the ability to pay sustained attention to the topic fades at about the 10-minute mark (Hartley and Davies, 1978). Each 10-minute module presents one main idea, the "gist" of a topic, that can be explained in one minute. The following nine minutes in the module contain details about the key idea that provide supporting evidence and clearly relate to the main idea. When the ten-minute module is complete, declining student attention is recaptured and boosted by presenting emotional hooks that are based upon case histories, anecdotes, narratives, and possibly even humorous material. It is important for these emotional breaks between modules to be relevant to the preceding modules to avoid the possibility of seeming "disjointed" or "patronizing". In other words, an off-topic joke is not desirable. An interesting example or anecdote that illustrates the lecture topic in an entertaining way is the goal. The emotional break is then followed by another ten minute module of educational content to start a new cycle. Throughout the class there are periodic reminders of the progress through the topics of the day to help keep students oriented in regard to how each module relates to the overall picture for the class. This pattern of regular switching from lecturing about course content to emotional hooks and then back again to course content helps to maintain a high level of student interest throughout the entire class period. This teaching method has not been explicitly tested, but it is based on research evidence and is also consistent with Bligh's recommendation for switching strategies during a lecture. Medina credits this "brain rule" understanding of human attention for his teaching success.

Powerpoint can help instructors follow this lecture-break-lecture-break pattern. Instructors can design powerpoint slide decks with regular break points in the lecture to avoid the monotony of a never-ending stream of facts. For example, the instructor could include a slide with a prompt that asks the students if they have any questions. Sometimes the instructor can dramatically illustrate key concepts with short video clips embedded in the powerpoint presentation. These video examples can be followed by a discussion that requires students to critically analyze the video content and make connections between the key terms and the video information. Yet another idea is to change from the lecture-based passive learning to a more active, hands-on type of learning through activities such as demonstrations, lab exercises, and working math problems. Short discussion exercises can also be quite effective (Bligh, 2000). The possibilities for brief alternatives to lecturing are nearly unlimited. Whatever the approach, the key idea is to intersperse the lecturing approach with other teaching approaches to maintain student interest in the topic throughout the class period.

Design Goal: Plan for the Limitations of Attention

Advertising firms that display ads on the Internet often discuss "eyeballs" as being a valuable resource. More ads viewed equals more products sold and more money made, which leads to a premium on getting people to view ads. This emphasis on the importance of "eyeballs" is, in many ways, similar to attentional issues that effective teachers must address. Students are only learning when their attention is actively engaged in the subject matter. Although attention is short, limited, and fickle, an understanding of how it works can produce effective teaching strategies that capture and maintain student attention while not overwhelming this valuable resource.

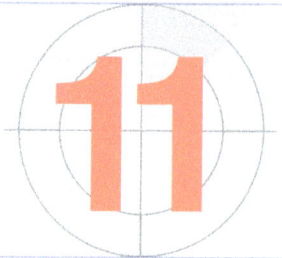

DESIGN FOR COGNITION I

Reaching the Student Mind

"If anything, Powerpoint, if used well, would ideally reflect the way we think." Steven Pinker

Teachers aim to improve their students' mental abilities, including conceptual knowledge, critical thinking, and problem solving abilities. The hope is that students will be more informed and enlightened thinkers when they finish their education, people who are awakened to new realities of the world. Cognitive science and the field of neurobiology have made numerous discoveries since the 1960s that have the potential to improve student learning. From this broad field, we will focus on topics in cognition that are the most relevant to improving the educational value of powerpoint presentations. Like Stephen Pinker suggests above, we will ideally find ways for our powerpoint presentations to match the inner workings of the mind and thereby stimulate the cognitive growth that teachers strive to achieve.

The Limitations of Short-Term Memory

The information processing model is a well-established view of human memory that was introduced in the late 1960s (R. C. Atkinson and Shiffrin, 1968). The model likens the human mind to a computer: information is entered, processed, and then stored for later use. The model proposes that long-term memory is gradually formed through three stages of processing. The first stage is sensory memory, which is a one- to two-second impression of sensory information. The second stage is short-term memory. This stage holds information for up to twenty seconds, a period just long enough to do something productive with the information. The capacity of short-term memory is very limited, with the classical description being 7±2 items of information (see also Baddeley, 1986; Baddeley, Thomson, and Buchanan, 1975). These first two stages of the model prepare information for the last stage, which is long-term memory storage.

As the information passes through these stages, a selective process takes place that eliminates the less important information. Vast amounts of sensory information enter the system, but relatively little information—only what is attended to—is eventually stored in long-term memory. The degree of data loss is huge. It has been estimated that each eye collects about 3,900 megabytes of information every second, which is enough information to fill six compact disks (Snowden, Thompson, and Troscianko, 2012). Most of this information never makes it past short-term memory. The vast majority of data is lost going from the earliest stages (megabytes) to the second stage (about seven items). This huge information loss may seem problematic, but it is, in fact, an important feature. The purpose of forgetting massive amounts of information is to prevent long-term memory from becoming filled up with unimportant details.

Cognitive scientists in the field of education have focused on the small capacity of short-term memory (sometimes called working memory) as being a key limiting factor for student learning (Baddeley, 1986; Paivio, 1990; Penney, 1989). Cognitive load theory proposes that the learning process places demands on the information processing capacity of students. When there is too much information, the limited cognitive capacity of short-term memory is exceeded and learning declines. Either the audience can be overwhelmed with too much information or the information may be presented in a manner that places too many demands on short-term memory. Cognitive load research in education has, in general, focused on finding teaching strategies that improve student learning by reducing the cognitive load on short-term memory.

At this point, it is worth noting that the key idea of limited cognitive capacity from memory research is quite similar to the research on attention described earlier. Both attention and short-term memory research suggest a very limited capacity in the human mind that can be easily overwhelmed by too much information. This evidence for limited attention and limited short-term memory capacity needs to be a guiding principle for the design of powerpoint presentations. The most effective educators aim to stimulate the minds of their students while simultaneously being careful to not overload them with too much information.

The Complementary Nature of Words and Visual Graphics

> On entering [the] room, we were struck at the appearance of an ample Blackboard suspended on the wall, with lumps of chalk on a ledge below, and cloths hanging at either side. I had never heard of such a thing before. There it was—forty-two years ago—that I first saw what now I trust is considered indispensable in every school—the blackboard—and there I first witnessed the process of analytical and inductive teaching. (May, 1855 as cited in S. C. Parker, 1912, p. 92).

The use of a chalkboard as a teaching technology may seem trivial and antiquated to modern teachers. We need to appreciate, however, that the use of chalkboards as an instructional aid is a relatively recent invention, going back to the early 1800s in the United States. Chalkboards enabled teachers to make key terms and outlines available to their students in a visual medium (i.e., not simply spoken). This change improved instruction by giving words a visual presence. It seems likely that chalkboards facilitated education, at least in part, by relieving a short-term memory limitation that students commonly face. A student who hears a purely spoken lecture must hold the key points of that information in short-term memory long enough to write down the information in their notes. A few words written on the board, however, improve the ability to process information by providing an external aid that reduces cognitive load.

Critics may be tempted to view powerpoint as being just an electronic version of chalkboard technology: a high-tech word delivery device. In fact, many educators held this attitude when powerpoint was introduced years ago, dismissing the then-new powerpoint technology as unnecessary. This view, however, errors by being too narrow. Just like great food combinations, the combination of visual and verbal information in a powerpoint presentation results in something more than the mere sum of the parts. Education has traditionally relied upon text to convey important ideas. With powerpoint, there is the opportunity to transcend the limitations of the written word by combining text with other rich sources of information. Seeing the topic material affords the students a more direct connection with the topic through images and video. This more immediate connection might facilitate student engagement much more than a chalkboard. The support of text with other visual information may also tap into deeper learning processes and thereby aid the teaching process.

The educational media used in today's classrooms has an information richness unimaginable in the 1800s due to the wide availability of pictures, diagrams, graphs, animations, and videos. This approach—words plus images—has been called a multimedia-based approach (Mayer, 2009). Multimedia educational research has compared the comprehension of text passages with or without the presence of visual images. The findings of these studies consistently show that combining words with visual information, such as instructional graphics, can have a beneficial effect on student learning from textbooks (Carney and Levin, 2002; J. R.

Levin, 1981; J. R. Levin, Anglin, and Carney, 1987). Later studies documented the positive effects of combining spoken words with animations and other high-tech visual media (Mayer, 2009). The complementary effects of visual and verbal information are the same regardless of the medium used to deliver this information to the students. This idea, which is variously called dual-coding theory or multimedia learning, is that visual and auditory information might work together in a complementary way to promote learning (Mayer, 2009; Paivio, 1990).

A number of ideas have been proposed to explain why using visual information plus spoken words promotes student learning. One explanation is that this improvement could occur because short-term memory uses separate brain areas for vision and hearing. These two separate channels of information processing might work together in a synergistic fashion (Horvath, 2014). A second possibility is that pictures themselves contain information and that this information richness might help overcome the limitations of short-term memory. Evidence suggests that information from visual aids may be processed more efficiently than text. Some studies also suggest that images such as diagrams may help students create mental representations of complex information (Glenberg and Langston, 1992; Mayer, 1989). Yet another possibility is that images help the learning process by directing attention or promoting information integration in ways that facilitate learning. The beneficial effects of pairing words with pictures may depend on all of these processes to some degree and may vary depending on the teaching situation.

Although combining words and images is positive, the research is very consistent in showing that not just any image will promote student learning. One test of this idea used eye-tracking technology to determine which parts of a slide received the most visual attention during a presentation (Slykhuis, Wiebe, and Annetta, 2005). The images that matched the slide instructional content received the most viewing time. In contrast, decorative images were viewed for much less time. These results show that students strategically allocate their mental resources in ways that will promote learning, such as close examination of images that provide some form of useful content.

Several image types are beneficial for learning. Carney and Levin (2002) describe and categorize some typical roles for pictures presented in context with text. Organizational images provide a framework for understanding the text content. For example, news stories about a particular region often include a map to help readers understand the geographical location of the news story. Node-link diagrams, such as organizational charts, also provide a visual representation of the organization and relationship between different elements (Dansereau and Simpson, 2009). Interpretational images such as diagrams, graphs, and instructional animations help the reader understand the text content by illustrating how complex systems work (Mayer and Gallini, 1990; Mayer and Moreno, 1998). Finally, transformation images contain memory aids like mnemonic devices that assist in the memorization of important points from the text.

Powerpoint seems like an ideal medium for multimedia instruction because it can display visual images to an audience in a way that can augment or complement the verbal message. This ability should allow educators to reach students in both an auditory and visual manner, which combine to facilitate learning.

Many presentations, however, do not take full advantage of multimedia learning possibilities because they rely too heavily on text and have few instructional images. Adding informative images to powerpoint presentations is an important practice for maximizing the learning potential that powerpoint offers.

From Short-Term Memory to Multimedia Learning

The relationships between multimedia and student learning have been extensively studied by Richard Mayer and his colleagues in an effort to find the optimal conditions for student learning. In their research studies, students learned about science or engineering topics from instructional passages that were accompanied by visual images or animated instructional graphics. The typical experiment was to compare students who had text accompanied by images (experimental group) to students who had just text (control group). Variations on this basic experimental approach were used to address a wide range of questions about the learning conditions that would promote or hinder learning. For example, would students learn more from an animation with narration alone or an instructional animation that has both narration and on-screen text? Would more learning occur with background music? Would students learn more if the subject content was accompanied by interesting stories? From these studies, a number of general principles were developed to guide instructional design (Mayer, 2009). These practical principles can be applied to make powerpoint presentations provide more effective education.

The Multimedia Principle

A multitude of studies show that the combination of verbal information with images produces stronger learning than verbal information alone (Mayer, 2009). Research from Mayer and other investigators tested this idea by comparing the performance of people who receive only narrative instruction to students who receive both narrative and image-based information. The combination of words and images produces superior performance in both recall and higher-order learning of the material. This superior learning is most likely to occur for topics that have a strong visualization component, such as scientific topics. The research findings that support multimedia learning are robust, with supporting evidence from studies of reading comprehension (for reviews, see Carney and Levin, 2002; Filippatou and Pumfrey, 1996; Levie and Lentz, 1982) and computer-based instruction (Mayer, 2009). Although most research in this area has not specifically focused on powerpoint presentations, it seems that powerpoint is well-suited to providing the visual component of the multimedia principle. Powerpoint images can provide representational, organizational, and explanative content that will support and enhance the speaker's message.

The Redundancy Principle

A research question related to the multimedia principle is whether the multimedia effects described above could be further improved by providing verbal information in two forms, both narration (auditory) and on-screen text (visual). To address this possibility, a number of studies by Mayer (Mayer et al., 2001; Moreno and Mayer, 2002) and other researchers (for reviews, see Sweller et al., 1998; van Merriënboer and Sweller, 2005) compared learning situations that had an instructional graphic plus narrative instruction to other learning situations that had instructional graphics, narration, and on-screen text. The results of these studies consistently show that students perform better when a graphical image is accompanied by narration without on-screen text. In short, providing the same words in both visual and auditory form hinders learning because providing too much information at one time creates a cognitive load problem.

The redundancy principle explains why the common presentation practice of reading a speech from a projected slide is problematic. The students in this situation receive a repetitious double-dose of the verbal message to the auditory and visual systems, which results in overloading short-term memory capacity. The redundancy principle suggests that educators would be better off by having a visual graphic plus narration accompanied by minimal or no on-screen text (see Chapter 9).

The redundancy principle is not meant to suggest that all of the text should be eliminated from a powerpoint slide. The typical source of the redundancy problem is displaying an excessive amount of text to the learner. The redundancy problem occurs in the laboratory when the entire narration and on-screen text are identical. Most powerpoint presentations, in contrast, only show brief bullet point items and do not follow this problematic pattern of excessive on-screen text. Some research shows that having brief phrases displayed to the students is beneficial. In particular, short word cues like captions that are strategically placed on a displayed graphic are often helpful because they cue attention to an important feature (Mayer and Johnson, 2008). The increased attention and organizational benefits from these useful cues in these situations outweigh the redundancy problem of the on-screen text.

The Coherence Principle

It seems very intuitive that adding human interest stories to educational content might assist instruction by increasing the students' emotional involvement. Although stories can be engaging, they sometimes have detrimental effects on learning when the stories have little relevance to understanding the topic. The research term for this phenomenon is seductive details: interesting yet irrelevant information producing harmful effects on learning. This seductive detail problem occurs because unimportant information consumes precious short-term memory resources, thereby leaving less cognitive capacity available in short-term memory for the important ideas (Mayer, 2009). The elimination of seductive details in some studies has helped to improve student learning (Mayer et al., 2001).

It might seem like the harmful potential of seductive details contradicts suggestions about the importance of emotions and stories from Chapter 5 and 6, but this is not necessarily true. The main suggestion from these chapters was that a presentation needs to have an overall storyline with story-like features that engage the audience (Duarte, 2010). Seductive details, in contrast, are small stories (not a storyline) that are only tangentially relevant to educational content. The seductive details problem occurs largely when these nonessential stories lack educational content and become emotional distractions that detract from important learning goals. Emotional features in presentations can be either helpful or detrimental, and here it is largely detrimental.

In powerpoint, one potential form of seductive details is the decorative images or content-free graphics that are meant to arouse emotion. Other sources of seductive details and unnecessary cognitive load may come from the nearly infinite number of design possibilities for fonts, colors, layouts, and animated special effects. From the perspective of multimedia learning, unnecessary or content-free features should be eliminated in order to decrease cognitive load and increase the short-term memory available for important learning objectives. The coherence principle suggests that students will do better if designers remove all of these unessential elements.

Undesirable cognitive load can also occur when a powerpoint slide deck has inconsistent design features. Significant design changes over the course of the presentation will create a situation in which each new slide will require a bit of extra effort from the audience to adjust to the new appearance. These design inconsistencies create a cognitive cost that may detract from student learning. Empirical support for this possibility comes from a study that deliberately manipulated slide design features to change during a presentation and thereby increase cognitive load or "interference" (Bradshaw, 2003). The results of this study showed better learning outcomes for the students who received slides that had a consistent design. In contrast, the students who received the inconsistently-designed slides had lower performance. Although this negative impact from inconsistent design is small, these results support the coherence principle. The practical implications are clear: Teachers should aim for a consistent slide design to reduce cognitive load and improve student learning.

The Signaling Principle

Topics that seem straightforward to experts can be overwhelming to novices because the novices cannot tell the difference between important information and unimportant details. Novice learners try to take in everything about a topic at one time, which leads to an information overload. The signaling principle proposes that effective instruction should use cues that highlight the most important points. The cues draw attention to the important features and help novice learners to organize information for the learning process. This is the practice of pointing out the most important features to the students. Examples of these cues can be outlines or headers that communicate how the topic is organized. The speaker's voice can also be used to emphasize certain points, such as the order of topics (first, second, third, etc.) or emphasizing a transition to a new subtopic. Vocal cues such as intonation or emphasis on certain words can also help listeners anticipate the organizational structure of a topic or presentation. Bullet point lists are commonly used in powerpoint presentations to cue the major points for students. Presentation graphics can also use signals that point out important information, such as arrows, highlighted text, or circles around a key point of interest. It seems likely that the signaling principle works by directing limited cognitive resources to the most relevant parts of the topic, which can decrease short-term memory load and promote the formation of new memories.

Several other multimedia learning principles might be useful for designing educational powerpoint presentations. The contiguity principle suggests that the placement of text in relationship to the graphics is important. Strategically placing text near the critical features of the graphical image (spatial contiguity) and together in time with the visual graphic (temporal contiguity) are best for learning due to easing cognitive load requirements for the students. These concepts are similar to the Gestalt law of proximity (see Chapter 8). The segmenting principle suggests that breaking a presentation into smaller parts and giving the learner control over the pacing of the presentation may facilitate learning. For further information about these and other principles of multimedia learning, please refer to comprehensive reviews of this topic (Mayer, 2009; Sweller et al., 1998; van Merriënboer and Sweller, 2005).

The multimedia learning principles described above are based upon the results of numerous laboratory experiments. A potential weakness is that the laboratory environment might be too artificial and produce results that are not effective for real educational situations. To address this possibility, several studies have tested the multimedia learning principles in powerpoint presentations given to real students. The good news from these studies is that the multimedia learning principles derived from laboratory studies are also effective in the classroom. One study reports that students learn better when powerpoint images and multimedia are combined with text, which supports the multimedia learning principle (Hallett and Faria, 2006). Two studies redesigned standard powerpoint slides to use formats suggested by multimedia learning principles. These studies documented improvements in student learning outcomes with the redesigned slides (Issa et al., 2011; Overson, 2014). Eliminating unnecessary slide elements and redundant text information also appears to be beneficial for learning (Wecker, 2012), as suggested by the coherence and redundancy principles. Overall, these findings show that the multimedia learning principles from laboratory research are effective when applied to powerpoint presentations used in real classroom situations.

As a final note, the use of instructional graphics has complex cognitive effects that are still being teased apart and may eventually yield important new insights. There are also controversies over contradictory experimental findings. Some studies in this area suggest that seductive details, which are those interesting yet irrelevant bits of information that might impair learning, can have neutral or even positive effects on learning in some situations (Park et al., 2015; Schneider et al., 2016). The emotional effects created by seductive details are apparently quite complex, with emotional content being beneficial in some situations and harmful in others. Another area of research focuses on cognitive load effects for short-term or long-term learning tasks. Under some conditions, overloading short-term memory may produce improved long-term learning, which is an effect that has been called "desirable difficulties" (Schweppe and Rummer, 2016). Yet another area of research interest has focused on individual differences in learners, such as comparing high-ability to low-ability students, novices to experts, or high school to college students. In general, novice learners seem to benefit more from multimedia instruction. More knowledgeable students may, in some situations, show impaired learning with multimedia instruction, which has been called the "expertise reversal effect" (van Merriënboer and Sweller, 2005). Altogether, these recent studies suggest that multimedia learning is complex. As Mayer (2009) has suggested, the principles derived from cognitive research are not absolute rules. These principles are more accurately understood as useful guidelines that are sensitive to a number of conditions.

A promising future possibility for multimedia education research is to explore the neurobiological mechanisms that might be responsible for the multimedia learning principles. Horvath (2014) attempts to explain multimedia learning in light of evidence from functional brain imaging studies. Horvath proposes that the redundancy principle (concurrent auditory and visual words decreases learning) occurs because the same auditory cortex areas in the temporal lobe are responsible for processing both silent reading and auditory speech perception. Situations that require reading and hearing words at the same time might create a competition between the two sources of information for access to a single brain area. This limited processing capacity for two streams of information thereby decreasing learning. In contrast, the multimedia principle (improved learning when images are combined with words) may occur because the images and the text are processed in parallel or side-by-side in different brain areas. The visual imagery is processed mostly in the occipital lobe and the ventral temporal lobe, whereas the text and auditory information is processed mostly in the superior temporal lobe. Thus, words and images can be processed in a complementary way in different brain areas, which avoids a conflict over a limited neural resource. This parallel or independent processing of visual and auditory information might explain why words and images can have synergistic, positive effects rather than interfering with each other. Neurobiological research on contextual cuing also suggests that having a consistent image size and location on a powerpoint slide, such as the assertion-evidence layout, might promote learning, possibly because the brain needs to expend less effort to analyze repeated visual scenes. The possibility of using brain imaging studies to gain further insights into the optimal powerpoint presentation display conditions is an exciting possibility. However, it is important to keep in mind that the current evidence is somewhat speculative. The wide gap between basic neuroscience research and applied teaching methods is difficult to bridge (Goswami, 2006).

Applying the Multimedia Principles to Powerpoint

Ironically, reading through all of these multimedia learning principles may be giving you a bit of cognitive overload by this point. It is challenging to understand how all of these multimedia learning principles will come together and make a good powerpoint presentation. Fortunately, Mayer has worked with Atkinson, the author of the book *Beyond Bullet Points* (C. Atkinson, 2011), to specifically apply multimedia learning principles to powerpoint presentations (C. Atkinson and Mayer, 2004). Their five recommendations provide practical suggestions for putting the research findings from cognitive psychology into practice. These recommendations are also a good review of the multimedia principles described above.

Their first recommendation is to make the slide titles more informative. This is achieved through using full sentences that explicitly state the main idea of the slide. Titles that are complete sentences explain and communicate better than the short phrase titles that are commonly used. This is an example of the signaling principle, which states that clear communication and organization facilitate better learning (see Chapter 9 on the assertion-evidence layout).

Their second recommendation is to use the slide sorter view of PowerPoint to organize the overall presentation into more easily digestible parts. Slides with too much information might be easily noticed in the slide sorter view. If there is too much information, then instructors can divide the slide contents across two or more slides. The presenter may also better evaluate the overall story line of the presentation in the slide sorter view. This practice works due to the segmentation principle, which advocates dividing complex information into smaller pieces to avoid the potential problem of overloading the audience with too much information on each slide.

The third recommendation is to reduce the amount of text on the slide, which is especially important for presenters who mistakenly attempt to place their entire speech on the screen. Reducing text benefits the audience by helping them to focus on hearing the speaker's words (narration only). If the speaker needs the text for delivering the speech, it can be put in the "notes" view of PowerPoint or possibly on paper or notecards. The general idea is that the presenter can see their speaking notes but the audience cannot, which reduces the cognitive load for the audience. This situation is an example of the modality principle: "People understand a multimedia explanation better when the words are presented as narration rather than on-screen text" (p. 12). The recommendation to reduce text may also be an example of the redundancy principle, which suggests that having the same words presented to both the visual and the auditory system at the same time is harmful for learning.

The fourth recommendation is to pair the text from the slide title with informative graphics. This combination of text plus a supporting image make a message more effective due to the multimedia principle. Descriptive titles plus relevant and informative instructional images should combine in a complementary way to enhance student learning. This recommendation is similar to the assertion-evidence layout slide (see Chapter 9).

Atkinson and Mayer's last recommendation is to declutter and simplify the appearance of powerpoint slides. Instructors should only use the essential instructional features. Content-free decorations are an avoidable and unnecessary burden on short-term memory, so instructors should eliminate these features. The recommendation to avoid unnecessary text, colors, decorations, and other design elements is based on the coherence principle, which is improved learning through the elimination of unimportant information.

Design Goal: Use Cognitive Principles to Improve Learning

The old view of how students learned has been characterized as an information transfer process. Information was moved from the mind of the teacher to the mind of the student in a manner similar to copying a file from one directory to another on a personal computer. Although this view is appealing, modern cognitive research has shown that this is simply not how the human mind works.

The modern view of student learning is that students must actively seek to understand information and develop new internal models (schemata) of how the world around them must work. This process takes effort. During this memory formation process, students can be easily overwhelmed by the amount of information that is being made available to them. Therefore, teachers must take the limitations of short-term memory into account when developing instructional materials. The key takeaway point is to deliver the right amount of information (not too much or too little) while simultaneously decreasing unnecessary details that might burden short-term memory. In addition, we should make strategic use of text and instructional images that complement each other in useful ways to promote student learning.

DESIGN FOR COGNITION II

Active Learning in Powerpoint Presentations

... [L]earning is an active, constructive, cognitive, and social process by which the learner strategically manages available cognitive, physical, and social resources to create new knowledge by interacting with information in the environment and integrating it with information that is already stored in memory. (Kozma, 1994, p. 8)

The old-fashioned view of education is that the teacher's role is to transmit important information to the students, who were treated like empty vessels that needed to be filled with information. The role of the instructor as an information provider was reasonable years ago when important information was contained in obscure books that students were unlikely to encounter. The instructor was the critical source of information in an information-limited environment.

The information-rich nature of the modern world has changed the focus of education. When information is easily available from the Internet and phone-based digital assistants, there is not as much need for the instructor to be the chief information provider. The critical cognitive skill is being able to use higher order thinking skills to evaluate information. As a result, modern educators view learning as an active process. The modern educator employs creative teaching strategies to facilitate this process of student exploration and understanding, rather than merely imparting information to an audience who has no other access to that information.

The focus of education has also changed dramatically as a result of educational theorists who have advanced a conceptual framework that advocates the need for deeper learning. Paulo Freire made the powerful argument that education once operated by a banking model, in which information was deposited into students like money was deposited in a bank (Freire, 2000). Such a learning approach was oppressive. In contrast, the true goal of education should be to empower students to think for themselves. Other educational theorists, such as Malcolm Knowles, Jack Mezirow, Donald Schön, and Stephen Brookfield, have also argued that educators need to aim for deeper, more meaningful forms of learning than simply memorizing information. Evidence from the fields of cognitive psychology and neurobiology is another possible contribution to the movement away from information transfer approaches to education. For example, cognitive psychology research on memory has shown that rote learning may be inferior to strategies that rely upon elaborative encoding of information, such as a more active learning process which relates new information to older, mastered understanding. Cognitive neuroscience research also suggests the existence for multiple forms of long term memory, such as procedural, semantic, and episodic memories. Altogether, our contemporary view is that a high-quality education needs to be much more than the simple transfer and storage of important information.

Although powerpoint is a modern technology, the inherent nature of powerpoint presentations is to gravitate toward passive learning approaches that emphasize information delivery. It seems that passive learning is a default mode of powerpoint presentations. This passivity is not surprising given that the modern powerpoint presentation has historical roots in older technologies associated with lecturing, such as chalkboards and overhead projectors. Teaching excellence with powerpoint will require, to some degree, going against the inherent tendency to use powerpoint for mere information delivery. To achieve active learning, the instructors will need to intentionally use powerpoint to promote active learning classroom situations (Vallance and Towndrow, 2007).

We will now explore the ways that powerpoint presentations can promote learning processes. Instructors can use powerpoint to provide support for active learning exercises, and thereby indirectly contribute to important course goals. Such methods include technologies and assignments that infuse a more active learning emphasis into powerpoint. Learning response systems that require student feedback and promote student-instructor interactions and student-authored powerpoint presentations are possible ways of encouraging active learning with powerpoint. There are many other possible approaches, all of which emphasize the stimulation of student cognition.

Adding Active Learning to Lectures

A key conclusion from the book *What's the Use of Lectures?* can be captured in a single sentence: "The lecture method alone is rarely adequate" (Bligh, 2000, p. 223). By extension, the standard powerpoint presentation that emphasizes information delivery and passive learning for an entire class period is a bad practice. Bligh cautiously points out that lectures are not always bad, even though educators sometimes view lectures with disdain. Bligh's view is that teachers should "[u]se lectures to teach information. Do not rely on them to promote thought, change attitudes, or develop behavioral skills if you can help it." (p. 20). Lectures become problematic when instructors overuse the lecture approach. To achieve teaching excellence, we will need to follow Bligh's advice to break up our traditional lectures with other teaching approaches that emphasize an active learning process. Active learning exercises are small parts of the big puzzle, activities that instructors can sprinkle throughout the class period to break up the monotony of a lecture approach. These activities can supplement the information-delivery focus of powerpoint presentations.

The active learning possibilities in powerpoint are very broad. Bligh recommended brief discussion activities during class to break the monotony of a continuous lecture. Burmark suggests using flashcards, digital photo essays, and writing prompts (Burmark, 2004). Berk suggests surveys, reading/interpretation, and reactions to music or video (Berk, 2011). Digital storytelling is another possibility (Robin, 2008). The general idea is that powerpoint slides do not need to always involve presenting information, even though information delivery is their typical function. The successful educational use of powerpoint is to realize that the slides can play a useful supporting role for promoting active learning.

Click to Active Learning

Powerpoint is like a one-way street: Information tends to move from the presenter to the audience. In some cases, powerpoint presentations may even discourage student feedback or interactions between the students and the instructor. This problem could be particularly strong in large lecture situations. Students in large lecture halls may feel uncomfortable asking questions during class due to the potential embarrassment that could occur when speaking in front of 100 or more people.

In the late 1990s, new wireless devices were introduced to promote more communication from the student to the instructor and thereby address an important weakness in the typical educational presentation. These wireless response systems go by a wide variety of names, with the most common term being "clickers." (Business professionals may use the term "clicker" to describe wireless remote control devices that advance a slide presentation, but in the field of education, the word "clicker" is typically used to describe student response systems.) Although a number of different vendors and possible features are available, the most essential characteristic is that this technology enables teachers to collect quick feedback on student learning.

Student response system technology is most commonly used for assessing content-based questions in large lecture classes. The instructor initiates the use of these devices by posing a question to the students on a powerpoint slide. The questions are often in a multiple choice or true-false format: A statement followed by several potential answers. The students answer this question through the student response system device by using buttons like A/B/C/D or Yes/No. Some educators ask their students to briefly discuss the best possible answer with their neighbor after they report their answer via the wireless remote device. The student responses are wirelessly transmitted to a receiver system that collects, tabulates, and displays the results on the computer. The powerpoint display can give students feedback on their answers and also project the classroom responses for the entire class to see. This information provides the instructor with a quick, real-time assessment of student learning. If students seem to be grasping the key concept, the lecturer can move on to new content. In contrast, poor student comprehension can be an important indicator that more class time is needed for the topic. The instructor can also use the student feedback for discussion purposes, for example, to comment on why particular student answers are correct or incorrect. This process typically repeats several times during the class period, with the instructor asking four to six content-based questions during a typical classroom period.

A recent trend in classroom response systems is favoring the use of smart phone apps over specialized hardware devices (Roll, 2017). This is a part of a general 'bring your own device' (BYOD) movement that involves personal phone use for business or institutional purposes. Examples of these smart phone apps include Poll Everywhere (see polleverywhere.com), Top Hat (see tophat.com), and Socrative (see socrative.com). Some response system manufacturers, such as Macmillan and Turning Point, are offering both hardware and phone app-based systems. Phone app responses systems offer the practical advantages of increased convenience and possibly lower cost. Student attitudes towards these systems are positive. The potential downsides include phone-based distractions, such as playing games during class, and dropped wireless connections (Miller Griffith and Roberts, 2013; Morrell and Joyce, 2015).

Learning strategies based upon student response systems, like content-based questions, effectively promote student learning, with only a few studies finding no benefits (for reviews, see Caldwell, 2007; Kay and LeSage, 2009; Keough, 2012). A good example study was done by Mayer, the multimedia learning expert whose work was discussed in the cognition chapter (see 11), and his colleagues (Mayer et al., 2009). In this study, a student response system group (student response system plus group questioning) was compared to two control groups (no student response system and no group questioning; no student response system with group questioning). The results showed a small but positive increase in the exam scores for the student response system group (83.4%) compared to the control groups that lacked this technology (80.3% and 80.2%).

Several possible reasons explain why student response systems and content-based questions might improve student learning. Mayer's interpretation is that this approach promotes generative learning, such as using attention, organization, and metacognitive skills that are beneficial for deep learning (Mayer et al., 2009). Another study suggests that the benefits may be due to testing effects and feedback (A. M. Shapiro and Gordon,

2013). Many other possible instructional benefits of using student response systems include increased student-teacher interactions, better assessment of student preparation, practice problems, and formative assessments (Caldwell, 2007). Student response systems also give students an opportunity to see how their performance compares to their classmates' (Dean, 2013). Let's say that two-thirds of a class answers an instructor-posed question correctly. The remaining students who got the answer wrong must face the uncomfortable truth that they were in the minority are, therefore, behind the rest of the class. This ability for the students to see where they stand in relation to their peers may put social pressure on the lagging students to work harder.

It seems natural to view the student response system technology as the source of important student learning gains in these studies, but this view is somewhat inaccurate. Several carefully designed studies suggest that the improved learning comes from questions, projects, assignments, and student discussions rather than the technology itself (Anthis, 2011; Christopherson, 2011; Fallon and Forrest, 2011; Zayac, Ratkos, Frieder, and Paulk, 2016). The learning gains are caused by posing questions or challenges to students that engage active learning (for examples, see Strauss, Corrigan, and Hofacker, 2011). In essence, the pedagogy is the real source of learning gains, not the technology. This understanding is useful because it suggests that there may be ways to capture many of the benefits of student response systems without the need to purchase and implement special technology. For example, student response system technology might be unnecessary in small classrooms in which students can use traditional means of responding, like raised hands. Focusing too much on the technology can lead educators astray by taking their focus away from the elements of teaching that are the most important for improving educational outcomes.

Both student and faculty perceptions of student response system technology tend to be positive. One review found that 89% of the student response system studies have an increase in student satisfaction (Keough, 2012). Most studies also show increases in perceived performance, attention, and attendance. Student response systems also increase student-faculty interactions, including ones not dependent on the technology. Increased interaction occurs because some students are more likely to use the response system for class participation compared to other means, such as asking questions, because the voting is anonymous and avoids the possibility of public embarrassment. Overall student engagement can be increased because voting on a question is a way that teachers can reach out to students and make them feel like they are involved in class activities.

For negatives, students may be concerned about the additional costs of these systems if they are required to purchase their own response system device or must access a phone app. Technical downsides can include broken or lost remote devices and possible system failures, such as dropped wireless connections. Some faculty members may be concerned about the increased preparation time it might take to incorporate these device activities into their powerpoint presentations. The amount of class time available for covering course content may also be decreased if more time is devoted to question-focused activities. These negative points may be small problems, but they are still important to consider for teachers who might use a student response system.

The use of content-based questions in large lecture classes is just one example of how student response system technology can be useful. A much wider range of creative possibilities are available. The devices can be used for interactive games, like the television game show *Jeopardy!* Some faculty use these devices to record attendance. Student response systems can also be used in conjunction with student discussion activities. For example, students can discuss the answers to a complex problem in small groups and then report their conclusion to the instructor via the response system technology. The devices could be used to vote for the winners of a debate contest. These ideas are only a small sampling of the possibilities that might be enabled by having a quick and efficient means of collecting responses and opinions from students in the classroom.

The present description of the potential benefits from active questioning methods and student response system technology is just a brief overview. For more, the interested reader should begin by reading review articles that cover the advantages and disadvantages of these systems (Caldwell, 2007; Kay and LeSage, 2009; Keough, 2012). The manufacturers of student response systems also have practical suggestions about how to maximize the educational gains from these systems.

Active Learning with Instructor-Provided Note Resources

It has become a common teaching practice to make powerpoint files available to students through learning management systems for use as a note-taking resource (see chapter 13). This practice is popular with students, but downsides exist, such as the promotion of passive note-taking. One idea for improving student note-taking quality is to provide a partial or incomplete resource to the students rather than the common practice of making the full slide decks available to students. The instructor-provided resources are partial because key terms are missing or important bits of information must be completed by the students during the class period. In most studies, using a partial resource in this manner produces better learning outcomes than either no notes or complete instructor notes (Annis, 1981; Cornelius and Owen-DeSchryver, 2008; Katayama and Crooks, 2003; Kiewra et al., 1988; but see also Stark-Wroblewski et al., 2006 for negative results).

The often beneficial, though not universal, effects of instructor-provided partial notes seem to come from a delicate balance between providing useful information and requiring active involvement. These incomplete notes provide enough information to be a guide for facilitating student note-taking, yet they are not so information-rich as to encourage a completely passive approach to note-taking and possibly poor class attendance. The need for student effort and engagement with partial notes presumably facilitates learning by requiring an effortful formation of memory and other cognition by providing useful scaffolding to help novices.

As a practical matter, the creation of partial note resources, notably, will require some additional effort from the instructor. At present, most teachers who make their powerpoint files available online are simply uploading the same file that they use during the class presentation. To make the note-taking resource incomplete, the instructor will need to go through the powerpoint file and remove information in critical spots. This creates gaps that the students must actively fill with their own notes when they are in class. Another possible way to make powerpoint slides into an incomplete resource is to save the outline as a text file without any images. Any information presented through the images or diagrams would need to be recorded by students as part of their note-taking activities.

Pardini and colleagues have proposed a different note-taking technique for online instructor-provided notes (Pardini, Domizi, Forbes, and Pettis, 2005). Their idea, which they call the parallel system, also involves active learning and was inspired by the split page or Cornell system for student note-taking. The system begins with the students downloading and printing the slide deck before class. On the back of each page, the students draw a vertical line two inches from the left side of the page. On the wider right side part of the page, the students take notes during class. This\\e information that the students record is done in parallel with the printed powerpoint resource. The narrow margin on the left side is used for annotations that reflect higher order thinking. These comments might include questions, synthesis, relationships, and possible comments about points that need further study. In other words, the left margin encourages a metacognitive assessment of issues and insights that are related to the content-oriented notes on the right.

This parallel note-taking system has several advantages. This system shows students an effective way to use instructor-provided slide decks plus student notes as a "hybrid text" (Pardini et al., 2005). The strategy communicates to students that instructor-provided resources are intended to guide learning, rather than replace the need for note-taking. Doing so gets away from the common view that students are passive recipients and recorders of information during a lecture. A teacher advantage is that this method does not require instructors to edit key terms out of their slides in order to provide a partial note student resource.

Student Presentations as an Active Learning Exercise

One of the best ways to learn about a topic is teaching the topic to others. Being a teacher puts social pressure on an individual to learn a topic thoroughly. You simply can't fake expertise when you are in front of an audience. The fact that understanding must precede teaching can make student presentation assignments a valuable method for promoting active learning. A presentation assignment requires students to take a careful inventory of what they know about a topic. During the development of the presentation, students will need to make critical decisions about the importance and relationships of the different aspects of their topic information. The use of powerpoint can play a strong role in this creative process by providing an organizing point for the presentation materials that will be shown to the audience.

Presentation assignments have a number of positive features (Marmienė, 2006). The projects are student-directed, which is an active, hands-on way to learn. Student presentations involve the integration of several abilities, including speaking, listening, writing, and analyzing. The development of the presentation includes elements of higher order learning from Bloom's taxonomy, such as evaluation and synthesis of information. Presentations can also provide opportunities for cooperative learning. Students may take more time and effort to impress their peers than they do their teachers, so the motivation to work hard on a presentation project can be quite high. Finally, presentations also provide a good opportunity for students to develop their public speaking skills, which is good preparation for future career activities.

The effectiveness of a present-to-learn teaching strategy is documented in several studies. In these studies, the assigned task was to make a presentation that included a powerpoint visual aid. When students in a present-to-learn group are compared to students exposed to a more traditional learning situation (no presentations), the group that was required to make presentations showed greater mastery of the subject (Gunel, Hand, and Gunduz, 2006; Gürbüz et al., 2010; Kisoglu, Erkol, Dilber, and Gurbuz, 2012; Siegle and Foster, 2001). Many studies of the present-to-learn approach emphasize cooperative learning as a natural fit to the practice of giving presentations. Teachers have reported successful collaborative presentations in a wide range of disciplines and age groups, including middle school students with disabilities (Kelly, 1999), middle school social studies students (Dils, 2000), undergraduate chemistry students (Pence, 1997), and MBA graduate students (M. A. Levin and Peterson, 2013). Student perceptions of a present-to-learn teaching strategy are also positive (Blake, Poranek, and MacCulloch, 2007; Kisoglu et al., 2012; Seo, Templeton, and Pellegrino, 2008).

Modern presentation software has online technology that can be particularly useful for presentations developed through a collaborative group effort. The newest versions of PowerPoint and some PowerPoint alternatives like Prezi enable each student to log into a cloud-based, online system to work on their own part of a presentation (Brock and Brodahl, 2013). In PowerPoint, online collaboration may involve using Microsoft's "OneDrive" cloud storage or SharePoint technology. These collaborative features should be useful for facilitating group work because the students do not have to share a file back and forth, such as sending email attachments several times between group members.

The slide formats used for preparing student presentations can significantly influence the degree of student learning in a present-to-learn strategy. One study compared undergraduate engineering students who were instructed to create a presentation using the assertion-evidence slide layout to another group of students who were allowed to design their slides in whatever manner they wished (Garner and Alley, 2016). The students in the latter group mostly designed slides with bullet point list characteristics. The students who made assertion-evidence slides performed better on a surprise quiz compared to the students in the other condition. The assertion-evidence slide format intriguingly had a significant positive impact on the presenter's mastery of the subject material.

Although student presentations have strong active learning possibilities, they also include significant downsides. A small number of students are extremely anxious about public speaking situations. It might be necessary, therefore, to have some kind of alternative assignment available for people who have extreme fears of public speaking. Poor attendance on presentation dates can be another significant problem. In one report, attendance fell to about 20% on the student presentation days (Dobson, 2006). The classroom logistics of having traditional, face-to-face student presentations can also be problematic. Student presentations can be time consuming, especially for larger classes, and this problem can be exacerbated by student presentations that run over the time limits. Valuable time might be wasted in the transition between different presenters.

Levin and Peterson suggest a creative solution to some of these student presentation problems based on a little-used PowerPoint feature (M. A. Levin and Peterson, 2013). Each student can make a presentation on their own time and use PowerPoint to record their voice as a narration (the "record slide show" function). This recording feature saves the narration along with the slides, which results in a digital presentation. The narrated slide deck can be electronically submitted to the instructor as a video file for grading. The recorded narration idea raises other instructional possibilities, such as peer-review grading of presentations or alternative presentation assignments for people with social anxiety problems. Narrated powerpoint presentations saved as digital files could also be useful assignments for online course formats.

Teachers who assign presentations will almost surely get problems related to powerpoint technology. Inexperienced student presenters often have common problems like bad slide themes, animated bullet points, and too much text. A good starting point to address these issues is to set limits and rules for acceptable presentations, such as rules against using gratuitous animations and slide transitions. Students also need rules on time requirements, like the minimum and maximum times, to guide the development of their presentation. In addition to rules, instructors can provide guidance by giving the students a slide template (default background and other formatting features) that will serve as the foundation for all of the student presentations. Doing so will help to prevent the use of unusual slide decorations and features, as well as setting a consistent appearance for the entire class. Some educators address these powerpoint technology problems by providing students with a brief instructional manual that explains a few basic ideas about how to use powerpoint (Downing and Garmon, 2001; Gareis, 2007). For an example of student presentation guidelines, please refer to Shackelford and Griffis, who thoroughly describe an assignment overview, learning objectives, definitions (e.g., software features), limitations, and requirements (Shackelford and Griffis, 2007).

The Pecha Kucha Format for Student Presentations

A drawback of student presentations is the time it can take to teach students good presentation practices. Developing presentation skills is desirable, but skill development is a secondary goal for most courses. Another problem is that student presentations often go over their allotted time limits, which creates logistical problems. Wouldn't it be nice if there was a straightforward way to quickly and easily prevent these bad presentation practices from occurring in student presentations? Some instructors have successfully implemented a specific style of powerpoint presentation that seems to accomplish these goals with very little work on the instructor's part.

The pecha kucha presentation places severe constraints on presenters with two very simple rules: twenty slides, and twenty seconds for each slide (20 x 20). This distinctive style of powerpoint presentation breaks with many presentation conventions. The pecha kucha format was invented by two architects, Astrid Klein and Mark Dytham, for the purpose of giving brief presentations to small audiences. The term "pecha kucha" is the Japanese equivalent of the English term "chit chat," which is consistent with its initial use for giving presentations to small groups. The pecha kucha style has grown into an international movement in which people gather in public venues for pecha kucha-style presentations, somewhat like open mic nights for poetry readings.

In a pecha kucha presentation, the slides are set to automatically advance every twenty seconds with no intervention from the speaker. This time limit fundamentally changes powerpoint presentations in ways that prevent many bad practices. The emphasis on brevity forces the presenter to get to the main point without meandering through digressions and off-topic musings. Long text passages and numerous bullet points must be avoided because these would be too long to read in twenty seconds. The emphasis in pecha kucha presentations is on graphical images, with text being used sparingly or not at all. The lack of text prevents speakers from using the slide as a teleprompter, which prevents another common presentation problem.

The pecha kucha format has features that make it well-suited to classroom use. The length of an entire pecha kucha presentation is just under seven minutes (20 slides x 20 seconds = 400 seconds or 6 minutes, 40 seconds). Students cannot run over their time limit because the timing is automatically controlled by the software. This helps the instructor with the logistics and planning for several pecha kucha presentations in a single class period. The constraints of pecha kucha benefits presenters by making them edit their message to focus on the essential ideas. The overall time limit of about seven minutes is short enough to make it easy for students to practice the presentation multiple times before the final presentation. All of these positive benefits are achieved without requiring the instructor to put significant time and effort into teaching students good presentation practices.

Pecha kucha presentations given by students are perceived as being more interesting and enjoyable than a traditional powerpoint presentation (Beyer, 2011). The pecha kucha format has been used successfully for student presentations in a wide range of academic disciplines, including business (Anderson and Williams, 2012; M. A. Levin and Peterson, 2013), psychology (Beyer, 2011), statistics (Wolverton, Butler, Martinson, and Thomas, 2014), and English (Gries and Brooke, 2010; Wolverton et al., 2014). Although the use of pecha kucha in a writing class might seem somewhat surprising, it is apparently very useful for teaching about powerful visual metaphors and the importance of the editing process in creative works (Gries and Brooke, 2010). The pecha kucha format does not result in higher learning scores compared to students who merely watch a presentation (Klentzin, Paladino, Johnston, and Devine, 2010), but the active learning involved in creating a pecha kucha presentation are rated by students as being a valuable learning experience (M. A. Levin and Peterson, 2013).

Teachers who are interested in using the pecha kucha style for class projects will need to invest some time into preparing the students for this format. It will take effort on the instructor's part to make the students clearly understand that pecha kucha is not the same as a typical powerpoint presentation. Showing an example pecha kucha presentation is a good way to start (many are available online; see www.pechakucha.org). Students may also need technical help with setting the slides to automatically advance every twenty seconds. Providing a template file with this feature enabled is a good way to address this need. The students also need to understand that pecha kucha-style presentations should be image-focused rather than the standard text and bullet points. Finally, the successful instructor will need to encourage students to rehearse the presentation, perhaps many times, to get comfortable with the up-tempo nature of this presentation style.

Many More Possibilities for Active Learning

There are numerous other ways that powerpoint could be used to promote active learning in the classroom. One possibility is to use powerpoint for organizing classroom discussion activities. The question that represents the focal point of discussion could be displayed on the projection screen at the front of the room. This facilitates discussion because the question has a visual persistence: It does not fade from memory like a question delivered by voice might. Students can refer back to this question as they form their responses. Other details about the discussion activity could also be listed on this slide. This might save the instructor from distributing paper handouts that describe the assignment or repeatedly announcing the activity requirements. Using powerpoint in this manner may have a beneficial effect by guiding the class through an active learning exercise.

In psychology, important phenomena can sometimes be directly conveyed to the students so that the students can experience it for themselves. There are examples of short term memory demonstrations and visual illusions that can be put into a powerpoint presentation. This direct experience with the subject matter may facilitate the formation of memories that are both verbal (from the powerpoint text) and experiential (from the demonstration).

Educators who teach science, math, or engineering may benefit from the highly visual nature of brief videos or animations that illustrate the movements of complex objects. Projection technology could be used to show students a live view of a microscopic image. In math classes, problems can be projected on to the screen for the students to solve. After this, the answers can be revealed on the following slide, along with an explanation. This approach requires student involvement and provides feedback on the answers (see Chapter 16 for an example).

A Spanish teacher shared a simple active learning exercise that she uses to promote active learning. The powerpoint displays short passages in Spanish on the screen. The students take turns reading these passages out loud to the rest of the class, which makes the students an active participant in the powerpoint presentation. The students benefit by getting feedback on their efforts. The rest of the class sees role models of good (and maybe not-so-good) pronunciations. Witnessing these examples from other students can form the basis of an observational learning process. Student involvement in this exercise is quite high because there is some social pressure to perform well. A similar approach will work well in other classes. In Sensation & Perception, I explain the different forms of monocular cues for depth perception to the students, along with examples. This is followed by a series of full-screen images from sites around the college campus. The students are asked to identify examples of the various monocular depth perception cues in the scene with a brief explanation of why this situation illustrates a particular concept. Powerpoint provides the means to accomplish this kind of rich active learning experience.

The important take-home idea is that the multimedia capabilities of powerpoint may facilitate active learning exercises. Embedded videos might serve as a launching point for an in-class discussion. The use of hyperlinks might help to organize information in a fashion that is organic and nonlinear. Links to different slide topics in the slide deck might be helpful to support learning processes. In this manner, powerpoint can be seen as a computer programming platform for educators. It enables instructors to assemble a rich assortment of information in creative ways to provide a stimulating experience that promotes active student learning. This medium can clearly be much more than overly simple lists of points that form the basis of most current powerpoint presentations. All that is needed is a creative learning approach, one that goes beyond a chalkboard-like use of powerpoint technology.

There are numerous ways to promote active learning with powerpoint, many of which may be specific to a particular topic or discipline. A common factor in all of these is to structure the powerpoint to provide students a challenge based upon the subject phenomenon. After this, it is up to the students to think deeply about the challenge, take action, and give an appropriate answer or response. The requirement of student involvement in these challenges should be interesting and beneficial to the learning process. It requires students to shift from absorbing information to actually using the new concepts in a realistic and productive manner. In addition, students can evaluate their own learning when they receive feedback on their responses to the challenge. There are also opportunities for interactions between students and observational learning from the examples seen by other students. These activities tend to be stimulating and have high student engagement.

Design for Active Learning Processes

The guiding spirit of this chapter is that the default role of powerpoint—information delivery—is not as important in modern education as it once was. Because the focus of modern education is more constructivist, the traditional use of powerpoint should be intentionally suspended at strategic moments during a lecture to make room for active learning. Doing so gives students a needed break from the task of absorbing more and more information. At these critical points, the teaching mission can switch from information delivery to active learning exercises that involve questions, discussions, or other activities. Lectures are good for information delivery, but teachers need to mix up the lecture approach with other learning strategies to promote the best educational outcomes.

Powerpoint is still a useful teaching technology even when it is not being used for information delivery. There are many ways that powerpoint can be used to promote active learning, such as student response system quizzes and present-to-learn approaches. Using powerpoint in these atypical ways must become a standard practice if we want to promote higher-order learning processes.

DESIGN FOR BEHAVIOR

Influences on Note-taking and Attendance

A few students were exceptionally thorough note-takers, but most did little more than to copy down the key terms and topic headings provided on the transparency. (Baker and Lombardi, 1985, p. 32)

An enlightening teaching experience happened to me many years ago, when I was just beginning to use powerpoint in my classroom lectures. My powerpoint presentations at that time were very basic, containing mostly headings and bullet point lists of key terms. They included only a few instructional graphics. The powerpoint presentations were essentially the same outlines that I once wrote on the chalkboard.

One day, a student pulled me aside just a few minutes before class to tell me that they would not be present in class due to an urgent personal situation. The student followed this information with a variation on the "Are we doing anything important today?" question. It's a question that frequently comes up in these situations. This question is annoying because it implies that most class meetings aren't really important. This student's variation was slightly different though, and it had a lasting impact on me.

"Are we just copying today?"

Thie question caught me off-guard. At first, it wasn't clear to me what the student meant, so I hesitated. I had never thought of my class as being a mere copying exercise. After a moment, I responded with something like "If you feel that this situation is urgent, you don't have to come to class today." The student was satisfied with this response, and I went ahead with teaching the class, just like usual.

The "copy" question stuck with me after this class period was over. It seemed that this student viewed my carefully prepared presentations as a simple information transfer exercise: The professor puts something up on the screen and the students copy it down. If this was true, the class required minimal note-taking effort and no active thought process. The question suggested disengagement from the course. This experience was a critical moment, one that makes a teacher deeply question their methods and search for finding a better way to increase student engagement. Perhaps this book can be viewed as the culmination of years of professional development towards answering this "copying" question. It sparked a search for finding powerpoint presentation techniques that would really engage students, stimulate thought, and produce a more authentic kind of learning.

After this episode, I began looking for signs of simple powerpoint copying. These signs can sometimes be detected while walking around a classroom and observing the notes that the students are taking. The following figure (13.1) is an example of student notes that seem to be a word-for-word copy of a powerpoint presentation. Even the bullet points have been recreated in the notes. The notes seem to exhibit no attempt to go beyond the content presented in the powerpoint slide.

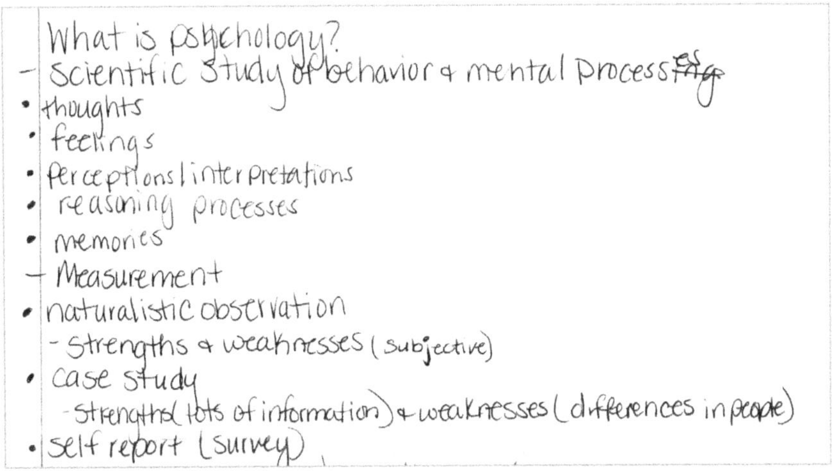

```
What is psychology?
- Scientific study of behavior & mental processing
• thoughts
• feelings
• perceptions/interpretations
• reasoning processes
• memories
- Measurement
• naturalistic observation
    - strengths & weaknesses (subjective)
• case study
    - strengths (lots of information) & weaknesses (differences in people)
• self report (survey)
```

Figure 13.1: An example of student notes based on a powerpoint presentation

This chapter focuses on how students react to the use of powerpoint. How does powerpoint influence student behavior, particularly student note-taking? A related topic is how making slide deck files available to students outside of class (e.g., uploading them to a course management system) influences both note-taking and attendance.

The Importance of Note-Taking

Recording notes during a class presentation has long been considered a positive student behavior. Both students and faculty agree that note-taking is helpful. In one study, students indicated a strong agreement with this question: "Overall, note-taking is very important to my academic success." (Williams et al., 2013, p. 96). However, the benefits of note-taking are not merely perceived; evidence from cognitive science research supports the utility of this practice.

One way note-taking helps students is by providing a form of information storage. Essential information can be recorded as notes and then studied at a later time. Students generally view note-taking as being important for information storage reasons (Badger, White, Sutherland, and Haggis, 2001). From a learning theory perspective, the use of notes as an information storage device suggests an information transfer model of learning. Information is moved from the teacher's mind to the student's notes and, eventually, the student's memory.

There is more to note-taking than simply storing information. A secondary role of note-taking involves the active selection and organization of important information from the presented material (Di Vesta and Gray, 1972; Hartley and Davies, 1978; Howe, 1974). During the note-taking process, students actively relate new information to ideas that they already understand in order to form a new level of understanding. This means that the activity of note-taking does more than simply store information on paper. Note-taking actually helps to form long-term memories and schemata (conceptual organization) in the brain. In cognitive psychology, this phenomenon has been variously called the encoding effect or the generative role of note-taking. In the field of education, this function might be called active learning, a term which implies more than just passive student listening, or constructivism, a term used to refer to a personal, subjective understanding of the course content. The encoding-related effects of note-taking may be small and may depend on a multitude of factors (for a review, see Kobayasi, 2005). In real educational situations, students likely benefit from both information storage and the encoding of new memory during the note-taking process.

Even though students understand the importance of taking notes, research studies of their behavior have clearly documented that students tend to be poor note-takers. In one typical study, students only recorded about 50% of the main ideas from a lecture (Baker and Lombardi, 1985). The range of recording critical information in notes is from 11% to 70%, with most studies reporting around 25% to 50% of the key ideas being captured (Kiewra, 1985). In contrast, most students believe that their note-taking skills are be very strong (Williams et al., 2013).

The low rate of recording important information in student notes is problematic for both the storage and the encoding functions of note-taking. If the goal of taking notes is information storage, then poor note-taking fails on that front because missing information cannot be used later to study for an examination. In addition, when students omit lecture information from notes, it suggests that they view this content as being unimportant, making it unlikely that the information was encoded into their long-term memory. Given these problems, a long-standing concern in the field of note-taking research has been to improve the quality of student notes. Better notes will hopefully translate into better study materials and a more active encoding of information into memory, eventually leading to better performance on examinations.

Powerpoint to the Rescue?

An important reason to use powerpoint in education is to highlight the key ideas in a presentation. If a concept is on the teacher's slides, the students will interpret this information as being important and will record it in their notes. In multimedia learning theory, this could be called a signaling effect: The presence of a key term on a slide communicates to students the importance of the idea.

Research on student note-taking provides strong evidence that students view the material presented in powerpoint slides as being important and, therefore, worthy of recording (Badger et al., 2001). Experimental studies also show that the use of powerpoint increased the quality of student notes (Austin, Lee, and Carr, 2004). One study compared students given different cues for recording information, such as powerpoint slides, verbal cues, or discussion cues. This study found a high rate of recording information from powerpoint slides, but much lower rates of recording information from the other sources (Huxam, 2010). This finding is consistent with earlier studies that were done with overhead transparencies and chalkboards (Baker and Lombardi, 1985; Locke, 1977). In one study, students recorded almost everything (88%) that was written on the chalkboard, but information not written on the chalkboard was recorded only 51.6% of the time (Locke, 1977). A similar study showed an even lower rate (27%) of note-taking for information that was not on the chalkboard (Locke, 1975). Overall, the research consistently shows that students are much more likely to record information presented to them in a visual rather than a spoken form.

These research findings show that powerpoint addresses the important note-taking problem of clearly communicating the key ideas from a lecture to the students. Anything that the instructor believes to be important should be put into the visual slide presentation. The visual presence in the slides sends a clear message to students that this material is important and worthy of being in the notes. Powerpoint use should help to increase the number of important points from a class that students capture in their notes.

Although powerpoint sends helpful note-taking cues, potential problems still exist with using powerpoint to guide student note-taking efforts. One problem is that some students record rather little in their notes, even when instructors use powerpoint to cue students about the important points (Huxam, 2010). A related problem is that much of the information that students record from a powerpoint slide could accurately be described as verbatim note-taking: Their notes are an exact replica of the slide information, such as Figure 13.1. The problem with verbatim notes is that such note-takers have made very little effort to understand key terms or make connections between concepts, both of which are crucial parts of the learning process. For example, one study found that only 22% of the notes were of sufficient quality to demonstrate understanding (Huxam, 2010). A third potential problem is that some students may still struggle with identifying the key ideas, even when these ideas are presented on the powerpoint slide (Haynes, McCarley, and Williams, 2015; Williams et al., 2016). Students may view all of the information from a powerpoint presentation as being of equal importance, even when this is clearly not true. If students' approach to note-taking involves simply copying information, this will not enable the student to distinguish more important material from less important material.

In sum, it appears that powerpoint provides a useful yet only partial solution to guiding student note-taking efforts. Instructors can use powerpoint to clearly signal the content and ideas that are important and encourage the recording of this information in notes. The problem, though, is that relying on powerpoint for these signals generally leads to low-quality records of the presented information which show little evidence of understanding or other higher-level thinking skills. Again, this problem is not unique to powerpoint (e.g., Locke, 1977); it may be more accurate to say that powerpoint is not a magical panacea for the problem of poor note-taking.

Making Powerpoint Files Available to Students

It has long been thought that instructors should try to enhance the quality of student notes by providing assistance that might improve note-taking efforts. One form of assistance takes the form of outlines of the lecture material, sometimes called 'partial notes' (Annis, 1981; Kiewra, 1985; Kiewra et al., 1988). The intent for providing this resource is to give students a framework for organizing the topic material. The students' job is to fill in the details of the framework with their own notes taken during class (see also Chapter 12). In general, these instructor-provided materials would meet two important needs of note-taking. First, the instructor-provided information would ensure the completeness and accuracy of the resources for storage and review, which fills the need for information storage. Second, since they were provided with key information, students would be free from the need to record lots of lecture information. Students could then direct their note-taking effort toward recording thoughts, reactions, and other kinds of active or constructive learning that might help the encoding of long-term memories.

A different type of solution, particularly if students are poor at recording information, is to give the students highly-detailed handouts (Katayama and Crooks, 2003; Kiewra, 1985; Kiewra et al., 1988). Full notes are somewhat helpful, but the students who are given these resources typically do not perform as well as students who receive partial notes. The complete notes decrease the students' need to work at note-taking, and the corresponding lack of student effort translates into lower grades. From a cognitive psychology perspective, it is possible to decrease the cognitive load too much, removing all need for effortful processing. The students clearly need to put some effort into recording notes in order to form new memories.

Although early studies showed that providing partial notes assisted note-taking, it was not widely adopted in practice. In the 1970s and 1980s, making paper copies of note-taking resources and distributing them before class was cumbersome. The transition to powerpoint technology dramatically changed this process by eliminating the need for paper copies altogether. It is now relatively easy for teachers to upload their powerpoint files or lecture outlines to an online course management system, such as Blackboard, Brightspace, or Moodle. Students can access the presentation files before or during class and then use these resources to augment their note-taking during the class presentation.

Students strongly approve of having online access to their teacher's powerpoint files (Badger et al., 2001; Worthington and

Levasseur, 2015). This information can serve as a guide to key ideas in the presentation, which is probably the biggest advantage of providing this access. The students do not have to copy down every word because some of the material is already available to them. Thus, the students can annotate the powerpoint file or print-out with their own thoughts, insights, possible exam questions, and issues for further clarification. Some students feel that access to the powerpoint slides is useful for keeping up with the rapid pace of a presentation and avoiding information overload (Sambrook and Rowley, 2010). Non-native English speakers and students with reading disabilities or hearing impairments may feel that the instructor-provided notes are valuable resources (Sambrook and Rowley, 2010). Students also like to use powerpoint files as a study guide when they prepare for exams. One student survey found that 69.2% of students "always" and 15.4% "usually" use instructor-provided powerpoint files as review material before tests (Debevec, Shih, and Kashyap, 2006).

There is another dimension to powerpoint that should also be considered, one that is broader than serving the note-taking needs of students. The modern use of powerpoint in our culture has two purposes. The first and most obvious purpose is to support presentations. The second purpose of powerpoint, which is newer and less obvious, is to preserve a record of information that was given during a meeting. This usually means storing the powerpoint slide deck file online or on a corporate network so the people in the audience can access it at a later time. This dual role of powerpoint—presentation and document—has become a standard practice in business and government (Knoblauch, 2012; Nathans-Kelly and Nicometo, 2014). Given this cultural standard, it would be a good practice to provide powerpoint files online in a course management system, as it will provide students with a good model for using powerpoint in their future occupations.

Although the practice of providing powerpoint files for students is now commonplace, it is worth examining whether or not having access to these files can really improve student performance on exams. Many studies have been conducted to address this question. Some of these studies employ an experimental approach (Does powerpoint file access cause better exam performance?) and some of these studies have taken a correlational approach (Is there a relationship or pattern between students downloading the slides and course grades?). The overall research findings are mixed. Out of fifteen reviewed studies, only six report a positive effect of providing powerpoint files online to students (Austin et al., 2004; Chen and Lin, 2008; Cornelius and Owen-DeSchryver, 2008; Frank, Shaw, and Wilson, 2008; Grabe, Christoperson, and Douglas, 2004; Hammonds, 2003). In contrast, seven studies found no improvement (Bowman, 2009; Debevec et al., 2006; Noppe, 2007; Nouri and Shahid, 2008; Stark-Wroblewski et al., 2006; Vandehey, Marsh, and Diekhoff, 2005; Worthington and Levasseur, 2015), and one study found a decline in grades (Weatherly, Grabe, and Arthur, 2002) for students who had powerpoint file access. One report had mixed results, with handouts leading to improvement in one experiment and no improvement in another (Marsh and Sink, 2010). Even when powerpoint file availability is beneficial, it seems that the benefits are small, with reported grade increases of only 3.5% to 6% across the entire class (Chen and Lin, 2008; Grabe et al., 2004). A research weakness in some studies is that correlations showing improved test scores associated with powerpoint file availability cannot be interpreted as demonstrating that powerpoint access *causes* better student grades (Cannon, 2011). It could be that students who download powerpoint files have other characteristics associated with greater academic success—such as being more organized or having more proactive study skills—that could cause them to do well on an exam with or without powerpoint file access.

A simple explanation for the weak educational benefits of slide deck availability is that many students do not use the available slide decks to guide their note-taking. Studies show that only thirty-five to fifty percent of students download slide decks before class, which is when this resource would be most beneficial for guiding note-taking efforts (Chen and Lin, 2008; Debevec et al., 2006; Grabe et al., 2004; Worthington and Levasseur, 2015). In one study, only eight percent of the students printed the slides before class to use as a note-taking resource (I. Wilson, 2016). Clearly, many students do not seem to take advantage of instructor-provided resources for improving their notes. Another problem is that the effectiveness of instructor-provided notes can be diminished if students do not understand how they should use instructor-provided resources. For example, students may be uncertain about whether they should add more information to the powerpoint file during class, or if they should just listen attentively to the instructor without writing anything down. Some students also complain that instructor-provided resources may have too much information or are poorly organized, which might decrease their educational effectiveness (Pardini et al., 2005).

Fortunately, the research literature in this area provides suggestions that may help instructors and students maximize the effectiveness of online powerpoint resources. A good starting point is whether or not the full slide deck should be made available. A number of studies suggest that partial notes, such as an outline, may be more beneficial than a more detailed set of notes (Annis, 1981; Cornelius and Owen-DeSchryver, 2008; Katayama and Crooks, 2003). Partial notes provide needed information and guidance, yet they still require a more active level of student involvement than full notes. Another decision when posting powerpoint files online concerns the resource format. Students seem to prefer text-based resources, such as bullet points, over image-based or audio-based resources (Garrett, 2015; Grabe and Christoperson, 2008). The student preference for text over images suggests that it might be worthwhile to convert a powerpoint presentation, particularly one that is image-heavy, to a text-only outline for sharing with the students. The timing of the resource availability is also important. Instructors should make these resources available before the class so the students will be able to use these resources as guides for their note-taking efforts during class. A possible variation is to make partial notes available before class (to help encoding and active learning) and full notes available after class.

Just as we should not assume that students naturally know how to take good notes, we also should not assume that students will naturally know how to use note-taking resources that the instructor provides. Less than half of the students will print the powerpoint file before class when this resource is available. This suggests that students may need direct encouragement or instruction to download and print powerpoint files before class. Students may also need help in using this resource to identify the most important ideas to record in their notes (Haynes et al., 2015; I. Wilson, 2016).

Powerpoint File Access and Student Attendance

> I missed classes thinking I could just look at the [online] notes, (then did bad on the test). . . . [S]tudents that have access . . . will probably assume that they can procrastinate, or only study a little because they have the answers right there (at least that's what I did, and it didn't work too well). Anonymous student from Stark-Wroblewski et al., 2006, p. 34

Class attendance is a student behavior that may be affected by powerpoint. This possibility is most relevant to college-level courses that may not have strict attendance policies. Since class attendance is known to be important for college success, any influence that powerpoint might have on attendance could be either helpful or harmful.

Several early studies found that attendance was improved in courses that used powerpoint presentations, presumably due to increased student motivation (Daniels, 1999; Evans, 1998 as cited in Szabo and Hastings, 2000; Susskind, 2005; Szabo and Hastings, 2000). Other studies, in contrast, have found that the use of powerpoint has no effect on student attendance, either positive or negative (Beets and Lobinger, 2001; Frey and Birnbaum, 2002; Sambrook and Rowley, 2010; Susskind, 2008). One interpretation of these mixed research findings is that powerpoint presentations may have boosted attendance when it was a new technology, but may not increase attendance at the present time because powerpoint is no longer a novelty to students (L. A. Burke and James, 2008). In one set of studies, students were more likely to self-report that they would attend a lecture with a powerpoint on a survey (Susskind, 2005), but a subsequent study based on actual attendance records was unable to confirm a real increase in attendance (Susskind, 2008). This difference between student perceptions and actual attendance records might also explain why some studies find increased attendance while other studies find no evidence of improved attendance. Altogether, the research findings suggest that using powerpoint in the classroom probably has no significant influence on student attendance or, at the very least, cannot provide a guarantee of increased attendance.

The possibility that powerpoint might change student attendance for the worse is relevant to the common practice of making powerpoint files available online to students. Concerns have been raised that students who can download a powerpoint presentation are less likely to attend class (e.g., Schuman, 2014). In particular, if students view a class lecture as a simple information transfer exercise (i.e., "copying"), then getting the key points from an online powerpoint file makes class attendance completely unnecessary. It would be much more efficient for students to simply download the file and not bother taking the time to attend class. To address this possibility, several studies have asked this question: Will classroom attendance decrease if powerpoint files are made available to students?

Again, the research evidence is mixed. A few reports of powerpoint use indicate decreasing class attendance. One professor observed a 20% drop in attendance when powerpoint files were made available to the students (Young, 2004), although this evidence is anecdotal and should be interpreted with caution. In one survey, students reported that they were less likely to attend class and were more likely to procrastinate if the instructor provided notes (Pardini et al., 2005). In another student survey, the students reported that having instructor-provided notes would not negatively affect their own attendance, but it might negatively affect the attendance of other students (Sambrook and Rowley, 2010).

In contrast, the majority of studies on attendance did not find decreased attendance when slide decks were made available to students. Ten empirical studies, based on varying research methodologies, report no adverse attendance effects from posting powerpoint slide decks online for student access (Bowman, 2009; L. A. Burke and James, 2008; Cornelius and Owen-DeSchryver, 2008; Debevec et al., 2006; Frank et al., 2008; Frey and Birnbaum, 2002; Grabe and Christoperson, 2008; Gurrie and Fair, 2008; Vandehey et al., 2005; Worthington and Levasseur, 2015). One study suggests that students with certain learning style preferences might be less likely to attend class if powerpoint slides can be downloaded, even though there was no overall decline in attendance for the class as a whole (Debevec et al., 2006). Several studies that failed to find a connection between powerpoint slide downloads and poor attendance did, however, find a general influence of attendance on grades. In other words, students who have poor attendance tend to do worse in class regardless of whether or not they have downloaded the powerpoint file (Bowman, 2009; Debevec et al., 2006; Worthington and Levasseur, 2015). Again, the real association at work here may be the influence of personal characteristics such as poor work ethic or ineffective study habits, which could affect both attendance and grades independently of powerpoint availability.

Most students seem to be aware of the importance of attending class. In one study, 17% of the students said that they were less likely to attend class when powerpoint was available online. However, the overall results suggested that most students felt that attendance was important and that online access to the powerpoint files was useful for note-taking activities (Gurrie and Fair, 2008). This pattern is likely true with many classes. Perhaps attendance is only a problem for a small proportion of students who are weakly motivated and who are at risk for doing poorly in class anyway. Powerpoint file access and regular attendance might still be valued by most of the class.

Some anecdotal evidence suggests that giving powerpoint file access to students causes lower attendance only when the teacher misuses powerpoint in a particular pattern. First, the powerpoint slides contain a large amount of text, which turns the powerpoint file into a stand-alone document. In other words, the powerpoint file by itself is sufficient to be understood without any commentary from the teacher. The second related condition is bad presentation practices, such as the teacher merely reading the text from the powerpoint display to the students, which most students find boring or even aggravating. When a detailed slide deck is available to students and is combined with a boring presentation style, the students might conclude that class time is simply not valuable. We should emphasize that this pattern does not describe good teaching practices. This pattern results in the dullest kind of class, and it seems likely that attendance might suffer in this kind of situation regardless of whether or not the powerpoint files were available outside of class sessions.

The overall picture from research studies suggests that making powerpoint slides available to students does not seem to cause a strong negative influence on class attendance. The majority of students believe that attendance is important and they will attend class regularly, even if the powerpoint slides are available online. Instructors who have reservations about sharing slides with students through online resources should not be too concerned about declining attendance. Still, instructors need to be vigilant about the possibility of lower attendance. The students may need to be informed that the purpose of class meetings and note-taking is more than just an information transfer process. In small classes, instructors can monitor attendance for signs of poor student engagement.

Design Tip: Make Powerpoint Files or Outlines Available to the Students

Powerpoint clearly can influence student behavior in various, though somewhat ambiguous, ways. Powerpoint may send important signals to students about the key ideas of a topic, but the downside is that powerpoint can promote the passive recording of information rather than deeper learning. Many instructors who make their slide decks available outside of class hope that doing so will help improve their students' note-taking skill by decreasing the need to merely transcribe information. In addition, students strongly approve of having access to powerpoint files. However, the availability of teacher slide decks is associated with, at best, only a modest improvement on student grades. Nevertheless, such availability does not seem to have a significant negative impact on attendance. Based on this evidence, a weak recommendation is to provide powerpoint files to students in the hopes that these resources may be beneficial for note-taking and study review efforts.

Because, again, students really prefer the text from powerpoint presentations, simply providing the text rather than the full powerpoint slides would be most useful. A text-only resource would be missing some information, which would make it similar to the partial notes conditions that produced the best learning outcomes in some notetaking studies. Student attendance and engagement would still be needed to fill in the gaps of missing information.

This chapter began with a story about how students might view powerpoint presentations as a mere copying exercise. This does not have to be the standard student experience. The use of better slide designs, such as using multimedia principles to guide slide construction, should result in a more engaging learning event. In addition, teachers need to ensure they use active learning methods as a part of the course. Taking these steps will ensure that students view class time as a meaningful and engaging learning experience, so they will hopefully make a strong effort to attend every class period.

TECHNOLOGY CHOICES

Evaluating PowerPoint and Similar Presentation Technologies

Microsoft PowerPoint has set the standard for office presentation software since it was introduced in 1990. The estimated market share of PowerPoint is over 90%, making it the undisputed leader of presentation software. This market dominance has thoroughly penetrated our culture as well. Whefn people think of presentations, they naturally assume that PowerPoint is the technology used for multimedia purposes.

Although Microsoft's PowerPoint is the clear leader, some teachers feel that that their needs are not fully met by this product. As we have seen, there are some concerns about the linear nature of slide decks and other limitations that PowerPoint imposes on users. There are numerous other software possibilities that can be used for delivering the multimedia component of presentations. One review of PowerPoint alternatives from 2017 described 36

PowerPoint-like applications (Croxton, 2017). In this chapter, the advantages and disadvantages of PowerPoint will be briefly reviewed. Several other possible alternatives to PowerPoint will also be explored to see if the needs of teachers can be better met with specialized products. Nontraditional distance learning uses of PowerPoint will also be considered.

Microsoft's PowerPoint: The King of Presentation Software

PowerPoint has a multitude of software features for designing and delivering presentations, such as slide templates, themes, and drawing tools. The advanced features include the creation of animations, editing photos, and embedding audio or video into slides. Altogether, the ability to organize a wide range of text, images, audio, and video makes PowerPoint a central organizing container for delivering various forms of multimedia resources during a class presentation. Many features are also available for controlling the delivery of the presentation.

Being the industry leader comes with numerous advantages. Most educators will have office and classroom computers that come with Microsoft Office applications, of which PowerPoint is an important component. There is a great convenience to using a software standard. PowerPoint users can feel confident that their presentations will work on almost any personal computer. There is an entire technology ecosystem that supports PowerPoint, including how-to instructional books and videos. Optional presentation hardware, such as remote presentation controls and student response systems, are typically designed to be used with

PowerPoint presentations, which eliminates potential headaches that might be caused by hardware incompatibilities.

There are a few downsides to PowerPoint. Having a multitude of software features is usually viewed as being positive, but it can occasionally be the source of problems. Users can become overwhelmed with too many software features, including features that may potentially harm the quality of presentations. For example, PowerPoint provides many possibilities for generic clip-art, overly fanciful slide templates, and unnecessary animations that most presentation experts warn against using. Another practical drawback is that the software can be expensive. This may not matter much to faculty who have computers provided by their schools, but the cost may be an important barrier to students who need to design presentations for classroom projects.

PowerPoint software has a long history compared to most contemporary computer technology. While a positive in many regards, this legacy or long tradition may also been seen as problematic. Standard features of PowerPoint may not be well suited to classroom use for a variety of historical reasons, such as being developed for business needs rather than educational needs. The original designers of PowerPoint were computer programmers who had no background in giving presentations. Fundamental aspects of PowerPoint slides, such as the emphasis on bullet points, can be viewed as a carryover from the limitations of the 1990s personal computers. These historical roots have created potentially problematic standards of emphasizing text over images in PowerPoint presentations. Another legacy hardware downside is that PowerPoint tends to favor files that are located on a local hard disk. This local storage inclination is at odds with the increasingly online nature of information such as web pages and videos. Current versions of PowerPoint have features for using links and cloud-based computer files, but these features can feel like awkward add-ons to a product that was originally intended for desktop computers. Most recently, Microsoft has begun to embrace the modern networked computing environment with web-based versions of PowerPoint in Office 365. Perhaps future versions will be friendlier to online information.

There are two notable software alternatives for desktop or laptop computers that closely match the features and capabilities of PowerPoint. For Apple computers, Keynote is a presentation application from the iWork office software suite. Keynote was used to develop and deliver the media presentations in Al Gore's award-winning "An Inconvenient Truth" documentary (see http://www.duarte.com/portfolio/an-irresistible-keynote/), which demonstrates the powerful potential of this software. A limitation of Keynote is that it only runs on Apple computer products. The second notable PowerPoint alternative is Impress from the LibreOffice/OpenOffice software suite. This application has almost all of the same features as PowerPoint, making it a workalike clone. Impress is available for free and runs on Windows, Apple, or Linux-based computers.

Having several software possibilities can be a downside because these technologies are incompatible with each other. Situations may arise in which a presentation was created in Keynote or Impress but the classroom projection system is based on PowerPoint. This is particularly likely to occur when students occasionally use these PowerPoint alternatives to create classroom presentations. Fortunately, there are easy solutions. Both Keynote and Impress can save or "export" files to the PowerPoint format (.ppt or .pptx on Windows computers). These exported presentation files can then be opened on systems that use PowerPoint. Another option is the web site cloudconvert.com. Upload the Keynote or Impress file to cloudconvert.com, select the desired file format, wait a moment, and then download the converted PowerPoint file. This service is free and does not require special software. Conversions to PowerPoint can be done quickly in a classroom situation, if needed, for facilitating student presentations.

Web-Based Presentation Applications

An important trend in computer technology over the last decade is the movement towards portability, such as smart phones, tablet computers, and so-called cloud storage of critical files (e.g., Dropbox, OneDrive, or Google Drive). This portability trend has increasingly emphasized online applications that are hosted on remote computers and accessed through a web browser on a hand-held device. This trend towards online computing resources is reflected in a number of web-based presentation applications, such as Microsoft's PowerPoint 365 (as part of the online Office365 application suite), Zoho Show, and Clearslide (formerly Sliderocket). The web-based PowerPoint alternatives usually have a feature/flexibility tradeoff. The upside of being web-based is that these applications can be accessed from any computer that is connected to the Internet. This might be a strong advantage if the presenter's goal is to give presentations from a wide range of computer platforms, post slides on the web, or give remote presentations. A chief disadvantage of online applications is that they tend to have fewer features than the desktop or laptop version of Microsoft's PowerPoint. Basic edits are possible with the online systems, but advanced features are usually lacking. For a comprehensive review of online presentation applications, please see Croxton's (2017) round-up of web-based alternatives to PowerPoint.

A flexibility advantage of PowerPoint 365 and many of the online presentation application is the ability to collaborate online with multiple authors during the creation of a slide deck. The authors have the freedom to separately log into the system and make slides at different times and different locations. This feature can be valuable for student presentations that require group collaboration. The ability to collaboratively author slide decks online may not be necessary for most teachers, but it could be a strong advantage for educators who assign presentation projects to their students.

Some online PowerPoint alternatives explicitly aim to break with potentially problematic PowerPoint conventions such as bullet point lists and linear slide decks. Of these, Prezi (prezi.com) has received the greatest degree of attention. Prezi is a free online presentation application that is somewhat like conventional PowerPoint yet has an innovative twist. The Prezi presentation begins with a large master slide—the infinite canvas—that works like a cognitive map of the overall presentation. The speaker can zoom into this canvas to reveal more details about a specific subtopic. The speaker can move through these subtopics in any desired order, which makes the flow of the presentation less confined than the typical linear order imposed by a conventional PowerPoint presentation. An unusual downside of Prezi is that the zooming effects can trigger nausea in some audience members: an effect that is called "Prezi sickness." The general recommendation is to avoid going too quickly through the presentation. The Prezi web site even has a special Prezi presentation on this topic—"Avoiding Prezilepsy"—that gives tips about ways to avoid motion sickness.

The educational view of Prezi is that this technology functions more like a graphical organizer or mind-map than the usual PowerPoint bullet list. A slide that starts with a map of Europe or an image of the brain is a good starting point to give the students a context. The instructor can then zoom into a particular region of Europe or the brain to reveal more details. This zooming feature might help students make connections between the whole (or context) and the parts of the topic.

Student perceptions of Prezi presentations are generally positive (Brock and Brodahl, 2013; Conboy et al., 2012; Virtanen et al., 2013). Some instructors feel that Prezi may hold audience attention better than the PowerPoint presentations. However, direct comparisons of Prezi to PowerPoint have not found that Prezi produces superior learning performance (Castelyn and Mottart, 2012; Castelyn et al., 2013; Chou et al., 2015). Prezi has also been successfully used for student presentation projects, although some students report that Prezi is more difficult and time consuming to use than PowerPoint (Brock and Brodahl, 2013; Conboy et al., 2012).

Another web-based presentation application is Haiku Deck, which was specifically designed to meet the needs of teacher and student presentations (Coget, 2015). The inspiration for this software comes from the Japanese haiku poetry tradition, which is characterized by a brief and simple elegance. Haiku Deck emphasizes simplicity through highly constrained options for creating basic slides. There are only four possible slide formats: title, bullet point, numerical list, and unformatted text. Each slide format also has limits, such as a five bullet point maximum, to help prevent clutter and information overload. Problematic features, like flying bullet point animations, are not available. The constraints force users to create a highly focused message, somewhat like Twitter (Coget, 2015) or possibly pecha kucha (see Chapter 12). The simplicity of this platform might also facilitate the creation of presentations on portable computing devices such as smart phones and tablets. The Haiku Deck system also has a classroom environment feature that enables students to easily create and share slide decks during class. Teachers can use the Haiku Deck system to quickly make basic presentations, which could help to increase teacher productivity. In regard to cost, Haiku Deck has a limited free trial offering of three presentations. A monthly or annual subscription fee is needed to access the full capabilities of this platform.

    A third noteworthy web-based PowerPoint alternative is the Slides application of the Google office suite. This application offers many features that are similar to PowerPoint, including slide authoring, style templates, and a presentation mode. The web-based nature lends itself well to a wide range of computing platforms, such as desktop or laptop computers, tablets, and smart phones. The key advantage for educators is that Slides is a component of Google's popular office software suite. Many teachers and students who are accustomed to Google's other educational services, such as Gmail-based email, Chromebooks, and Google Classroom, may find it convenient to create and present their presentations within the same environment. The Slides application might be particularly useful for students due to the web-based advantages: Portability, compatibility, and online collaboration with other students. This application is available for free, another feature that should greatly appeal to students.

Broadly speaking, the computing environment has changed dramatically over the last decade, with a movement away from desktop computers towards smaller, more portable devices like smart phones and tablets. PowerPoint and similar software applications are no exception to this trend. The capabilities of web-based presentation applications have been greatly improved and expanded over the last several years. It seems quite likely that online, cloud-based technology is the future direction of presentation software, with the flexibility and other advantages that web-based software has to offer. Another possibility is that a traditional/cloud hybrid model will emerge, in which presentations are authored on desktop computers but are presented with cloud-based technologies.

PowerPoint for Distance Education

A second important long term trend in the field of education is the increase in distance education delivered via the Internet. PowerPoint has shown a remarkable ability to adapt to these newer online needs. Powerpoint-style presentations are increasingly given through a variety of online technologies in which the educator does not need to be in the same physical space as the student.

One approach to making an online powerpoint presentation is to record the spoken component of a presentation as a narration that can be integrated into the slide presentation. The end product is a powerpoint presentation that can be watched over the Internet without the instructor's presence. In PowerPoint, voice-over narrations can be created through the "Slide Show" tab, then "Record Slide Show" button. The resulting dialog box that pops up has checked radio buttons for "Slide and animation timings" (for recording the slide transitions) and "Narrations, ink, and laser pointer" (for recording voice and other features). The "Start recording" button begins a normal slide presentation while recording the speaker's voice from a microphone and the slide transitions with either mouse buttons or keyboard inputs. After finishing, the resulting presentation with the voice-over narration can be saved as a PowerPoint file or it can be saved as a video file format, such as mpeg-4 (file extension .mp4) or Windows media video (.wmv). The video formats are the best choice for online courses. These video files display the slides and play the audio recording for each slide as the slide deck advances, giving the presentation a stand-alone quality that eliminates the physical presence of the teacher.

Narrated PowerPoint files can also be used for whiteboard-like functions. These might be particularly useful for doing basic math or similar kinds of demonstrations. For this feature, begin by inserting a blank slide at the point in the presentation that requires the whiteboard. The "Record Slide Show" option for record "Narration, ink, and laser pointer" must be checked. During the recording, the keyboard command of control-p (for pen drawings) can be used to draw on the blank slide, just like a whiteboard. The control-l (for laser pointer) key combination can also be used for pointing out key areas of interest on the slide.

These drawings and laser pointer movements are saved on the PowerPoint presentation just like the narrated voice. For further technical information, please search for instructional videos on Youtube.com with the terms "powerpoint record voice narration."

Some educators opt for more powerful video creation and editing software. Camtasia is a popular video creation application that can combine voice narration, screen captures, media files like PowerPoint, and more to create a unified video product that can be shared with students through online learning management systems. Camtasia and similar products can combine media sources in a much richer manner than PowerPoint, such as including videos of the instructor obtained via a web cam as part of the powerpoint presentation.

Narrated PowerPoint presentation videos can be used in a variety of ways. Some instructors upload these files to online courses. The students in these online courses watch the powerpoint presentations in a manner that is similar to an in-class presentation. A well-known example of instructional lecture videos is the video offerings available at Khan Academy (see khanacademy.org). Salman Khan, the founder of Khan Academy, had the insightful idea that video lectures would be a powerful tool for students, who would be empowered to use lecture material in a manner that was based upon their instructional needs. For example, students who miss a particular idea during the video presentation could replay the key part of the video to watch it a second time. The Khan Academy web site hosts a multitude of short educational presentations that cover a wide range of topics.

Another possibility for recorded presentations that is gaining in popularity is the "flipped" classroom model. This teaching strategy aims to reverse the traditional roles of the classroom and homework by moving the lecture parts of a class to an online environment. The cycle of flipped instruction begins by assigning short video lectures online before class to prepare for the classroom experience. Other educational content and activities, such as participation in discussion boards, may also be assigned as part of the classroom preparation. In the classroom, the emphasis is on hands-on learning activities, like working math problems, or interactions with other people, such as discussion activities. The teacher's role during the class meeting is to provide feedback and assistance to students rather than delivering educational content like traditional lectures. In brief, the general flipped teaching strategy is to move course content, which might possibly include recorded powerpoint presentations, to an online environment and use face-to-face classroom time for engaging learning activities rather than information delivery. There is currently considerable enthusiasm among educators for the flipped classroom approach. However, the overall effectiveness and best methods for flipped classroom teaching have not been clearly established yet (Abeysekera and Dawson, 2015; O'Flaherty and Phillips, 2015).

Some distance educators use special applications to give live powerpoint presentations online in real time, just like a face-to-face presentation. These applications are similar to popular video conferencing applications like Skype, Google Hangouts, or Apple Facetime, but they have additional features that support teaching activities. Many of these applications can share Microsoft Office files, including PowerPoint, and interactive white board spaces with the audience. Some of these software products are aimed at the needs of business professionals (example: Citrix GoToMeeting), but a few products are specifically designed for educational needs (example: Blackboard Collaborate). The practice of giving live online presentations is sometimes described as "synchronous" because the presenter and audience must agree to meet online at the same time. An advantage of having a simultaneous meeting time is that the students and instructor can freely interact in a quick fashion, such as the instructor answering student questions as part of the presentation. A drawback is that some students may not be able to meet at a particular time. Online students, in particular, may feel that the requirement for a synchronized meeting time defeats the scheduling flexibility that is a highly desired component of online courses.

Designing for Pedagogy Needs During Times of Changing Technology

Moore's Law is an observation that computer technology doubles in power about every two years. The implication is that a two-year-old computer is obsolete, which demonstrates the speed of these technology changes. New technologies are sometimes described as "disruptive" or "paradigm shifts" to express how new technologies can revolutionize a field in a relatively short period of time Powerpoint-style presentations are no exception. These presentation technologies are likely to see continuing innovation in the upcoming years, particularly in regard to web-based delivery and distance-learning needs. Perhaps today's standard, Microsoft PowerPoint, will be dethroned in a few years by a new technology that cannot be currently imagined.

Although the technology may evolve, current trends suggest that supplementing spoken intstruction with powerpoint-style, multimedia components will continue to be a standard feature of classroom presentations for the future. The main feature of these technologies—combining a speaker's voice with slide-based information—is the shared multimedia presentation strategy across all of these technologies. The Microsoft PowerPoint alternatives described above do not substantially break the multimedia instructional standard of supplementing the spoken word with text and graphical images. It's true that some of these newer technologies have innovative features, such as Prezi-style zooming transitions and nonlinear slide order, but these innovations do not render multimedia learning approaches obsolete. The powerpoint presentation style is more of a social standard for modern presentations rather than being a specific technology produced by a single company (Knoblauch, 2012). There seems to be no emerging new technology that will trigger a radical break or paradigm shift away from the cultural standard for multimedia presentations.

The wide-ranging technology possibilities combined with the rapid rate of change in the technology world can feel overwhelming at times. It can be difficult to keep up with the fast pace of change. Educators who feel this way can take heart by maintaining a focus upon human beings and the learning process rather than technology. The highly visual modern style of presentation capitalizes on the information processing strengths of human vision and the cognitive advantages of combining words and images in synergistic manner. These human strengths are timeless when compared to the ever-changing trends in technology.

Accordingly, the pedagogical needs of students will continue to be the paramount need for educators to consider. Educators need to ask themselves how they can best combine words and images for their students, rather than becoming carried away to with the latest technology fad. The investment of time and effort put into designing effective multimedia presentations will result in an important teaching skill that will not become obsolete over time. This emphasis on designing for multimedia learning needs will help educators keep up with endless technology changes.

Tips and Tricks for Slide Presentations

"There can be infinite uses of the computer and of new age technology, but if teachers themselves are not able to bring it into the classroom and make it work, then it fails." Nancy Kassebaum

Teachers need to focus on the learner rather than teaching technology, as experts in the field of educational psychology have recommended (R. E. Clark, 1983). However, we must not forget that an important part of being a successful teacher is the handling of practical matters. Sometimes, educators with good intentions fail when they cannot execute the technical demands of powerpoint presentations in the classroom. Indeed, student surveys about classroom technology often express frustration with classroom technology failures or the inappropriate use of presentation technology. We will, therefore, now focus on practical technology skills that are important to educators and students. A secondary goal is to provide tips that might help teachers work in a faster or more effective manner. I present these ideas in the order that it would take to develop a classroom presentation. For a few topics, I mention software instructions for Microsoft PowerPoint, but I have kept this coverage brief in order to maintain focus on best practices rather than specific software features.

The Basic Slide Appearance

Many books and articles make recommendations about best practices for the appearance of powerpoint slides (Alley, 2013; Ball, 2009; Durso, Pop, Burnett, and Stearman, 2011; Giles and Kinniburgh, 2014; Stryker, 2010). The font characteristics are a good starting point. The general recommendation is to use fonts from a sans serif font family, such as Calibri, Arial, or Helvetica. The sans serif fonts are distinguished by the lack of small curly endings or strokes at the ends of the letters (Figure 15.1), rendering them "visually simple" (Kosslyn, 2007, p. 68). Sans serif fonts are generally preferred for computer screen monitors and similar situations because they are more easily read than other font families. Sans serif fonts are also higher-rated in regards to having a professional appearance (Mackiewicz, 2007a). The default PowerPoint fonts are usually for sans serif fonts like Calibri, so staying with a default font is usually a good choice.

Figure 15.1: A serif font (Times New Roman; left) compared to a sans serif font (Calibri, right)

An important general principle is that fonts must be a fairly large size in order to be visible to the audience. The sizes recommended commonly range from 22- to 44-points, depending on parameters such as classroom size and student distance from the screen. Michael Alley recommends the following settings for assertion-evidence formatted slides: left justification, bold weight, and 28-point. It is also noteworthy that Microsoft's PowerPoint 2016 has a default 28-point size for bullet point text items. Keep in mind that the largest fonts, like 44-points for titles, will force the presenter to use short phrases that can be vague or ambiguous.

The degree of contrast between background and text is also important. Dave Paradi's web site thinkoutsidetheslide.com has a tool for evaluating color and contrast (see "Free Resources"). The user enters the background and text colors as RGB values, which is similar to the color values used for the design of web pages. The calculator simulates the colors in a sample slide and makes a recommendation about whether or not there is a sufficient degree of contrast. Some of these issues were already covered in Chapter 7, but the information in that chapter does not eliminate the need for real-world testing of color schemes.

Most teachers and other presenters simply pick a pretty slide format from the gallery of possibilities that the software maker provides. Using built-in templates is convenient, but it may not be the optimal approach for teaching because these templates often contain undesirable colors, graphics, and layouts. It would be more effective for teachers to take the time and effort to create their own slide styles and layouts, especially if they intend to use the assertion-evidence formatted slide. Fortunately, there is a way to make slides without having to obsess about all these formatting and appearance details every time a new presentation is created. PowerPoint has a feature called the "master slide template" that can be used to set the default layouts, fonts, colors, and other formatting characteristics. The creation of a slide template with a personalized custom appearance can be a bit time-consuming, but the long term benefit is that the template can be used repeatedly, saving teachers from the hassle of setting the appearances for each new presentation.

The Shape of Computer Displays

Television and computer monitors had the same shape for several decades. They were slightly rectangular, being a little bit longer in the horizontal plane. In 2003, the conventional shape of these displays started changing to a more overtly rectangular shape with a noticeably longer horizontal dimension. Most displays are now based upon this newer standard. Many people have noticed this difference on newer high-definition, widescreen televisions. Current television shows will fill the entire screen. In contrast, older television shows fit into the center of the display while leaving blank spaces on the left and right sides of the screen.

The technical term for the shape of television screens and computer monitors is called the "aspect ratio." This is a ratio of the width to the height of the display area. A display that is four units wide and three units tall (or multiples of these) would have an aspect ratio of 4 units to 3 units, or 4:3. The two most common aspect ratios are the older, nearly square shape of 4:3 and the newer, more rectangular shape of 16:9 (Figure 15.2). On televisions, these aspect ratios are called "standard" and "widescreen," respectively, so we will adopt this terminology for the sake of convenience. Most computer displays now use the widescreen format (16:9), although some businesses and schools might still use the older standard display (4:3).

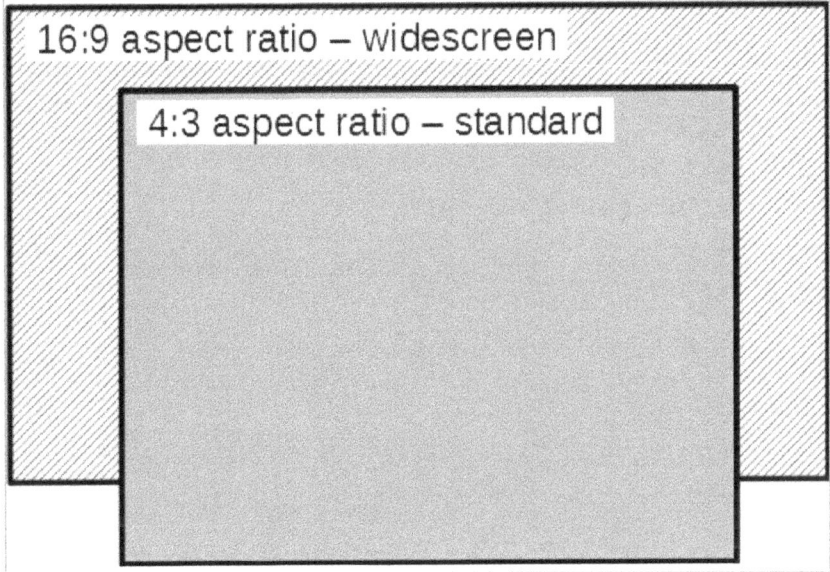

Figure 15.2: Display aspect ratio examples

Outstanding presenters need to have a basic understanding of aspect ratio in order to design presentations that fit the available projector technology. The older standard format of 4:3 is the most conservative choice in that it will run well on either older or newer projection hardware. For this reason, many powerpoint slides are still formatted with the standard aspect ratio dimensions. In contrast, if a classroom projector has widescreen capability, presenters might as well take advantage of the entire screen by using the widescreen format. In PowerPoint, teachers can select aspect ratios by going to the "design" tab, then selecting "slide size" ("page setup" in older versions). The selection possibilities are for standard (4:3), widescreen (16:9), or custom sizes.

Prefabricated Powerpoint Files from the Textbook Publisher

Many textbook publishers for college-level courses offer teachers prepared powerpoint presentations as an ancillary resource. The advantage of these prepared slide decks is convenience. The downside is that prepared slide decks tend to be text-heavy repeats of material from the textbook. It's also possible that these resources may have been prepared by someone with little expertise in the subject matter, meaning that important concepts are not effectively identified or displayed. Prefabricated slides also encourage teachers to not prepare for their lectures, which ultimately leads to presentations that stumble through an unfamiliar slide deck. This possibility has led to the criticism that prefabricated slides are contributing to a "de-skilling" of faculty, who are reduced to a commentators role on someone else's slides (Gabriel and Griffiths, 2005, p. 372). Given these problems, it would seem to be best to avoid using powerpoint presentations from textbook publishers.

Prepared slide decks may still be a valuable resource in spite of these problems. The images in these files can be easily copied into instructors' own powerpoint presentations, saving the instructors valuable time that would otherwise be spent hunting down images online or scanning textbook images into the computer. Discussing textbook images in class can also be appropriate for situations with textbook errors or confusing information. Doing so can offer the opportunity to walk the class through a difficult topic.

Another possibility is to use publisher-provided powerpoint files as a base for customization. In some cases, altering the content on an existing slide to one's own specifications may be more time-efficient than creating a collection of new slides from scratch, although this is somewhat of a judgment call.

Focusing on the Story Line

Most presentation experts recommend that a presentation's organization should begin on paper rather than on the computer. The thoughts and organization can be composed on paper, then transferred to the software when the ideas are complete. This recommendation is similar to practices used in other disciplines. For example, the traditional approach for developing a film is to use story boards that show the composition of scenes and their overall order. A similar idea for powerpoint is to use post-it notes, with one post-it representing each slide (Duarte, 2008, pp. 28–29). The post-it notes can be physically edited and rearranged into a desirable order before the slides are created.

PowerPoint also has features to help presenters perceive the overall feel and order of the slide deck. The "slide sorter" feature shows a comprehensive overview of the presentation, with each slide represented by a small thumbnail view. This view allows the presenter to examine the overall impression of the slide presentation and make any necessary changes in slide order, appearance, or content. Using this feature can be helpful for identifying global organization problems prior to the presentation delivery, although testing the presentation in the actual setting is the only way to ensure effectiveness.

Designing for Accessibility

Educators have an obligation to educate everyone in their classroom, including students with sensory disabilities. Powerpoint is primarily a visual medium, so the main accessibility concern is making the slide information available for students who may have vision deficits.

As mentioned in Chapter 7, a minor yet common visual disability is insensitivity to the colors red and green. A good design principle for addressing this problem is to avoid or minimize the use of critical slide elements that are either red or green. For example, red arrows might seem like a good choice for highlighting important aspects of a diagram, but perceiving the color red may be problematic for some people. Blue, green, or yellow would be better color choices for highlighting purposes. If presenters have concerns about color visibility, the web site Vischeck.com has a tool for testing how color insensitive people experience images. The web site allows users to upload images and view them without certain colors in a manner that simulates color blindness. Teachers can use this feedback to determine whether or not critical information might be unavailable to color insensitive students.

Students with severe visual disabilities may need assistive technologies that convert powerpoint deck text into speech, thereby enabling the student to listen to the slide deck. An important part of this technology is that the slide deck must be properly designed to make the text-to-speech conversion process work well. Images and hypertext links should include "alt" tags (short for "alternative") that contain brief explanations that document the purpose or key idea. The assistive technologies use the text of these alternative tags to describe the image or hyperlink in an audible form. Teachers can insert this alt image tag into PowerPoint by right clicking on an image and selecting "format image," then the "alt text" option. A second feature to prepare slide decks for use with assistive reading technologies is setting the proper order of elements on each slide. This setting tells the reading technology which element of the slide must be read first, second, and so on. Teachers can use this PowerPoint feature by starting at the "home" tab, then clicking on the "arrange" button and selecting "selection pane." For each slide, this window will show the elements on the slide. Teachers can modify the order of slide items by moving the various slide components up or down in the sequence.

Microsoft PowerPoint versions 2010 and later have an "accessibility checker" tool that makes recommendations for accommodating disabilities. To run the accessibility checker, go to the "file" tab, select "Info," then the "Check for issues" button, and then "Check accessibility." The tool analyzes the slide deck and displays the accessibility recommendation results in a new window. Running this tool near the end of the slide deck development process will help presenters catch potential problems that people with low vision might encounter when they use assistive technologies.

Preparing the Slide Deck for Student Notes

Teachers often make their slide decks available to students to assist student note-taking efforts (see Chapter 13). Many educators simply upload the PowerPoint file to their learning management system or distribute these files to their students via email. A problem with sharing the PowerPoint files is that students may not have the correct software to open the file, which can be an expensive problem to solve. Another problem is that PowerPoint files are formatted in a manner that makes them poor candidates for printing hard copies. A 44-point title font on a full-page slide, for example, is enormous on a printed page. Students may waste paper if they simply print the file without reformatting it.

Teachers can improve on the common practice of simply sending out the powerpoint files without much additional effort. Nathans-Kelly and Nicometo recommend that the archival format for powerpoint presentations should be an Adobe Acrobat document (sometimes called "pdf" for "portable document format") rather than the original PowerPoint format (Nathans-Kelly and Nicometo, 2014). These pdf documents are less software-bound because pdf software is available for free from Adobe. Most modern web browsers, such as Google's Chrome, can open pdf files without needing any additional software. This makes it nearly effortless for students to open these files from a web-based learning management system. Another pdf file advantage is their smaller size, which makes the files easier to post on a web site or send as an email attachment. In general, the pdf document file format is better suited than PowerPoint for the creation of paper-based documents that might be used for note-taking or studying efforts.

There are three possible methods to create a pdf document from a PowerPoint presentation. If the Adobe Acrobat software is installed on your PC, an Adobe pdf file can be created by going to the "file" tab and selecting "print" (or simply select control+P on the keyboard). To make a pdf file, the "printer" setting must be set to "Adobe pdf" for the output rather than the usual printer driver. Selecting "Adobe pdf" as the printer output will save the document to the computer's hard drive as a pdf file instead of sending the slides to the actual printer. A second method for creating pdf file is to select the "file" tab, then "save as", then "save as type." Choose pdf for the output option. A third method is through the "file" tab, then "export", then "create Adobe pdf." The first two methods provide options for formatting the presentation in student-friendly formats like handouts, slides with notes, or outlines. It is well worth the small amount of extra effort to prepare these nicely formatted pdf files for students.

Another useful tip for archiving PowerPoint files is to put documentation that might be too detailed for the presentation into the "notes" part of the slide deck (Nathans-Kelly and Nicometo, 2014). During the slide deck creation, the teacher might enter important information, such as context or references, in the notes part of the slide where it cannot be seen by students during the presentation. Other possibilities for the notes area include direct quotes or brief explanations about the purpose of the slide. This practice prevents the presentation slides from being cluttered by details during the presentation but still preserves these important details for an information-rich handout. To view these notes, the students would need to receive a paper handout or a pdf file that has been formatted to include the notes along with the slide thumbnails. This approach is a clever way to strike a balance between the need to keep a visually simple presentation appearance, yet still give the students an information-rich take-home document with more details.

Navigating Through a Powerpoint Presentation

Most teachers know that powerpoint presentations can go full-screen and that the slide presentations can be advanced by using the arrows on the computer keyboard. As mentioned earlier, the presentation can enter full screen mode in PowerPoint through the "slide show" tab or by pressing the F5 key. The arrow keys on the keyboard can advance or go backwards through the slide deck. If the presentation must be terminated before the end, pressing escape will return the software to the author view mode.

PowerPoint has many other features that can also be used during presentations. These features are accessed through keyboard commands because the on-screen buttons are not displayed during a presentation. Using these keyboard commands may take some practice, but they are easy and powerful once a teacher becomes accustomed to using them. A list of the most useful commands is shown in Table 15.1.

Start presentation:	F5 for starting a presentation from the beginning Shift+F5 starts from the current slide
Advance:	n (next), enter, right arrow, down arrow, page down, spacebar
Previous:	p (previous), left arrow, up arrow, backspace
Display blank:	b or period (for black), w or comma (for white)
Pen tool:	Control+P
Highlighter tool:	Control+I
Erase annotations:	Control+E
Laser pointer tool:	Control+L
Jump to a slide:	Control+S
Go to slide:	Slide number then enter
End presentation:	Esc (escape)

Table 15.1: Keyboard shortcuts for presentation navigation and effects (PowerPoint 2013 and later)

Having the right hardware setup enables a special presentation mode that gives the audience and the presenter different views of the slide presentation (Figure 15.3). The PowerPoint "presenter view" gives the audience the full screen slide display. The presenter, in contrast, sees a smaller version of the slides along with more information and additional options, such as notes, navigation buttons, and a timer. The essential requirement for using the presenter view is that the projection setup must have two separate monitors, one for the presenter and a projector for the audience, that have two separate connections to the computer.

The advantage of using the presenter view is that the presenter has a rich feature set of navigation tools and other tools available on their display screen. Seeing the next slide in the queue can help smooth the transitions between slides. Presenters will be less likely to forget the content of the next slide or skip a few slides ahead. The availability of the notes view can be valuable to remind the speaker of important points or information that needs to be shared with the students yet would be too excessive to put on to the projected screen.

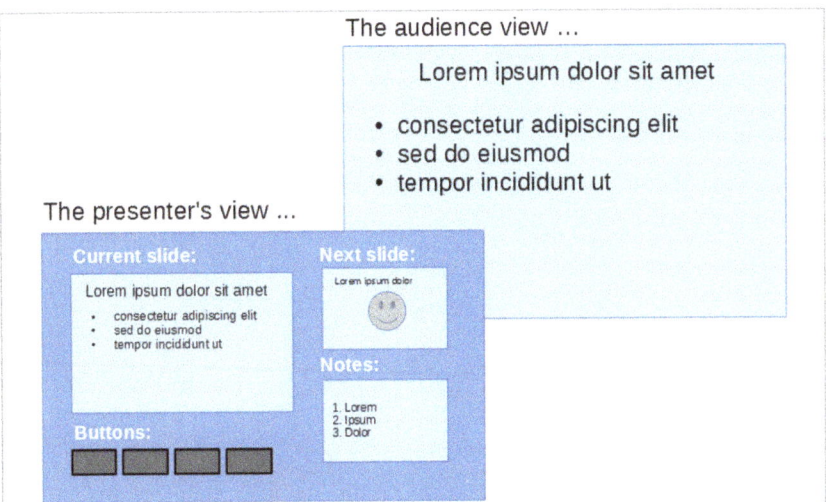

Figure 15.3: A comparison of the audience view and the presenter view

The presenter view is very useful, but it can be tricky to use at times. Care must be taken to not rely on the presenter view feature too much. Overreliance can bind the presenter to the monitor and take the presenter's focus away from the audience (Kosslyn, 2007). Another potential problem is that the links or buttons shown in the presenter view are just images, rather than real links. This can be confusing and lead to errors during the presentation.

An expert-level tip for using the presenter view mode is to think of the presentation as having two screens that are positioned side-by-side. The presenter's view is on the left and the audience view is on the right. These screens, however, are linked and continuous with each other. The mouse is not restricted to one screen and can be moved to the other by going either left or right. For example, activating a button on the PowerPoint presentation might require the presenter to move their mouse from the left to the right, off the presenter's screen and on to audience screen, in order to make it extend over into the view that the audience sees. Once in the audience, view the mouse cursor can click on buttons to activate them. A similar process can be used to display information in another window. For example, a Youtube.com video that is open in a web browser window may need to be shown to the audience. This window can be selected and then dragged from the left presenter screen rightward to the projected screen for the audience. When done, the browser window will need to be selected on the right in the audience's view and dragged from right to left to move it back to the presenter's view. This process of moving from one screen to the other by moving left-right can be somewhat tricky, but with practice, these kinds of transitions can be mastered.

The full screen slide-show mode is rich with possibilities for taking presentations to the next level. Learning to use these features will make presentations seem polished and professional, making it well-worth the time to learn a few keyboard shortcuts and the presenter view.

Continuous Slide Development for the Long Run

At times, teaching feels like a constant battle to stay just one step ahead of where the students are in the course. This is especially true for new teachers who often struggle to develop content materials for their courses. Therefore, teachers need a long-term strategy in order to overcome the urgency of developing materials at the last minute.

Teaching the same courses repeatedly year after year offers faculty members a chance to continuously improve their course presentations and see these presentations gradually evolve over several semesters. Sometimes, a teacher might randomly find a good example or activity to use for a future class. Powerpoint can function like a filing cabinet for saving these new materials and ideas. It can store all of the interesting ideas or information in the relevant slide deck until the next time the presentation is needed. The text on the slides and the images are obvious ways to organize the pertinent information. Multimedia resources can also be collected as links, such as links to Youtube-based video clips. Comments can be inserted like post-it notes to document future changes that might be worthwhile. Another possibility is to save information in the "notes" option for each slide. This practice of storing new information in the appropriate presentation file organizes these new materials in an efficient manner so they will be ready to use for the next presentation.

When the course content is ready to be taught again, take time to review the past feedback on the slides. The outstanding teacher makes any necessary changes that were noted from the last presentation and uses the improved presentation to further their course.

To be clear, the idea of reuse is not to recommend being like the stereotypical old college professor who uses the same lecture notes they made thirty years ago. Rather, the spirit is more of a slow but continuous improvement to the slide deck over time. The small additions and improvements instructors make from semester to semester serve to keep furthering and reinvigorating the course so that it gets better each time they teach the topic.

The Hide Slide Feature

Slide decks for a given topic tend to grow over time when a presentation is repeatedly given. This can occasionally produce the problem of having too much content. This problem of having too much presentation material is especially serious when teaching time is lost due to school cancellations for inclement weather or other problems. A presentation that typically covers topics X, Y, and Z might need to be reduced to just topics X and Y in order to fit into the shrunken time window. A simple solution would be to delete the extra slides from topic Z, but the loss of slides would create a new problem for future semesters when topic Z might need to be covered again.

The elegant solution to having too many slides for the available time period is the "hide slide" feature. This feature renders selected slides invisible to the audience without actually deleting them from the slide deck. The slides that need to be skipped are selected by right clicking on the undesired slide thumbnail images and then choosing the "hide slide" command from the pop-up menu. The ability to hide slides as needed can be a quick way to customize a presentation to fit a shorter time period, without sacrificing the long-term structure and content of a carefully prepared slide deck.

Good Teaching Requires Technical Excellence

Good educational presentations are a kind of performance art, just like a concert or a play. The information, ideas, and intentions are important starting points, but they ultimately count for nothing if the final product cannot be delivered in front of an audience. Teachers must be able to effectively implement the technology in the classroom in order to succeed.

The numerous ideas outlined here may seem somewhat overwhelming at first. However, instructors need not implement all of these ideas in order to achieve better presentations. They can pick and choose the strategies and technical elements that seem to be the most important. Also worthwhile is thinking of powerpoint-use as a technical skill that can be developed slowly over time. Consistently following this approach over a few years will lead to a dramatic improvement in presentations, one that may result in recognition on campus for being a masterful speaker.

A Classroom Presentation Example

"Example isn't another way to teach, it is the only way to teach." Albert Einstein

After reviewing a wide range of possibilities to improve the educational quality of powerpoint presentations, we will now consider how to put these ideas into practice. To do so, I will show an educational powerpoint presentation, accompanying it with commentary describing the reasoning behind each slide's design. This approach will assemble various ideas into a single example that illustrates important ideas about designing slides for students.

This slide deck comes from my Psychological Statistics class. I chose Statistics and the specific topic, which is variability, because it seems to be the epitome of a boring class that students dread taking. Rather than considering it a hopeless topic, we can view this situation as a challenge. Let's see if it is possible to breathe some life into a dull topic by using powerpoint in an effective manner.

Setting the Stage for Student Interest

The beginning of a successful presentation must accomplish two important goals. The first goal, which is arguably the most important, is to spark student interest in the topic. A second goal of the opening is provide students with an overview of the topic. This preview may have cognitive benefits by preparing the students for the direction that the class will take.

Let's begin with a brief summary of the guiding principles that went into the general design of this presentation. For high-contrast visibility, the slides have black text on a white background (Figure 16.1). I used the assertion-evidence layout for most of the slides in order to provide complete ideas to the students rather than fragmented phrases. The main message of each slide is positioned at the top of the screen to maximize the visibility in a classroom setting. The font formatting of the slide titles follows the recommendations for evidence-assertion layouts: Calibri font (from the sans-serif font family), 28-point size, and bold weight (Alley, 2013). Formatting the shape of the slide for a widescreen aspect ratio (16:9) takes advantage of all of the space on the classroom screen.

The opening slide is a "two content" type layout in PowerPoint terminology (Figure 16.1). On the left, the slide contains the title of the topic, plus an overview of what students can expect. On the right, an image of students from my university appears. This graphic, which is from the university web site, has an attribution below the image to document the source. Students find these local images to be interesting. The students may even know a few of the people in the photo. The unstated point of this graphic is that students have a wide variety of characteristics: sex, race, size, clothing, hair style, etc. This image sets the stage for the topic, which is describing human variations with statistics.

Figure 16.1: Introductory slide with overview and interesting image

The class might start with a brief reminder announcement or two, followed by a verbal description of what variability is about. The title slide image can help make a quick point about variability: Students can have many different characteristics that distinguish them from each other. Discussing a simple example prepares the students for the more quantitative methods that will follow. This point about the importance of human variability can be followed by a short overview of where the class is headed.

The timing of this opening slide is also important. The aim is to start displaying this slide a few minutes before the actual class lecture begins. While the students are waiting for class to start, they can begin looking at the slide and start wondering about the topic. This is an effortless way powerpoint can help draw the audience into the presentation topic (Kosslyn, 2007).

The opening slide is important for sparking some interest in the topic, but it is rarely sufficient by itself to really set the stage for learning. We need to go a little bit deeper to lay a foundation with the students about why this topic is interesting and important. For the topic of variability, I ask the students to do a simple thought experiment: What would the world be like if everyone was exactly the same, down to the smallest detail? This second slide (Figure 16.2) illustrates the question's concept by showing an image of identical gingerbread man cookies. The idea is to ask students to think about the opposite of variability, a world in which everyone is identical, just like cookies stamped out by a cookie cutter. The typical student reactions to this thought experiment is that a world with identical people would be quite boring. Human variability is special and valued.

This slide has an assertion-evidence structure with the important idea stated at the top. The evidence part of this slide is an image of gingerbread men that are identical, which provides the visual means to reinforce the verbal message. This image helps the students grasp the concept of my thought experiment. It also helps to make an emotional point about the thought experiment, which might help to make it more memorable. Almost everyone likes cookies. Maybe some of these positive associations transfer to the topic of statistics by showing a slide that pairs them together.

Figure 16.2: Establishing why the topic is important. This free image is from publicdomainpictures.net.

The conclusion of this thought exercise is that variability is an important reason why we must use statistics. The assertion part of the next slide (Figure 16.3) provides the key term "variability" and a definition of the key term (individual differences between people). The evidence part of the slide is a large family from South Africa that has a wide range of skin tones. It's quite a contrast from the preceding slide with the identical gingerbread man cookies. I chose this image because this simple physical evidence can quickly and easily make an important point about human variability. This image can also serve as a jumping off point for class discussions. An instructor could ask the class for other examples of human variability that are occurr in this image. They could also discuss how we can only see physical differences in this image. The social or psychological differences between these family members must be equally large.

Figure 16.3: Establishing importance, with documentation and notes.

This visual evidence makes a compelling point that human variability is important. The combination of the definition with a powerful supporting image is a good use of multimedia learning. The two sources of information combine in a synergistic way to make a strong and memorable impression on students. This feature is arguably powerpoint's strongest: It provides the opportunity to combine words and images in ways that are informative, emotional, and memorable. This slide helps to establish the idea that describing variability is an important part of a statistician's mission.

The image for the slide in Figure 16.3 came from Wikipedia, which only uses images that have open licenses for sharing and reuse. The presenter's notes document this source information

(Figure 16.3, bottom). Again, this note area hides content from the audience during a presentation. The teacher can benefit from this documentation, especially in future semesters. The notes can serve as a memory aid to help the teacher recall why this image fits this slide's purpose. In future semesters, the teacher can revisit the source information to see if an update might be needed. In addition, the students who read these notes on a handout (see below) will get an idea of the image's importance in relation to the slide's topic. In this way, the handout will be more informative than simply providing the same slides that were shown during class.

Using Transitions

The introduction ends when the discussion about the variability example is complete. This transition from the introduction to the body of the presentation may be useful to mark. It can be helpful to the audience as they mentally track the progress of the presentation.

The teacher could use vocal cues to notify the class of this transition. Let's be more dramatic though and use powerpoint to send a clear signal about the transition to a new topic. The slide in Figure 16.4 shows a simple transition that marks a turning point in the course. Only a few seconds will be needed to communicate that a shift in purpose is about to occur. The formatting of this slide is different from the assertion-evidence format. The text is positioned in the center and is highlighted differently from the other slides. These subtle visual cues inform the students that this slide does not contain important content and does not necessarily need to be recorded in their notes.

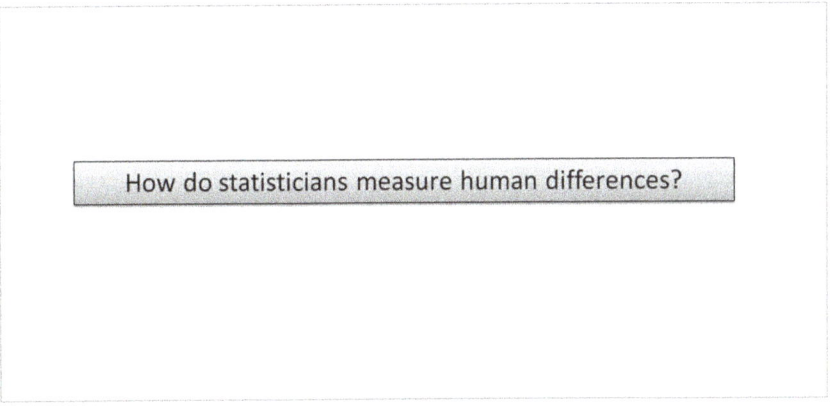

Figure 16.4: Transition slide to a new part of the presentation

The use of a special slide to mark presentation transitions may not be absolutely necessary, but some cognitive benefits may be derived by marking these topic changes. It sends the clear signal that the introduction is over and the body of the presentation is about to start. The segmentation principle from multimedia learning suggests that it is beneficial to break down educational content into groups or chunks (Mayer, 2009). Doing so will help to prevent the possibility of overloading the audience with too much information. The audience will also appreciate knowing the transition points in a presentation (Duarte, 2010). Another transition possibility is to show the outline from the opening slide again and cue the new subtopic to show students the overall progress through the topic.

Establishing a Key Concept

The body of the presentation begins by relating new ideas to concepts that were covered in a previous class to provide some background. The next two slides (Figures 16.5 and 16.6) are aimed at establishing this relationship. Figure 16.5 is a brief review of topics—central tendency and frequency distributions—from the previous class period. Figure 16.6 shows the same image (a frequency distribution graph) but adds new information about variability. This slide sequence shows the students where the new topic fits into their existing understanding and gradually builds the students' cognitive schemata about statistics. The brief repetition of material from a previous class may also be helpful for strengthening the memory for this previous topic.

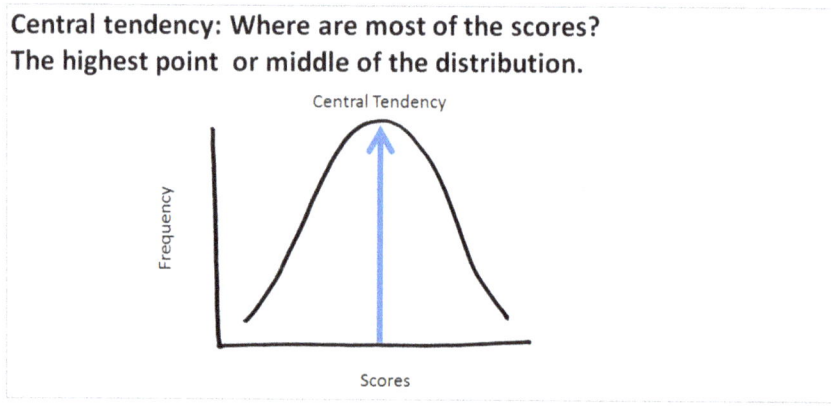

Figure 16.5: Establishing context: A refresher of ideas from the previous class

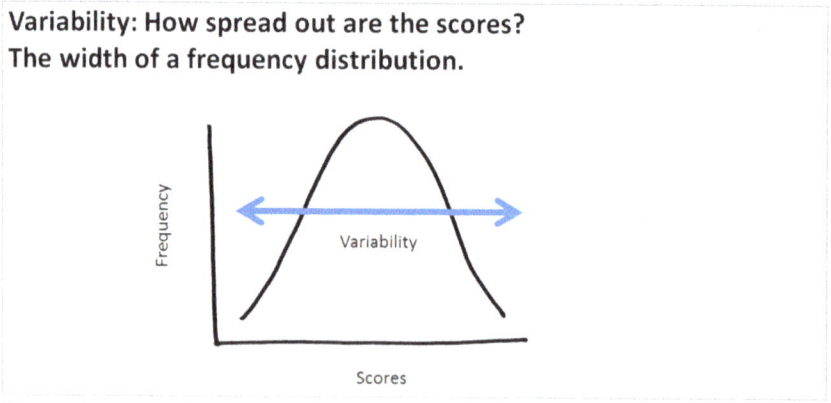

Figure 16.6: Establishing context: The current topic in relation to the previous class

Because no commercially available images exactly capture the ideas these slides are trying to convey, my simple solution was to hand draw a special graphic for this situation (Figures 16.5 and 16.6). I drew the basic graph design with a Sharpie pen on regular printer paper, scanned the drawing into the computer with an inexpensive scanner, and then inserted it into the powerpoint file. The black/white scanned image blends seamlessly into the black/white theme of the slide. I added the terms like "frequency," "central tendency," and "scores" to the scanned image in powerpoint. Because it's the key concept for this slide, I placed the term "central tendency" at the top of Figure 16.5. I colored the arrows blue to help draw student attention to key features of the graph. The color blue minimizes potential problems for people with red-green color insensitivity might experience. Creating this image might seem like a lot of extra work, but it involves little more work than drawing a diagram on a chalkboard. The benefit of putting this diagram in powerpoint is the availability for future classes.

Critics might fault images like the ones in Figures 16.5 and 16.6 for looking amateurish or homemade. They might also look down on using images from web sites like Wikipedia that have open licenses for sharing. These are valid opinions. It is undeniable that hand-drawn images lack the professional quality of images made by expert artists and graphic designers. My opinion, however, is that teacher-made resources like these are certainly acceptable for classroom use. Moreover, I feel that such do-it-yourself graphics are commendable for expressing teacher creativity and special efforts to promote learning. Most educators simply do not have enough time to make highly polished artwork on the computer. They may lack the specialized hardware, software, and training that might be required to make publication-quality graphics. Therefore, the guiding spirit for classroom content should be a pragmatic approach that emphasizes the quick and easy creation of effective teaching materials over the painstaking production of professional-looking graphics. It is sufficient to scan a drawn diagram or take a picture and highlight key areas, if these materials are successful in promoting student understanding. It is unrealistic to expect that every instructional aid will have the professional polish of textbook graphics. The students, who are the real audience, will appreciate these homemade creations even if they look less than perfect. They understand that their mission is to learn rather than being art or design critics. My overall suggestion is to not worry about graphic perfection in classroom materials unless you are creating materials for publication. Teachers should design powerpoint presentations as an individual expression of teaching creativity without worries about having the appearance look like textbook-quality images. The examples in this chapter follow this creative spirit to show teacher creativity in action.

Multimedia Instruction through Informative Images

The beginning of the presentation body covered the basic concept of variability through the use of pictures. I avoided numbers because they might be more difficult (and potentially scary) to some math-phobic students. This next part of the body aims to establish a more abstract understanding of variability. Fortunately, this purpose can be achieved through visual images as well. We can rely on frequency distribution graphs to communicate concepts about variability without having to do any mathematical operations yet. Doing so keeps the topic on an intuitive level because the images are much easier to understand. The mathematical operations are saved for later in the presentation.

Figure 16.7 shows graph examples that represent two frequency distributions that differ in regard to variability (low or high). Using the techniques described above, I made the frequency distribution graphs as freehand drawings. One difference is that I made these graphics entirely by hand, including the labels on the graphs. Doing so sped up the development time a bit, although the downside is that the images are more crude. The students don't seem to mind that these were drawn by hand. Again, it's a practice not much different than drawing on a whiteboard.

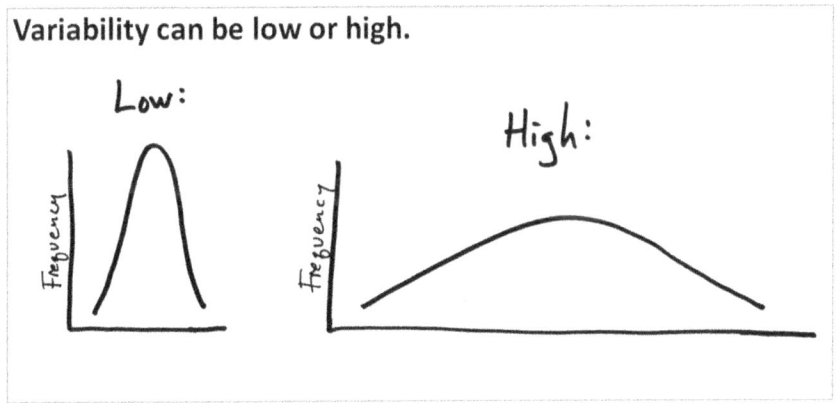

Figure 16.7: Visualizing the Main Concept

Figure 16.8 shows that one way to understand variability is to think of it as the opposite of consistency. These are the same graphs as Figure 16.7, but they now have the labels "consistent" and "inconsistent" on the bottom. The aim is that teaching the same concept in a slightly different manner might help some students to better grasp the concept of variability. In Figure 16.9, the same images are used again, but with a new terminology to describe the spread of distributions (kurtosis). The same graphs work again to provide two examples that differ in degrees.

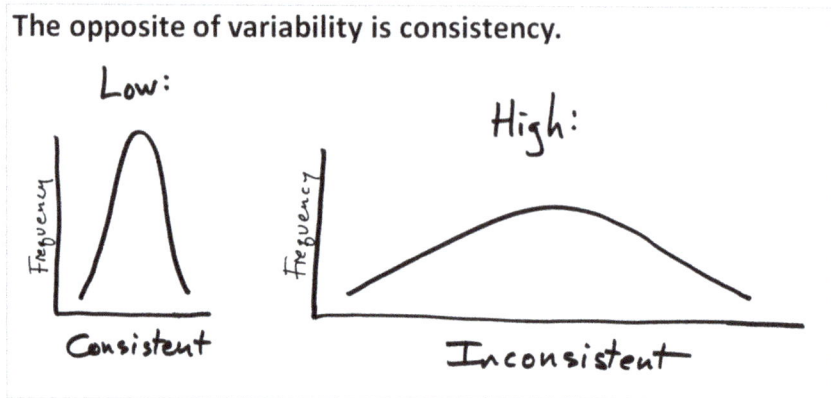

Figure 16.8: A variation that builds the concept from the previous slide

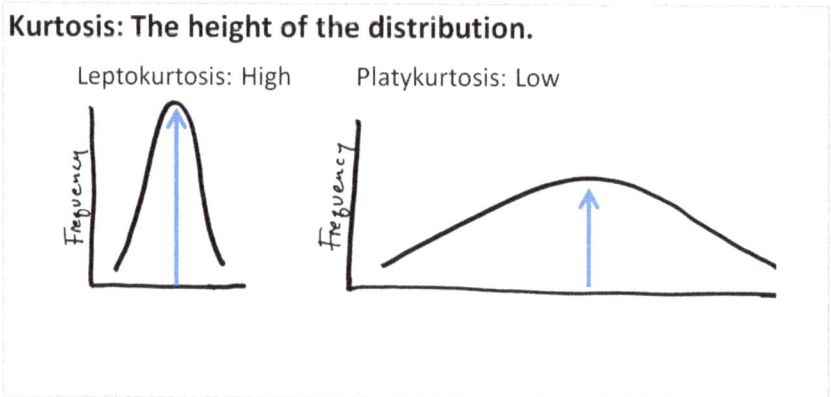

Figure 16.9: New key terms related to the preceding concept (Figure 16.8)

The intention of the layout designs in Figures 16.7 through 16.9 is to help students understand the topic. The side-by-side layouts help students see the differences between low and high variability, consistency, and kurtosis. These key terms are closely related, and the repeated graphics hopefully help students understand this close degree of relationship. A second educational feature of this slide sequence is the gradual build of information. We are taking the same basic graphs and progressively adding more or different characteristics over the course of several slides. The progressive nature breaks down the complexity into smaller pieces that are far more manageable to learn. This strategy helps avoid the information overload problem.

The term platykurtosis refers to flat frequency distributions. This term is unusual and rarely used, so students might have difficulty remembering it. The joke in the next slide (Figure 16.10) is that a platykurtic distribution is shaped like a platypus. This joke usually gets some eye rolling and a few groans, but the students seem to appreciate the attempt to introduce humor to the topic. Although this joke may seem like pointless fun, it has a serious reason behind it. The combination of emotion with the information, as well as the association with a familiar and distinctive animal, should strengthen student memory for an obscure technical term. The use of humor should also help maintain student engagement with the presentation.

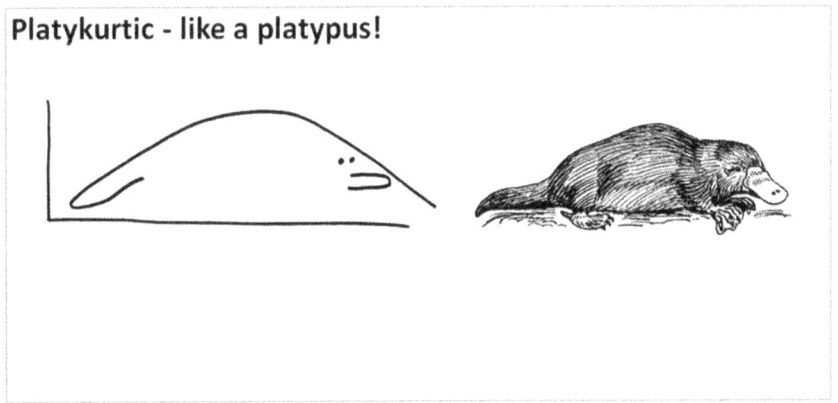

Figure 16.10: Making a memorable point with humor. The platypus image was made by Pearson Scott Foresman and downloaded from commons.wikimedia.org.

We will skip the remaining part of the presentation body in order to keep this chapter brief, but a few more slides will be discussed to exemplify good practices. One slide from the body of this presentation concerns the coverage of complex topics, which is spread out over multiple slides to prevent information overload. Figures 16.11 and 16.12 cover the concept of deviation scores in two ways. The first approach is graphical in nature (Figure 16.11). The assertion part of the slide defines the concept of a deviation score, while the evidence part of the slide illustrates what this concept looks like in regard to a frequency distribution. The next slide (Figure 16.12) shows what deviation score calculations will look like in a simple data set. Overall, the use of two different methods—visual and numerical—to illustrate the same idea should improve student understanding.

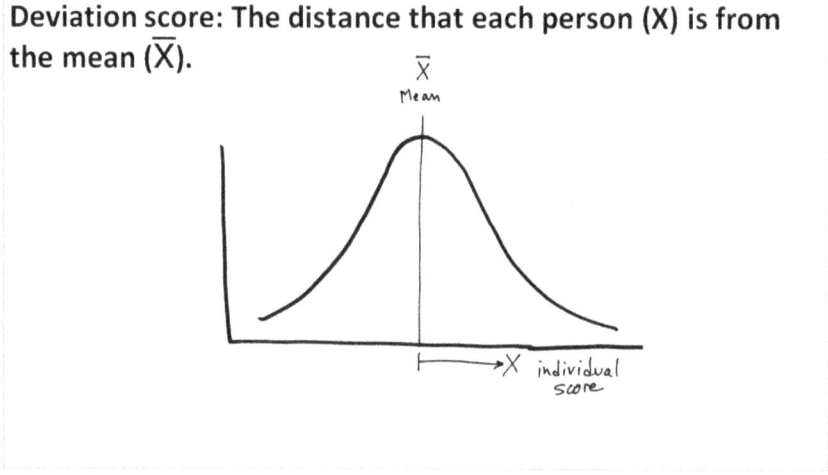

Figure 16.11: Deviation scores explained by a graphic illustration

Subtract the mean score from each individual's score.

$$\bar{X} = \frac{\Sigma X}{n} = \frac{30}{5} = 6$$

X	X - X̄
2	2 – 6 = -4
4	4 – 6 = -2
6	6 – 6 = 0
8	8 – 6 = 2
10	10 – 6 = 4
ΣX = 30	

Figure 16.12: Deviation scores explained by numerical example

The graphics in Figures 16.11 and 16.12 were created for this presentation, with the graphic in Figure 16.11 being inspired by a textbook illustration that was useful but somewhat ambiguous. I made the graphics in Figure 16.12 with PowerPoint's formula and table tools. The deviation score part of the table in Figure 16.12 uses color (yellow) to direct attention to the most important part. Because it is the only color shown on the slide, the highlighting effectively draws attention. Using black and white for the basic formatting allows any color to stand out to the viewers, so applying color intentionally can highlight key features of the graphic.

The body of the presentation finishes with an example that involves calculations. This example takes the information that was presented and illustrates how it should be worked. This part of the class involves modeling the behavior that students will need to do on the exams. It also provides a practical application of the concept covered during the body of the lecture.

Moving to an Active Learning Exercise

The body of the presentation is a lecture that walks the students through the basic concepts and finishes with an example of calculating standard deviation. This part of class takes about forty minutes, which is all the statistics lecturing that most students can handle. During this part, the students have been taking notes and occasionally participating by asking questions. They have seen an example of the calculations. Most of the students have been nodding their heads up and down throughout the lecture, suggesting that they understand the class content (although experienced teachers know that this nodding can be deceiving). They have not, however, been challenged very much.

This is a good time to shift the pedagogy strategy away from lecturing and towards active learning. The general strategy for my statistics course is to begin by lecturing and then follow-up with active learning exercises when student attention is nearly exhausted. After the lecture part, the students must do the same calculations by themselves to see if they can master the topic. This is the student-centered, active learning part of the class. This general approach of mixing lecturing with other kinds of active learning exercises is well supported by research studies (Bligh, 2000). This active learning part of the class provides important feedback to the students about their understanding of the topic. Students who are struggling can get assistance from their colleagues or the instructor.

At this point, I distribute a handout that contains short exercises similar to the example covered in the lecture. These exercises also correspond with computational questions students will find on future examinations, so it is important for them to be proficient in this exercise. The handout is the major focus during this part of the class, but powerpoint will still play a useful and supportive role. The slide in Figure 16.13 signals to the class that the instruction method has changed over to the hands-on learning activity. This slide briefly summarizes the goals of the handout and informs students about what they should be doing. This slide remains on the screen while the students are working on their handout problems. Students will find the specific information they need for the exercise, such as the exam scores from six students, on the handout that complements the powerpoint slide.

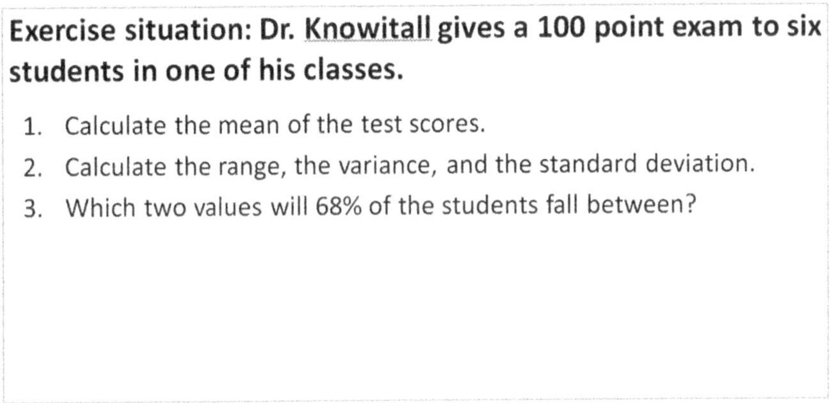

Exercise situation: Dr. Knowitall gives a 100 point exam to six students in one of his classes.

1. Calculate the mean of the test scores.
2. Calculate the range, the variance, and the standard deviation.
3. Which two values will 68% of the students fall between?

Figure 16.13: Challenging the students with an active learning exercise

After the students complete their work, they see feedback about the handout problems on the next presentation slides (Figure 16.14). After creating the graphic in this slide by doing the handout in pencil, I scanned the relevant part of the handout into the computer. This is, once again, an example of teacher creativity in action. A quick but effective graphic was made to satisfy the educational need rather than typing all of these details into the computer. A potential benefit beyond the time savings is that the students perhaps feel some reassurance in knowing that their professor also does these problems by hand. Spreading the computation feedback over several slides gradually builds this information. Once again, the powerpoint slide supports the active learning exercise during this feedback stage by enabling an instructor to provide the answers to the entire class.

Exercise answers:

Student	Test Scores (X)	$X - \bar{X}$	$(X - \bar{X})^2$
Freddy Freshman	73	-7.5	56.25
Suzie Sophomore	85	4.5	20.25
Jonny Junior	68	-12.5	156.25
Samantha Senior	94	13.5	182.25
Franklin Fifthyear	86	5.5	30.25
Alicia Auditor	77	-3.5	12.25
$N = 6$	$\Sigma X = 483$		$\Sigma(X - \bar{X})^2 = 457.5$

Figure 16.14: Feedback for the active learning exercise

Seeking Closure at the End of the Class

The class ending needs to finish in a meaningful way. Perhaps summarizing the lecture with its essential take-home message will work. Maybe we could loop back to the starting message and see how our new information answers a critical question. For some classes, this ending might be a good occasion for a take-home point or possibly even a humorous example. Yet another possibility is briefly describing upcoming events, such as assignments, quizzes, and exams. The important part, though, is that we should not just stop suddenly at the end of the main content. Closure is needed to make the most of the lesson.

For the present example, the main goal of the class was to find ways of describing human variability. After spending some time on calculating standard deviation, the students need to know more about what we could possibly do with this statistical tool. The slide in Figure 16.15 shows that standard deviation is useful for describing where the scores of most people in a group are located. The hope is that this slide can establish the usefulness of what we have accomplished in class. Figure 16.16 shows that standard deviation can also be used as a form of measurement. This slide uses Shaquille O'Neal as an example of someone who is extremely tall and thus reinforces the concept of his being an outlier, which is a concept that was introduced in the previous class period. The new wrinkle at the end of this lecture is that his height could be expressed with standard deviation as a form of measurement. This topic will be covered in a future class, so introducing it briefly here will help prepare students for an upcoming idea, which is an example of foreshadowing.

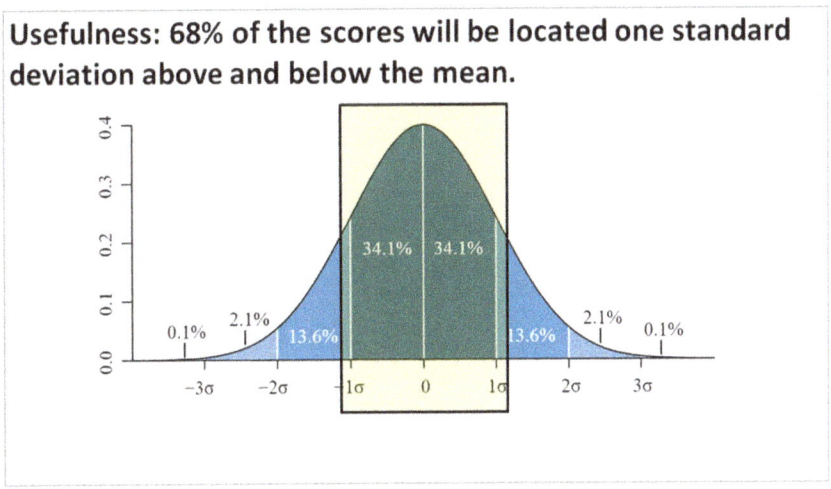

Figure 16.15: Closure at the end of the lecture

Standard deviation can also be used as a unit of measurement; Distance above or below the mean.

Example: Shaq's height is about three standard deviations above the mean.

Figure 16.16: Foreshadowing a new topic

The slides in Figures 16.15 and 16.16 follow an assertion-evidence layout with open-licensed images from Wikipedia. I highlighted the key part of the graph in Figure 16.15 by drawing a box with a yellow fill, with its transparency set to 80% in order to allow the underlying graph to show through. This method effectively highlights a particular feature in a complex object. The text box next to Shaquille O'Neal explains why he is relevant to the assertion used in this slide.

Handouts as the Second Life of the Slide Deck

The powerpoint slide deck is often provided to the students as a file in an online course management system to support note-taking activities or to review before an examination. Student access to the presentation slide deck is particularly helpful in Statistics to provide the students with the details from the classroom examples without the need to copy down all of this information. I converted the present slide deck into an Adobe pdf file for the students by printing the PowerPoint presentation to the pdf printer driver. To give the students access, I uploaded the subsequent pdf file to the course management system. This upload comprises the second life of the powerpoint presentation as a document.

An example of a handout for the current presentation appears in Figure 16.17 for the slide that defines variability. This particular handout was printed with the "notes page" option to put the presenter's notes on the handout. Providing this additional information gave the slides a context that would help students understand the key point of the slide after the presentation. Another useful function of the slide notes is, again, to provide documentation for the images or other information. The documentation for this image was not shown to the students on the projection screen, though it is available in the handout. A possible indirect benefit of including the documentation for the image is that it sets a good example to students about the importance of documenting the information sources, and thereby helps to communicate expectations for academic writing. The notes feature might also be useful for other kinds of documentation, like technical details or citing page numbers from the textbook. Plenty of space is available at the bottom of the page for students to add their own notes.

Figure 16.17: An example slide from a handout pdf document that was printed with the "notes page" option

Some teachers might not use or need the "notes" feature. For this situation, it would probably be best to print the presentation as a handout, with three or four slides per page. In Figure 16.18, the appearance of this handout for "3 slides" illustrates what the same slide deck would look like in a handout format. The "3 slides" option has the nice feature of providing an area that is specifically formatted for handwritten notes. The blank lines may help communicate to students that they are expected to take their own notes that go beyond the information on the slides.

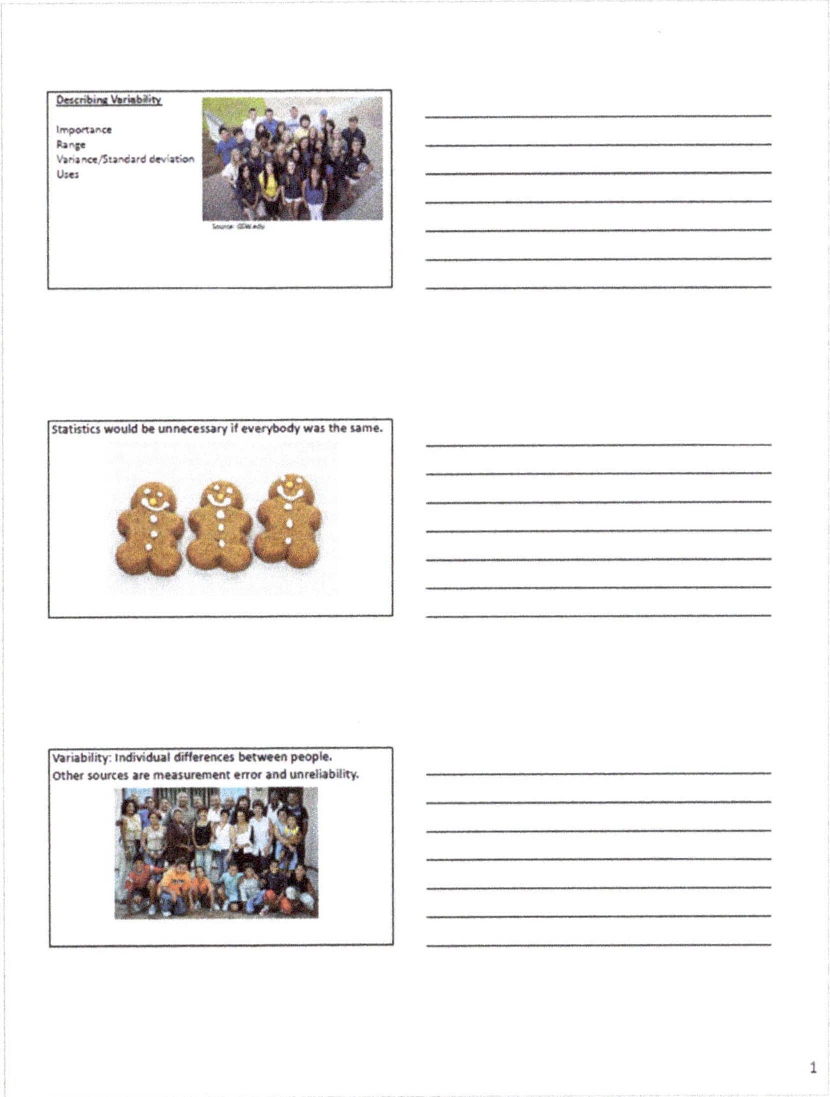

Figure 16.18: The slide deck printed with a "3 slides" handout format

The Successful Classroom Presentation

Let's summarize the overall goals to see how they were achieved in the above presentation. The first goal of high visibility was achieved through a black/white color combination, large sans-serif font, and positioning the most important text high on the slide. A second goal was to direct student attention to areas of the slide that were particularly important. It was achieved by using arrows, colors, and highlighting. A third goal was to maintain emotional engagement throughout class. Using images that were visually interesting yet relevant and informative were achieved this goal. Humor, sparingly used during the lecture, alleviated the tedium of a strictly-lecture approach. Switching from lecturing to an active learning exercise was used to increase student engagement at a time when the students' ability to maintain attention on the lecture reached a low point. In regard to behavioral goals, the slides were made available as an Adobe pdf file before class for students to use as a note-taking resource. Using the "notes" feature of powerpoint provided context for the slide and documented the sources of the images.

The overall structure of the class is also worthy of review. The first slide, which is on-screen before the lecture begins, is a critical point for getting the class started by stimulating interest in the topic. This first slide introduces the topic, lays out a roadmap for the class, and stimulates student interest through an intriguing picture. After this, two introductory slides aim to establish the importance of the topic. The body of the presentation focused on the key ideas that were presented in a logical sequence. Complex information in this part of the lecture distributed over several slides gradually built student understanding. The lecture part transitioned into an active learning situation followed by feedback. The class ending emphasized important take-home ideas, including some ideas that students will encounter again in future classes. Altogether, a presentation like this has a coherent, logical story line. It gently leads the students through a topic that most people find to be difficult and uninteresting.

The most important goal of any class is to improve student cognition. In this example, powerpoint features used in strategic ways effectively helped promote understanding of content that students often struggle with. The assertion-evidence slide layout in most of the slides provided text complemented by relevant instructional graphics. In this example, a mathematical concept (variability) was often illustrated with graphs exemplifying this concept. Some of the graphics appeared side by side so as to facilitate comparisons. Complex topics, like calculating variance and standard deviation, were broken down into smaller parts that were gradually introduced to students over a sequence of several slides. Using this gradual build approach prevented cognitive overload. Powerpoint also supported an active learning exercise by communicating instructions and providing feedback on student answers.

The format and structure of this powerpoint example uses multimedia learning principles to help students make important connections. The assertion-evidence structure pairs statements with visual images, which is an example of multimedia learning (or dual coding). Some of these images were used to stimulate student interest, but most served to support and reinforce the concepts stated in the title of the slide. The signaling principle was used to point out features of interest with arrows or colored highlighting. In a few instances, applying the spatial contiguity principle effectively provided useful labels in close association to the graphic features that they represented. The information was carefully segmented by spreading the information over multiple slides. The use of transition slides also segmented the parts of the presentation into related groups. An effort was made to avoid using the slides as a teleprompter, which follows the redundancy principle. Finally, the slides in this example presentation have only the minimal features needed for education: text and instructional images. Leaving out unnecessary colors, decorations, animations, and transitions exemplifies the coherence principle.

At this point, some readers may be having a negative reaction: This is the most boring slide deck ever! It had no colorful slide themes, no zooming bullet points, and no exploding slide transitions. For these concerns, consider the potential benefits of the Spartan slide deck. The absence of these commonly used and abused powerpoint features makes the critical information stand out on the slide, which focuses student attention. Every single feature on the slide is prominent because it has no extraneous information to compete with. All of the slide elements are carefully and intentionally planned in order to contribute in some meaningful way to student learning. The positive result is that the slide deck has an effortless and transparent quality which focuses on learning rather than on superficial presentation gimmicks. Powerpoint technology only needs to support the goals of teaching. Anything else is superfluous and detracts from the educational value of the presentation.

The example in this chapter shows how much more can be done with powerpoint than simply listing information. The powerpoint presentation had an important organizing function for coordinating class activities, including supporting active learning exercises. It paired images and text synergistically to benefit student comprehension. Some of the graphics were created by me, the instructor, to clarify specific ideas to students rather than merely describing them with words. The student note-taking efforts benefitted from handouts that were information-rich or had spaces to take notes. There are also benefits for the instructor, such as space in the "notes" area to document sources and make useful comments. This medium offers abundant means for instructors to be creative and find new ways to promote student learning. Part of the fun of using powerpoint is coming up with creative new ways to illustrate ideas and engage student thinking.

THE BRIGHT FUTURE OF POWERPOINT IN EDUCATION

"Everyone has sat through a presentation in which the presenter's knowledge of the subject was far greater than their ability to design and produce an effective message.... To enhance our presentations, we need to improve our understanding of visual design and use of the technology we have available." (Shackelford and Griffis, 2007, p. 19)

Throughout this book, I have carefully evaluated powerpoint presentations from the perspective of the student. In order to see how they might be influenced by powerpoint presentations, I examined psychological functions such as vision, emotion, attention, cognition, and behavior. From this student-centered focus, I derived some practical recommendations for improving the educational effectiveness of powerpoint. Through the intentional and skillful design of powerpoint slide features, the accomplished instructor should be able to enhance the necessary components and thereby achieve the optimal slide deck for student learning. The design recommendations here should, hopefully, avoid the dreaded "death by powerpoint" experience in the classroom.

Powerpoint presentations have some positive attributes, but the quality of the actual presentations often falls short of the potential that this medium has to offer. The challenge, then, is to harness these positive features and use them intentionally to support student learning. Altogether, it seems that the future of powerpoint in education is not as dark as some critics have suggested. Multimedia presenations have an amazing educational potential provided that we use it in a skillful way. The future of powerpoint and multimedia-based learning in education is really quite optimistic.

In order to offer now some big-picture thoughts about powerpoint and the future of powerpoint in education, I will start with future directions for research, which is needed to better understand how powerpoint works in an educational setting. Next, I will consider the standards that surround powerpoint with the aim of going beyond the current standards, which are often weak presentation practices. I will close with thoughts about the relationship between powerpoint and pedagogy and the potential of powerpoint as a medium for creative teaching.

Productive Directions for Further Research

No academic review project would be complete without looking towards the future. New research will be essential for making improvements and providing further guidance to educators.

When powerpoint was introduced to the classroom, a wave of studies compared the new powerpoint technology to older classroom technology, typically blackboards and overhead projectors. These initial comparison studies produced a mixed bag of results, with most studies showing no measurable improvement (see Chapter 3 and Appendix A). It would be somewhat inaccurate to say that these studies demonstrated that powerpoint had failed in the classroom. Rather, these media studies were misguided by focusing too much on technology, rather than concentrating on the teaching methods that the technologies supported (R. E. Clark, 1983, 1991). A general fault of these studies is their tendency to say very little about the pedagogy, such as the details of how the instructors used powerpoint to teach students. Clearly, we need no further media comparison studies (see Appendix A) or surveys about students' general feelings towards powerpoint presentations (see Appendix B). When combined, at least 140 studies have been published on media effectiveness and/or student attitudes towards powerpoint. It seems unlikely that further studies of this nature will reveal anything useful.

A powerpoint research area that needs more attention is the understanding of how different slide layouts might affect learning. Clearly, an endless stream of slides with numerous bullet point lists is very ineffective. In spite of this common knowledge, relatively little progress has been made towards making slides with better designs. Research on the assertion-evidence slide layout suggests it is more effective than the usual bullet point list, but more work needs to be done in this area. The use of instructional images in support of reading has been thoroughly examined by educational psychologists, but a corresponding analysis of images in presentations seems lacking. We need a new generation of powerpoint studies that focuses specifically on the structure, layouts, and images used in powerpoint slides and how these might help or hinder learning. Diving into the details of slide formatting might seem rather dull and technical, but this area is the most likely source for the greatest possibility of future educational gains.

A second area for future research concerns the research methodologies employed in the study of powerpoint. A desirable approach would be to use highly focused outcome measurements that are more sensitive than global assessments (e.g., quizzes or exam scores) to gain a higher degree of sensitivity. Research on effectiveness could achieve such higher sensitivity through fine-grained analyses of how educational slides directly impact specific questions on examinations. For example, a study by Diesel and colleagues used seventeen multiple-choice questions (that were individually analyzed in a comparison of standard slides) to slides with the assertion-evidence format (Diesel et al., 2006). This item-level analysis allowed the investigators to make specific conclusions about how a topic from a particular slide impacted the correct response rate on the quiz item related to that slide. This kind of highly focused link between specific slides and specific quiz questions might be much more sensitive—and hopefully more illuminating—than making global comparisons from overall quiz or exam scores.

A third possible area for future research might lie in what the medical research community calls translational research. These research efforts attempt to bring ideas out of carefully constructed, artificial laboratory environments and apply them to solving problems in the real world. In education, a wealth of research has been conducted in the lab, particularly in cognitive psychology. However, the results from this research have not had much impact on educational uses of powerpoint. The results from a few translational research studies are promising (Garner and Alley, 2013; Issa et al., 2011; Overson, 2014), but clearly we need more work in this area.

Past studies on powerpoint in education seem to have been hampered by misguided research questions and insensitive outcome measures. Fortunately, some signs of progress point in the direction of possibilities that might make powerpoint presentations more productive. We can hope that the combination of focusing on specific issues, such as slide layouts and instructional images, in carefully designed experiments and classroom-based studies will yield new insights into the best practices for using powerpoint.

Fixing Our Slides

Most educators can use powerpoint software with little training, yet they often do not know much about making powerpoint presentations work well. This lack of knowledge and training causes the average teacher to passively follow the default settings of powerpoint, which is the path of least resistance. These defaults invisibly guide teachers and other presenters into presentation practices that may be counterproductive (C. Adams, 2006, 2009; Alley, 2013). Most presenters assume that following the default settings of powerpoint will lead to a good presentation, but their assumption is mistaken.

The widespread adoption of powerpoint in our culture is another form of a powerpoint default. The ubiquity of powerpoint presentations in modern culture has defined the conventions for presentations to follow (Knoblauch, 2012). The previous powerpoint presentations that a teacher has witnessed sets expectations and standards—use bullet point lists!—that teachers may unconsciously copy when they author their slide decks.

When these software and cultural defaults combine, the end result is a conglomeration of ineffective practices: too much text, too many bullet points, and—unfortunately—too many students who fall asleep during a presentation. Fortunately, we have a cure for powerpoint mediocrity. If we want to improve our presentations, we must overcome the ineffective, default ways of using powerpoint. The following is a brief summary of problematic powerpoint defaults in order to to reinforce our awareness of these sometimes implicit guides that influence powerpoint presentations.

1. The default settings. The typical uses of powerpoint, like bullet point lists, are based on historical standards, such as the text-focused computers of the 1980s (Alley, 2013). These standards were neither designed by presentation experts, nor scientifically tested for effectiveness. Bullet point lists have their place, but the overuse of this feature leads to mediocrity.
2. Unnecessary decorations. A common default approach of using powerpoint is the idea that colors, decorations, and lots of motion will make our presentations better by exciting the audience. The truth, however, is just the opposite.

3. Presenting too fast. The third powerpoint default is the tendency to go too fast. Powerpoint does not cause teachers to slow down like the more organic chalkboard. A related possibility is that powerpoint might encourage an attitude that instructors must achieve maximum efficiency in every teaching moment (C. Adams, 2009), which could promote a fast pace and impatience with student questions.
4. Being too linear. Powerpoint imposes a rigid order on the presentation, which makes the presentation default to a linear progression through the slide deck. Instructors may need to break with the predetermined order to encourage nonlinear exploration of a topic, especially in regard to student questions.
5. Tired bullet point lists. The default powerpoint slide layout is a bullet point list. The problem, however, is that presenters often overuse bullet points or use them in an ineffective manner. Educators can benefit from replacing the overused bullet point lists with slides based upon the assertion-evidence format, which combines statements and informative graphics. Slides that focus on instructional images rather than text may also be an improvement. Bullet point list layouts can have a beneficial role, but presenters must be careful to avoid making every slide follow this structure.
6. Overreliance on lecturing. The default teaching mode of many college professors is the lecture method, and powerpoint-use may encourage this style of teaching. Overuse of lecturing leads to the problem of student inattention and passive learning. Accordingly, the successful powerpoint lecture

needs to be supplemented with active learning as a part of the overall instructional plan.

7. Student expectations. Modern students expect their teachers to use powerpoint in the classroom, as well as make the slide decks available online. The modern educator needs to pay close attention to how powerpoint might be affecting the students. Does powerpoint seem to encourage a joyless march through a fact-filled slide deck? Does attendance decline because students are just downloading the slide deck? If powerpoint seems to be having adverse effects, it might need to be changed in some substantive way to make it more effective.

As the above examples show, powerpoint users—both presenters and audiences—are subtly guided by the software defaults and social expectations that surround the medium. These guiding expectations are often invisible to teachers, who uncritically accept these defaults. The end result is mediocre powerpoint presentations that are similar to everyone else's mediocre powerpoint presentations. In contrast, excellence in using powerpoint requires us to go beyond these defaults. Users must use powerpoint in a thoughtful and intentional manner. With careful evaluation and intentional design, it's possible to make presentations with a higher educational value than the current standards. It simply takes a knowledge of design issues and the effort to do more than settle for the current standards.

The Need to Emphasize Pedagogy Over Technology

A long-standing trend in education is to view the latest communications technology as a force that will revolutionize learning. As we saw with the 1960's, many educators thought television would revolutionize the field of education. More recently, the introduction of personal computers and the Internet have received much attention and enthusiasm from educators. Perhaps this viewpoint—that technology will be an educational game-changer—is itself a default cultural value in the field of education. We continuously search for the next silver bullet technology that will improve education. One thing that psychology research tells us, though, is that this search may be futile because certain human-based aspects of the educational context, such as visual perception and cognition, have remained constant despite these changes in technology.

The use of powerpoint is certainly an example of the enthusiasm for technology in the field of education. However, even though powerpoint technology has advantages, it does not necessarily lead to better instruction. The potential for improved instruction is there, but it needs to match with the fairly constant human potential to learn.

The cautious conclusion we must always keep in mind is that powerpoint and related technologies are simply tools. There is no teaching magic in the technology. Powerpoint is not a panacea for the various challenges teachers face in their classes. Powerpoint technology is simply an instrumental means for achieving particular educational goals. Therefore, educators must always place their pedagogy and instructional methods first when it comes to intentional design approached for instructional use. The technology tools, in contrast, should be a secondary consideration. The ideal powerpoint presentation does some heavy lifting in regard to achieving instructional goals, yet its use should be intuitive, effortless, and almost invisible to the students. The powerpoint presentation can be a canvas for the expression of ideas. We should not, in contrast, notice the canvas itself.

The overemphasis of technology solutions in education suggests a needed practical change in regard to how teachers work. Sitting down at the computer and typing out the powerpoint presentation may seem natural if our default way of thinking equates the technology as the center of instruction. It may be better to begin preparing for a class by thinking about the educational goals of the day, and how to best achieve those goals. Once instructors establish these goals and methods, then it might be worth considering how powerpoint would support the instruction. In other words, powerpoint slide development should be the third or maybe even the fourth step in preparing for a class.

Making technology the star of the educational show creates a technological dependency, but little emphasis is often given to training the teachers who run the technology. University or school administrators often believe that purchasing technology completes the objective of integrating technology into the classroom. The teacher training is an afterthought that is typically given no time, attention, or funding. However, purchasing technology is only the start of the process. Powerpoint software is relatively easy to use, especially for people who have some background in office-related software programs, like Microsoft Word. They are presumed to have software training already, so many educators are forced to learn about the technology on their own. The end result is that the majority of powerpoint users learn the most basic features, but then fail to develop any further mastery of the software. They remain perpetual beginners in the use of powerpoint. It seems peculiar to focus on the technology, yet ignore the training of the human beings who run it. Nevertheless, teacher training is relatively neglected.

To improve the effectiveness of powerpoint presentations, we must begin to treat this situation in a different manner. It's not enough to assume that teachers will master complex technologies on their own. This situation can only be improved by emphasizing more training for educators, so they can use the software features to their fullest potential. In the future, training educators to make the most out of the existing technology may be the area in need of emphasis most.

A parting idea is to approach powerpoint technology with enthusiasm, but still appreciate that it must always be in the back seat of the educational car. Pedagogy must be in the driver's seat. We can hope that educational researchers and professionals begin approaching technologies like powerpoint with a more sophisticated appreciation of what the technology can and cannot do for us.

The Bright Future of Powerpoint in Education

This thoughtful investigation of powerpoint presentations began with a paradox. Powerpoint seems to have so much potential, yet it is often used in counterproductive or ineffective ways. Powerpoint presentations have received strong words and condemnation, with some critics even calling for a complete ban. As we have seen, powerpoint in education is sometimes criticized as being a teacher-centered technology that promotes mere information delivery and passive learning. This technology may diminish the instructional dialogue between teachers and students, so that students ultimately submitting to the authority of powerpoint, merely transcribe information from powerpoint slides. Teachers are left offering little more than a modern, boring, traditional lecture.

These views of powerpoint presentations are rather dark. Fortunately, it doesn't have to be this way.

First, it is important to acknowledge that computer technology has played a progressively increasing role in our society over the last several decades. We spend much of our contemporary life looking at computer screens in some form or another, such as televisions, tablets, smart phones, and computer displays. In this cultural context, we should expect that computer-based information displays will play an essential role in the classroom environment. Suggestions to eliminate powerpoint in order to get "back to the basics" seem woefully out-of-step with our computer-based society. Powerpoint presentations may have their faults, but there are more advantages than problems. Computer technology is simply not going to disappear from the classroom.

The next step in this powerpoint revolution is to admit that we have been using powerpoint in all the wrong ways. Death by powerpoint occurs because our cultural expectation for presentations have gradually changed. The previous standard for presentations was to use 3 x 5 inch notecards to provide memory cues for the speaker. The audience did not see this information. These memory cues were restricted to the presenter. With powerpoint, the presenter's notes generally turned into bullet points for the audience to see. As we have seen, this new standard fails due to placing too much text on the projected slide, which leads to a cognitive overload. Reading from the slide also conflicts with the students' attempt to listen to their instructor's spoken words. And the presenter typically ends up facing the screen instead of the audience, another presentation failure. These changes in our cultural expectations for presentations have led to a decline in the overall quality of modern presentations.

The path forward to better powerpoint presentations should now seem clear. Eliminating unnecessary slide features and decreasing the amount of text will be useful. For content, students will benefit from presentations that express entire thoughts as statements. These statements should be accompanied by supporting visual evidence. Instructional images may promote efficient processing of information and promote student interest more than text-based information. The effective learning environment will need to switch from pure information delivery to other methods that promote more active pedagogy. Incorporating question points and seeking student feedback (either by raised hands or by response systems) will promote better communication between the teacher and the students. Instructors can encourage better note-taking by sending students unambiguous indicators of the important material they need to learn. The annotation of slides from a handout may be helpful for the note-taking process. These are some of the many ways we can better use powerpoint in the classroom than our current standard.

These positive changes will not happen easily or quickly. The defaults of powerpoint and our cultural expectations of this medium combine to easily make ineffective presentations. We will need to actively aim our efforts and overcome these easy approaches in order to achieve more engaging and educationally sound presentations. It's not just needing to change our own ineffective habits. We also need to gradually change the cultural standards and expectations for good presentations.

Overall, the future of powerpoint in education is rather bright. Using practices based in research evidence will show us the way forward. We can use powerpoint effectively as a tool to support our pedagogical techniques and ultimately leads to better learning. It is up to us to work together and help make this positive future come about.

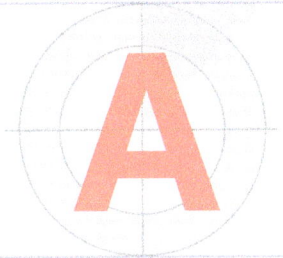

Appendix A

Efficacy Studies

Students learning outcomes with powerpoint were better/same/worse when compared to traditional forms of instruction (chalkboards, projectors, or no technology).

Better outcomes

Blalock & Montgomery, 2005

Blokzijl & Andeweg, 2005

Erwin & Rieppi, 1999

Evans, 1998

Hove & Corcoran, 2008 Kunkel, 2004

Lowry, 1999

Mantei, 2000

Massery, 2008

Morrison & Vogel, 1998

Szabo & Hastings, 2000 Weinraub, 1998

Neutral or mixed outcomes

Ahmed, 1998

Apperson et al., 2006

Avila, Biner, Bink, & Dean, 1995

Bartlett & Strough, 2003

Beets & Lobinger, 2001

Brewster, 1995

Buchko, Buchko, & Meyer, 2012

Bushong, 1998

Butler & Mautz, 1996

Carrell & Menzel, 2001; #1 and #2

Chou et al., 2015

Daniels, 1999

DeBord, Aruguete, & Muhlig, 2004; #1

Forsyth & Archer, C.R., 1997

Hardin, 2007

Jandaghi & Matin, 2009

Koeber, 2005

Kunkel, 2004; Crime Theory

Larson, 2001

Luna & McKenzie, J., 1997

Meo et al., 2013

Nouri & Shahid, 2005

Pippert & Moore, 1999

Prabhu, Pai, Prabhu, & Shrilatha, 2014

Rankin & Hoaas, 2001

Ricer, Filak, & Short, 2005

Seth, Upadhyaya, Ahmad, & Kumar, 2010

Sidman & Jones, 2007

Smith & Woody, 2000

Stoloff, 1995

Susskind, 2005, 2008

Swati, Suresh, & Sachin, 2014

Szabo & Hastings, 2000; #1, #3

Wecker, 2012

Worse outcomes

Amare, 2006

Bartsch & Cobern, 2003; #1

Casanova & Casanova, 1991

deSa & Keny, 2014

El Khoury & Mattar, 2012

Rokade & Bahetee, 2013

Savoy, Proctor, & Salvendy, 2009

Sosin, Blecha, Agarwal, Bartlett, & Daniel, 2004

Appendix B

Perception Studies

Student attitudes towards powerpoint lecture presentations from survey research.

Positive attitude

Ahmadi, Dileepan, & Raiszadeh, 2007

Amare, 2006

Apperson et al., 2006

Atkins-Sayre, Hopkins, Mohundro, & Sayre, 1998

Bartsch & Cobern, 2003

Beets & Lobinger, 2001

Blokzijl & Naeff, 2004

L. A. Burke & James, 2008

L. A. Burke, James, & Ahmadi, 2009

Cassady, 1998

J. Clark, 2008

D'Angelo & Woosley, 2007

Daniels, 1999

Daniels et al., 2008

Davis, 1998

DeBord et al., 2004; #1

Erdemir & Topcu, 2012

Feldkamp, 2008

Ferrell & Ferrell, 2002

Fifield & Peifer, 1994

Forsyth & Archer, C.R., 1997

Frey & Birnbaum, 2002

Gurrie & Fair, 2008

Harknett & Cobane, 1997

K. E. James, Burke, & Hutchins, 2006

Kahraman, Cevik, & Kodan, 2011

Koeber, 2005

Kumar, 2013

Lavin, Korte, & Davies, 2010

Loisel & Galer, 2004

Lowry, 1999

Luna & McKenzie, J., 1997

Luttig, 1998

Mantei, 2000

McConnell, 1996

Milliken & Barnes, 2002

Morrison & Vogel, 1998

O'Dwyer, 2008

O'Quigley, 2011

R. E. Parker, Bianchi, & Cheah, 2008

T. Perry & Perry, 1998

Pippert & Moore, 1999

Rickman & Grudzinski, 2000

Roehling & Trent-Brown, 2011

Sammons, 1995

Savoy et al., 2009

Seth, Upadhyaya, Ahmad, & Kumar, 2010

Shittu, Basha, Ahmad, & Liman, 2011

Shuell & Farber, 2001

Simpson, Pollacia, Speers, Willis, & Tarver, 2003

Sugahara & Boland, 2006

Susskind, 2005, 2008

Swati et al., 2014

Szabo & Hastings, 2000; #1

Tang & Austin, 2009

Thareja, Jayjee, Dhawan, & Singla, 2011

Treleven et al., 2012, 2014

Weinraub, 1998

I. Wilson, 2016

Neutral or mixed

El Khoury & Mattar, 2012 Hardin, 2007

Jandaghi & Matin, 2009 Nouri & Shahid, 2005 Prabhu, Pai, Prabhu, & Shrilatha, 2014

Rosenthal et al., 2002 Selimoglu & Arsoy, 2009 Seth, Upadhyaya, Ahmad, & Moghe, 2010

Shallcross & Harrison, 2007 Thomas & Raju, 2012 Yilmazel-Sahin, 2009

Negative attitude

Abdelrahman, Attaran, & Hai-Leng, 2013

Bushong, 1998

deSa & Keny, 2014 Hashemzadeh & Wilson, 2007 Kardes & Poroy, 2009

Mann & Robinson, 2009

Novelli & Fernandes, 2007 Rokade & Bahetee, 2013

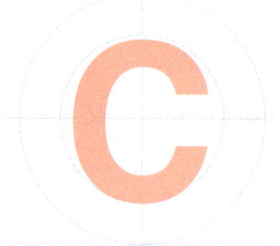

Appendix C

Resources

Recommended Readings

Critical evaluation of PowerPoint shortcomings

Tufte, Edward R. *The Cognitive Style of PowerPoint: Pitching Out Corrupts Within*. 2nd ed. Cheshire, Connecticut: Graphics Press LLC, 2006.

Developing an emotionally compelling message

Duarte, Nancy. *Resonate: Present Visual Stories that Transform Audiences*. Hoboken, NJ: John Wiley & Sons, 2010.

PowerPoint recommendations from a design expert

Duarte, Nancy. *Slide:ology: The Art and Science of Great Presentations*. Canada: O'Reilly Media, 2008.

Recommendations for scientific and engineering presentations

Alley, Michael. *The Craft of Scientific Presentations: Critical Steps to Succeed and Critical Errors to Avoid*. 2nd ed. New York: Springer, 2013.

Applying cognitive psychology to PowerPoint

Kosslyn, Stephen M. "Graphics and Human Information Processing: A Review of Five Books." *Journal of the American Statistical Association* 80 (1985): 499–512.

A comprehensive review of multimedia learning principles

Mayer, Richard E. *Multimedia learning*. 2nd ed. New York: Cambridge University Press, 2009.

A review of student response system technology studies

Keough, Shawn M. "Clickers in the Classroom: A Review and a Replication." *Journal of Management Education* 36 (2012): 822–847, https://doi.org/10.1177/1052562912454808

Powerpoint design recommendations based on multimedia learning research

Atkinson, Cliff and Richard E. Mayer. *Five Ways to Reduce PowerPoint Overload*. PDF: https://cit.duke.edu/wp-content/uploads/2012/07/atkinson_mayer_powerpoint.pdf

Web sites

Assertion-evidence.com
   Examples and guidelines for using the assertion-evidence slide format.

Cloudconvert.com
   Converts Apple Keynote and other file formats into PowerPoint files and vice versa.

Images.google.com
   Search for images. Try using "tools" and "usage rights" for "labeled for reuse" to find images with open licenses for reuse.

Pechakucha.org
> Examples of the pecha kucha presentation style.

Pixabay.com; publicdomainpictures.net
> Images with open licenses for reuse.

Thinkoutsidetheslide.com
> Free resources for evaluating color, fonts, and more.

Accessibility

Vischeck.com
> Evaluates color images by simulating color blindness.

www.section508.va.gov/support/tutorials/powerpoint/index.asp
> U.S. Department of Veterans Affairs guidelines for creating accessible documents with PowerPoint 2010.

www.ncdae.org/resources/cheatsheets/#msppt
> Quick guides to PowerPoint accessibility from the National Center on Disability and Access to Education.

References

3M. *A Century of Innovation: The 3M Story*. 3M, 2002, http://multimedia.3m.com/mws/media/171240O/3m-coi-book-tif.pdf

Abdelrahman, Limia Ali Mohomed, Mohammad Attaran, and Chin Hai-Leng. "What Does PowerPoint Mean to You? A Phenomenological Study." *Procedia - Social and Behavioral Sciences* 103 (2013): 1319–1326, https://doi.org/10.1016/j.sbspro.2013.10.462

Abeysekera, Lakmal and Phillip Dawson. "Motivation and Cognitive Load in the Flipped Classroom: Definition, Rationale and a Call for Research." *Higher Education Research & Development*, 103, no. 1 (2015): 1–14, https://doi.org/10.1080/07294360.2014.934336

Adams, Catherine. "PowerPoint, Habits of Mind, and Classroom Culture." *Journal of Curriculum Studies* 38, no. 4 (2006): 389–411, https://doi.org/10.1080/00220270600579141

———. "PowerPoint and the Pedagogy of Digital Media Technologies." In *Annual Proceedings on the Practice of Educational Communications and Technology* (vol. 2). Louisville, KY: 2009.

Adams, Scott. *"PowerPoint" poisoning* [Cartoon]. August 16, 2000, http://dilbert.com/strip/2000-08-16

Ahmadi, Mohammad, Parthasarati Dileepan, and Farhad Raiszadeh. "Is PowerPoint Evil? Students' Perceptions." *Review of Business Research* 7 no. 4 (2007): 15–19.

Ahmed, Christine. "Powerpoint versus Traditional Overheads. Which is more Effective for Learning?" Presented at the Conference of the South Dakota Association for Health, Physical Education and Recreation, Souix Falls, SD, 1998.

Alley, Michael. *The Craft of Scientific Presentations: Critical Steps to Succeed and Critical Errors to Avoid*. 2nd ed. New York: Springer, 2013.

Alley, Michael, Madeline Schreiber and John Muffo. "Pilot Testing of a New Design for Presentation Slides to Teach Science and Engineering." In *ASEE/IEEE Frontiers in Education*, S3G–7 to SG3–12. Indianapolis, IN: IEEE, 2005.

Alley, Michael, Madeline Schreiber, Katrina Ramsdell and John Muffo. "How the Design of Headlines in Presentation Slides Affects Audience Retention." *Technical Communication* 43 (2006): 225–234.

Altman, Rick. *Why Most PowerPoint Presentations Suck and How You Can Make Them Better*. 3rd ed. Pleasanton, CA: Harvest Books, 2012.

Amare, Nicole. "To Slideware or to not Slideware: Student Experiences with PowerPoint vs. Lecture." *Journal of Technical Writing and Communication* 36 no. 3 (2006): 297–308.

Anderson, Joe S., and Susan K. Williams. "Pecha Kucha for Lean and Sticky Presentations in Business Classes." In *Working Paper Series—12-03*. Flagstaff, AZ: Northern Arizona University, 2012.

Annis, Linda Ferrill. "Effect of Preference for Assigned Lecture Notes on Student Achievement." *Journal of Education Research* 74 (1981): 179–182. https://doi.org/10.1080/00220671.1981.10885306

Anthis, Kristine. "Is it the Clicker, or is it the Question? Untangling the Effects of Student Response System Use." *Teaching of Psychology* 38(2011): 189–193, https://doi.org/10.1177/0098628311411895

Apperson, Jennifer M., Eric L. Laws, and James A. Scepansky. "The Impact of Presentation Graphics on Students' Experience in the Classroom." *Computers and Education* 47(2006): 116–126, https://doi.org/10.1016/j.compedu.2004.09.003

Atkinson, Cliff. *Beyond Bullet Points: Using Microsoft PowerPoint to Create Presentations that Inform, Motivate, and Inspire*. 3rd ed. Redmond, WA: Microsoft Press, 2011.

Atkinson, Cliff and Richard E. Mayer. *Five Ways to Reduce PowerPoint Overload.* PDF: https://cit.duke.edu/wp-content/uploads/2012/07/atkinson_mayer_powerpoint.pdf

Atkinson, Richard C. and Richard M. Shiffrin. "Human Memory: A Proposed System and its Control Processes." *Psychology of Learning and Motivation* 2 (1968): 89–195, https://doi.org/10.1016/S0079-7421(08)60422-3

Atkins-Sayre, Wendy, Sonya Hopkins, Sarah Mohundro, and Ward Sayre. "Rewards and Liabilities of Presentation Software as an Ancillary Tool: Prison or Paradise?" Presentation at the Annual Meeting of the National Communication Association, New York, NY: 1998.

Austin, Jennifer L., Melissa Lee, and Jeffrey P. Carr. "The Effects of Guided Notes on Undergraduate Students' Recording of Lecture Content." *Journal of Instructional Psychology* 31 (2004): 314–320.

Avila, Ramon A., Paul M. Biner, Martin L. Bink, and Raymond S. Dean. "Course Materials Presentation Using Video-Based Technologies: An Evaluative Study of College Student Performance and Attitudes." *Psychology in the Schools* 32(1995): 38–45, https://doi.org/10.1002/1520-6807(199501)32:1<38::AID-PITS2310320107>3.0.CO;2-F

Baddeley, Alan. D. *Working Memory*. New York, NY: Oxford University Press, 1986.

Baddeley, Alan D., Neil Thomson, and Mary Buchanan. "Word Length and the Structure of Short-Term Memory." *Journal of Verbal Learning and Verbal Behavior* 14 (1975): 575–589.

Badger, Richard, Goodith White, Peter Sutherland and Tamsin Haggis. "Note Perfect: An Investigation of how Students View Taking Notes in Lectures." *System* 29 (2001): 405–417, https://doi.org/10.1016/S0346-251X(01)00028-8

Baker, Linda and Bruce R. Lombardi. "Students' Lecture Notes and Their Relation to Test Performance." *Teaching of Psychology* 12 (1985): 28–32, https://doi.org/10.1207/s15328023top1201_9

Ball, Corbin. "Avoiding Death by PowerPoint." *Public Management* 91 no. 6 (2009): 26–27.

Bartlett, Robin M. and JoNell Strough. "Multimedia versus Traditional Course Instruction in Introductory Social Psychology." *Teaching of Psychology* 30 (2003): 335–338, https://doi.org/10.1207/S15328023TOP3004_07

Bartsch, Robert A. and Kristi M. Cobern. "Effectiveness of PowerPoint Presentations in Lectures." *Computers and Education* 41 (2003): 77–86, https://doi.org/doi:10.1016/S0360-1315(03)00027-7

Beets, S. Douglas and Patricia G. Lobinger. "Cyber Dimensions: Pedagogical Techniques: Student Performance and Preferences." *Journal of Education for Business* 76 (2001): 231–235, https://doi.org/10.1080/08832320109601316

Berk, Ronald A. *Professors are from Mars, Students are from Snickers: How to Write and Deliver Humor in the Classroom and in Professional Presentations.* Sterling, Virginia: Stylus Publishing, 2003.

---. "'PowerPoint Engagement' Techniques to Foster Deep Learning." *Journal of Faculty Development* 25 (2011): 45–48.

Beyer, Alisa Miller. "Improving Student Presentations: Pecha Kucha and Just Plain PowerPoint." *Teaching of Psychology* 38 (2011): 122–126, https://doi.org/10.1177/0098628311401588

Birch, Jennifer. "Worldwide Prevalence of Red-Green Color Deficiency." *Journal of the Optical Society of America A* 29 (2012): 313–320, https://doi.org/10.1364/JOSAA.29.000313

Blake, Kim, Ada Poranek, and Kate MacCulloch. "Structured Clinical Case PowerPoint Presentations for Distributed Learning." *Medical Education* 41 (2007): 512–513.

Blalock, M. Gale and Robert D. Montgomery. "The Effect of PowerPoint on Student Performance in Principles of Economics: An Exploratory Study." *Journal for Economics Educators* 5 no. 3 (2005): 1–7.

Bligh, Donald A. *What's the Use of Lectures?* U.S.A.: Jossey-Bass, 2000.

Blokzijl, Wim and Bas Andeweg. "The Effects of Text Slide Format and Presentational Quality on Learning in College Lectures." In *2005 IEEE International Professional Communication Conference Proceedings*, 288–299, 2005.

Blokzijl, Wim and Roos Naeff. "The Instructor as Stagehand: Dutch Student Responses to PowerPoint." *Business*

Communication Quarterly 67 no. 1 (2004) 70–77, https://doi.org/10.1177/1080569903262046

Bowman, Laura L. "Does Posting PowerPoint Presentations on WebCT Affect Class Performance or Attendance?" *Journal of Instructional Psychology* 36 (2009): 104–108.

Bradshaw, Amy C. "Effects of Presentation Interference in Learning with Visuals." *Journal of Visual Literacy* 23 no. 1 (2003): 41–68.

Brewster, JoAnne. "Teaching Abnormal Psychology in a Multimedia Classroom." *Teaching of Psychology* 23 (1995): 249–252, https://doi.org/10.1207/s15328023top2304_15

Bridges, Cecil C., Jr. "An Attention Scale for Evaluating E.T.V. Programs." *Journal of Educational Research* 54 (1960): 149–152.

Brock, Sabra and Cornelia Brodahl. "A Tale of Two Cultures: Cross Cultural Comparison in Learning the Prezi Presentation Software Tool in the U.S. and Norway." *Journal of Information Technology Education: Research* 12 (2013): 95–118.

Brock, Sabra and Yogini Joglekar. "Empowering PowerPoint: Slides and Teaching Effectiveness." *Interdisciplinary Journal of Information, Knowledge, and Management* 6 (2011): 85–94.

Buchko, Aaron A., Kathleen J. Buchko and Joseph M. Meyer. "Is There Power in PowerPoint? A Field Test of the Efficacy of PowerPoint on Memory and Recall of Religious Sermons." *Computers in Human Behavior* 28 (2012): 688–695, https://doi.org/10.1016/j.chb.2011.11.016

Bumiller, Elisabeth. "We Have Met the Enemy and He is PowerPoint." *New York Times*, April 27, 2010, p. A1.

Burke, Deirdre and Alan Apperley. "PowerPoint and Pedagogy." *Learning and Teaching Projects 2003/2004*. (2003): 77–82. Center for Teaching and Learning: University of Wolverhampton.

Burke, Lisa A. and Karen E. James. "PowerPoint-Based Lectures in Business Education: An Empirical Investigation of Student Perceived Novelty and Effectiveness." *Business Communication Quarterly* 71 (2008): 277–296, https://doi.org/10.1177/1080569908317151

Burke, Lisa A., Karen E. James, and Mohammad Ahmadi. "Effectiveness of PowerPoint-Based Lectures Across Different Business Disciplines: An Investigation and Implications." *Journal of Education for Business* 84 (2009): 246–251, https://doi.org/10.3200/JOEB.84.4.246-251

Burmark, Lynell. "Visual Presentations that Prompt, Flash & Transform." *Media and Methods* 40 (2004): 4–5.

Bushong, Sarah. "Utilization of PowerPoint Presentation Software in Library Instruction of Subject Specific Reference Sources." (Master's thesis). Kent State University, 1998.

Butler, Janet B. and Mautz, R. David, Jr. "Media Presentations and Learning: A Laboratory Analysis." *Issues in Accounting Education* 11 (1996): 259–280.

Caldwell, Jane E. "Clickers in the Large Classroom: Current Research and Best-Practice Tips." *CBE - Life Sciences Education* 6 (2007): 9–20, https://doi.org/10.1187/cbe.06-12-0205

Cannon, Edmund. "Comment on Chen and Lin 'Does Downloading Power-Point Slides Before the Lecture Lead to Better Student Achievement?'" *International Review of Economics Education* 10 (2011): 83–89, https://doi.org/10.1016/S1477-3880(15)30039-6

Carney, Russell N. and Joel R. Levin. "Pictorial Illustrations Still Improve Students' Learning from Text." *Educational Psychology Review* 14 (2002): 5–26, https://doi.org/10.1023/A:1013176309260

Carr, Nicholas G. "Is Google Making Us Stupid? What the Internet is Doing to Our Brains." *The Atlantic* 302 (August 2008): 56–63.

---. *The Shallows: What the Internet is Doing to Our Brains.* New York: W.W. Norton & Company, 2010.

Carrell, Lori J. and Kent E. Menzel. "Variations in Learning, Motivation, and Perceived Immediacy Between Live and Distance Education Classrooms." *Communication Education* 50 (2001): 230–240, https://doi.org/10.1080/03634520109379250

Casanova, J. and S. L. Casanova. "Computer as Electronic Blackboard: Remodeling the Organic Chemistry Lecture." *Educom Review* 26 (1991): 31–39.

Cassady, Jerrel C. "Student and Instructor Perceptions of the Efficacy of Computer-Aided Lectures in Undergraduate University Courses." *Journal of Educational Computing Research* 19 (1998): 175–189, https://doi.org/10.2190/XY1K-0BET-JF6C-WTPL

Castelyn, Jordi and André Mottart. "Presenting Material via Graphic Organizers in Science Classes in Secondary Education." *Procedia - Social and Behavioral Sciences* 69 (2012): 458–466, https://doi.org/10.1016/j.sbspro.2012.11.434

Castelyn, Jordi, André Mottart, and Martin Valcke. "The Impact of Graphic Organizers on Learning from Presentations." *Technology, Pedagogy, and Education* 22 (2013): 283–301, https://doi.org/10.1080/1475939X.2013.784621

Chen, Jennjou Tsui-Fang Lin. "Does Downloading PowerPoint Slides Before the Lecture Lead to Better Student Achievement?" *International Review of Economics Education* 7 (2008): 9–18.

Chou, Pao-Nan, Chi-Cheng Chang, and Pei-Fen Lu. "Prezi versus PowerPoint: The Effects of Varied Digital Presentation Tools on Students' Learning Performance." *Computers and Education* 91 (2015): 73–82, https://doi.org/10.1016/j.compedu.2015.10.020

Christopherson, Kimberly M. "Hardware or Wetware: What are the Possible Interactions of Pedagogy and Technology in the Classroom?" *Teaching of Psychology* 38 (2011): 288–292, https://doi.org/10.1177/0098628311421332

Clark, Jennifer. "PowerPoint and Pedagogy: Maintaining Student Interest in University Lectures." *College Teaching* 56 (2008): 39–45.

Clark, Richard E. "Reconsidering Research on Learning from Media." *Review of Educational Research* 53 (1983): 445–459.

---. "When Researchers Swim Upstream: Reflections on an Unpopular Argument About Learning from Media." *Educational Technology* 31 (1991): 34–40.

Coget, Jean-Francois. "Haiku Deck: A Minimalist, High-Impact Alternative to PowerPoint." *Journal of Management Education* 39 (2015): 422–438.

Conboy, C., S. Fletcher, K. Russell, and M. Wilson. "An Evaluation of the Potential Use and Impact of Prezi, the Zooming Editor Software, as a Tool to Facilitate Learning in Higher Education." *Innovations in Practice* 7 (2012): 31–42.

Cornelius, Tara L. and Jamie Owen-DeSchryver. "Differential Effects of Full and Partial Notes on Learning Outcomes and Attendance." *Teaching of Psychology* 35 (2008): 6–12, https://doi.org/10.1080/00986280701818466

Creed, Tom. "PowerPoint, No! Cyberspace Yes." *The National Teaching and Learning Forum* 6, no. 4 (1997): 1–5.

Croxton, Justin. "40 Presentation Software & Powerpoint Alternatives For 2017." *CustomShow*, September 3, 2017. Retrieved September 29, 2017, from https://www.customshow.com/best-powerpoint-alternatives-presentation-programs/

D'Angelo, Jill M. and Sherry Ann. "Technology in the Classroom: Friend or Foe?" *Education* 127 (2007): 462–271.

Daniels, Lisa. "Introducing Technology in the Classroom: PowerPoint as a First Step." *Journal of Computing in Higher Education* 10 (1999): 42–56.

Daniels, Lisa, John C. Kane, Brian P. Rosario, Thomas A. Creahan, Carlos F. Liard-Muriente, and Mary Ellen Mallia.

"The Impact of PowerPoint on Student Performance and Course Evaluations in Economics Courses: An Experiment at Six Institutions." *Social Sciences Research Network,* 2008, http://papers.ssrn.com/sol3/papers.cfm?abstract_id=1090662

Dansereau, Donald F. and Dwayne D. Simpson. "A Picture is Worth a Thousand Words: The Case for Graphic Representations." *Professional Psychology: Research and Practice* 40 (2009): 104–110, https://doi.org/10.1037/a0011827

Davis, Mark S. "The Electronic Biology Classroom: Implementation and Student Opinion." Presentation at the Teaching in the Community Colleges; Online instruction: Trends and Issues II, 1998, http://www.eric.ed.gov/contentdelivery/servlet/ERICServlet?accno=ED449976

Dean, David. "The Clicker Challenge: Using a Reader Response System in the (British) History Classroom." *The History Teacher* 46 (2013): 455–464.

Debevec, Kathleen, Mei-Yau Shih, and Vishal Kashyap. Learning Strategies and Performance In a Technology Integrated Classroom. *Journal of Research on Technology in Education* 38 (2006): 293–307.

DeBord, Kurt A., Mara S. Aruguete, and Jeannette Muhlig. "Are Computer-Assisted Teaching Methods Effective?" *Teaching of Psychology* 31 (2004): 65–68.

deSa, Sunita B., and Mukundraj S. "PowerPoint versus Chalkboard Based Lectures in Pharmacology: Evaluation of Their Impact on Medical Student's Knowledge and Their

Preferences." *International Journal of Advanced Health Sciences* 1 (2014): 10–14.

Di Vesta, Francis J. and Susan G. Gray. "Listening and Note Taking." *Journal of Educational Psychology* 63 (1972): 8–14, https://doi.org/10.1037/h0032243

Diesel, E., M. Alley, M. Schreiber and M. Borrego. "Improving Student Learning in Large Classes by Incorporating Active Learning with a New Design of Teaching Slides (p. T2G11-16)." Presentation at the ASEE/IEEE Frontiers in Education Conference, San Diego, CA, 2006.

Dils, Keith A. "Using Technology in a Middle School Social Studies Classroom." *The International Journal of Social Education: Official Journal of the Indiana Council for the Social Studies* 15 (2000): 102–112.

Dobson, Stephen. "The Assessment of Student PowerPoint Presentations-Attempting the Impossible?" *Assessment and Evaluation in Higher Education* 31 (2006): 109–119, https://doi.org/10.1080/02602930500262403

Doumont, Jean-Luc. "The Cognitive Style of PowerPoint: Slides Are Not All Evil." *Technical Communication* 52 (2005): 64–70.

Downing, Joe and Cecile Garmon. "Teaching Students in the Basic Course How to Use Presentation Software." *Communication Education* 50 (2001): 218–229, https://doi.org/10.1080/03634520109379249

Driessnack, Martha. "A Closer Look at PowerPoint." *Journal of Nursing Education* 44 (2005): 347.

Duarte, Nancy. *Slide:ology: The Art and Science of Great Presentations*. Canada: O'Reilly Media, 2008.

---. *Resonate: Present Visual Stories that Transform Audiences.* Hoboken, NJ: John Wiley & Sons, 2010.

Durso, Francis T., Francis T. Durso, Vlad L. Pop, John S. Burnett, and Eric J. Stearman. "Evidence-Based Human Factors Guidelines for PowerPoint Presentation. *Ergonomics in Design: The Quarterly of Human Factors Applications* 19 (2011): 4–8, https://doi.org/10.1177/1064804611416583

El Khoury, Rim M. and Dorine M. Mattar. "PowerPoint in Accounting Classrooms: Constructive or Destructive?" *International Journal of Business and Social Science* 3 (2012): 240–259.

Ellington, Aimee J. "A Meta-Analysis of the Effects of Calculators on Students' Achievement and Attitude Levels in Precollege Mathematics Classes." *Journal for Research in Mathematics Education* 34 (2003): 433–463.

Elliot, Andrew J. and Markus A. Maier. "Color Psychology: Effects of Perceiving Color on Psychological Functioning in Humans." *Annual Review of Psychology* 65 (2014): 95–120, https://doi.org/10.1146/annurev-psych-010213-115035

Erdemir, Naki and Mustafa Sami Topcu. "The Impact of Presentation Graphics on Preservice Science Teachers' Attitudes towards Physics." *Journal of Baltic Science Education* 11 (2012): 141–152.

Erwin, T. Dar and Ricardo Rieppi. "Comparing Multimedia and Traditional Approaches in Undergraduate Psychology Classes." *Teaching of Psychology* 26 (1999): 58–61, https://doi.org/10.1207/s15328023top2601_18

Evans, L. "Preliminary Study: Lectures versus PowerPoint 4.0." (1998): http://www.kcmetrocc.mo.us/longview/lect_ppt.HTM

Fallon, Marianne and Stacey Forrest. "High-Tech versus Low-Tech Instructional Strategies: A Comparison of Clickers and Handheld Response Cards." *Teaching of Psychology* 38 (2011): 194–198. https://doi.org/10.1177/0098628311411896

Feldkamp, John K. "The Effectiveness of Electronic Whiteboards and PowerPoint Lessons in the Mathematics Classroom." (Senior Honors Thesis). Eastern Michigan University, 2008, http://commons.emich.edu/honors/144/

Felleman, D. J. and Van Essen, D. C. "Distributed Hierarchical Processing in the Primate Cerebral Cortex." *Cerebral Cortex* 1 (1991): 1–47, https://doi.org/10.1093/cercor/1.1.1

Ferrell, O. C., and Ferrell, Linda. "Assessing Instructional Technology in the Classroom." *Marketing Education Review* 12 (2002): 19–24.

Fifield, Steve and Rick Peifer. "Enhancing Lecture Presentations in Introductory Biology with Computer-Based Multimedia." *Journal of College Science Teaching* 23 (1994): 235–239.

Filippatou, Diamanto and Peter D. Pumfrey. "Pictures, Titles, Reading Accuracy and Reading Comprehension: A Research Review (1973-95)." *Educational Research* 38 (1996): 259–290, https://doi.org/10.1080/0013188960380302

Fisk, Gary D. "Using Animation in Forensic Pathology and Science Education." *LabMedicine* 39 (2008): 587–592, https://doi.org/10.1309/LM2MP23DKGWWCCPJ

Forsyth, Donelson R. and C. Ray Archer. "Technologically Assisted Instruction and Student Mastery, Motivation, and Matriculation." *Teaching of Psychology* 24 (1997): 207–212, https://doi.org/10.1207/s15328023top2403_17

Frank, Jonathan, Lewis Shaw, and Elizabeth Wilson. "The Impact of Providing Web-Based Powerpoint Slides as Study Guides in Undergraduate Business Classes." *Journal of Educational Technology Systems* 37 (2008): 217–229, https://doi.org/10.2190/ET.37.2.g

Freire, Paulo. *Pedagogy of the Oppressed*. New York, NY: Bloomsbury Publishing, 2000.

Frey, Barbara A. and Birnbaum, David J. (2002). "Learners' Perception on the Value of PowerPoint in Lectures." (2002): http://www.eric.ed.gov/contentdelivery/servlet/ERICServlet?accno=ED467192

Frommer, Frank. *How PowerPoint Makes You Stupid: The Faulty Causality, Sloppy Logic, Decontextualized Data, and Seductive Showmanship That Have Taken Over Our Thinking*. U.S.A.: The New Press, 2012.

Gabriel, Yiannis and Dorothy S. Griffiths. "Against the Tyranny of PowerPoint: New Avenues for Passionate Learning?" In The Passion for Learning and Knowing: Proceedings of the 6th International Conference on Organizational Learning and Knowledge. Vol. 2, 371–378. University of Trento, 2005.

Garber, Angela R. "Death by PowerPoint." *Small Business Computing*. April 1, 2001, http://www.smallbusinesscomputing.com/biztools/article.php/684871/Death-By-Powerpoint.htm

Gareis, Elisabeth. "Active Learning: A PowerPoint Tutorial." *Business Communication Quarterly* 70 (2007): 462–466.

Garner, Joanna K. and Michael P. Alley. "How the Design of Presentation Slides Affects Audience Comprehension: A Case for the Assertion-Evidence Approach." *International Journal of Engineering Education* 29 (2013): 1564–1579.

---. "Slide Structure Can Influence the Presenter's Understanding of the Presentation's Content." *International Journal of Engineering Education* 32 (2016): 39–54.

Garner, Joanna K., Michael P. Alley, Allen F. Gaudelli, and Sarah Elizabeth Zappe. "Common Use of PowerPoint versus the Assertion-Evidence Structure: A Cognitive Psychology Perspective." *Technical Communication* 56 (2009): 331–345.

Garrett, Nathan. "PowerPoint Outside Class: The Impact of Slide Design on Student Use." *Journal of Educational Technology* 44 (2015): 69–85, https://doi.org/10.1177/0047239515598521

Gaskins, Robert. "PowerPoint at 20: Back to Basics." *Communications of the ACM* 50, no. 12 (2007): 15–17.

Gazzaley, Adam and Larry D. Rosen. *The Distracted Mind: Ancient Brains in a High-Tech World.* Cambridge, MA: MIT Press, 2016.

Gazzaniga, Michael S. "Cerebral Specialization and Interhemispheric Communication: Does the Corpus Callosum Enable the Human Condition?" *Brain* 123 (2000): 1293–1326.

"Gestalt Psychology." *Wikipedia.* Retrieved December 14, 2016, https://en.wikipedia.org/wiki/Gestalt_psychology

Gilbert, Rick. *Michael Alley We Can Do Better.* PowerSpeaking, Inc., 2015. Retrieved from https://www.youtube.com/watch?v=EK76KwaP8J8

Giles, Rebecca M. and Leah H. Kinniburgh. "Putting PowerPoint in Its Place." *The Teaching Professor* 28 (2014): 1–2.

Glenberg, Arthur M. and William E. Langston. "Comprehension of Illustrated Text: Pictures Help to Build Mental Models." *Journal of Memory and Language* 31 (1992): 129–151, https://doi.org/10.1016/0749-596X(92)90008-L

Godin, Seth. "Really Bad PowerPoint (and How to Avoid It)." 2001, http://www.sethgodin.com/freeprize/reallybad-1.pdf

Goswami, Usha. "Neuroscience and Education: From Research to Practice?" *Nature Reviews Neuroscience* 7 no. 5 (2006): 406–413, https://doi.org/10.1038/nrn1907

Grabe, Mark and Kimberly Christoperson. "Optional Use of Online Lecture Resources: Resource Preferences, Performance, and Lecture Attendance." *Journal of Computer Assisted Learning* 24 (2008): 1–10, https://doi.org/10.1111/j.1365-2729.2007.00228.x

Grabe, Mark, Kimberly Christopherson, and Jason Douglas. "Providing Introductory Psychology Students Access to Online Lecture Notes: The Relationship of Note Use to Performance and Class Attendance." *Journal of Educational Technology Systems* 33 (2004): 295–308.

Gries, Laurie and Collin Gifford Brooke. "An Inconvenient Tool: Rethinking the Role of Slideware in the Writing Classroom." *Composition Studies* 38 (2010): 9–26.

Guadagno, Rosanna E., Nicole L. Muscanell, Jill M. Sundie, Terrilee A. Hardison, and Robert B. Cialdini. "The Opinion-Changing Power of Computer-Based Multimedia Presentations." *Psychology of Popular Media Culture* 2 (2013): 110–116, https://doi.org/10.1037/a0031072

Guernsey, Lisa. "PowerPoint Invades the Classroom." *The New York Times*. May 31, 2001, http://www.nytimes.com/2001/05/31/technology/31POWE.html?src=pm&pagewanted=1

Guetig, Meredith. "Harness the Power of PowerPoint." *PM Network* (September 2011): 50–54.

Gunel, Murat, Brian Hand, and Sevket Gunduz. "Comparing Student Understanding of Quantum Physics when Embedding Multimodal Representations into Two Different Writing Formats: Presentation Format versus Summary Report Format." *Science Education* 90 (2006): 1092–1112, https://doi.org/10.1002/sce

Gunn, Robert and Betsy Raskin Gullickson. "Forget Slides, Project Confidence." *Strategic Finance* (June 2005): 8–10.

Gürbüz, Hasan, Mustafa Kisoglu, Mehmet Erkol, Ali Alas, and Sakip Kahraman. "The Effect of PowerPoint Presentations Prepared and Presented by Prospective Teachers on Biology Achievement and Attitudes Towards Biology." *Procedia - Social and Behavioral Sciences* 2 (2010): 3043–3047, https://doi.org/10.1016/j.sbspro.2010.03.462

Gurrie, Chris and Brandy Fair. "Power Point--From Fabulous to Boring: The Misuse of Power Point in Higher Education Classrooms." *Journal of the Communication, Speech and Theater Association of North Dakota* (2008): 23–30.

Hallett, Terry L. and Geraldine Faria. "Teaching with Multimedia: Do Bells and Whistles Help Students Learn?" *Journal of Technology in Human Services* 24 (2006): 167–179, https://doi.org/10.1300/J017v24n02_10

Hammes, T. X. "Essay: Dumb-Dumb Bullets." *Armed Forces Journal*. (2009): http://armedforcesjournal.com/essay-dumb-dumb-bullets/

Hammonds, Steve. "Impact of Internet-Based Teaching on Student Achievement." *British Journal of Educational Technology* 34 (2003): 95–98, https://doi.org/10.1111/1467-8535.00310

Hanke, J. "The Psychology of Presentation Visuals." *Presentations* 12 no. 5 (1998): 42–51.

Hardin, Erin E. Presentation Software in the College Classroom: Don't Forget the Instructor." *Teaching of Psychology* 34 (2007): 53–57, https://doi.org/10.1080/00986280709336652

Harknett, Richard J., & Cobane, Craig T. "Introducing Instructional Technology to International Relations." *PS: Political Science and Politics* 30 (1997): 496–500.

Hartley, James and Ivor K. Davies. "Note-Taking: A Critical Review." *Innovations in Education and Training International* 15 (1978): 207–224.

Hashemzadeh, Nozar and Loretta Wilson. "Teaching with the Lights Out: What Do We Really Know About the Impact of Technology Intensive Instruction?" *College Student Journal* 41 (2007): 601–612.

Haynes, Jeremy M., Nancy Mccarley, and Joshua L. Williams. "An Analysis of Notes Taken During and After a Lecture Presentation." *North American Journal of Psychology* 17 (2015): 175–186, https://doi.org/10.1037/t05257-000

Heavens, A. "Death by Bullet Points." *The London Times*, June 28, 2004, http://business.timesonline.co.uk/printFriendly/0,2020-13469-1161635-13469,00.html

Hill, Andrea, Tammi Arford, Amy Lubitow, and Leandra M. Smollin. "'I'm Ambivalent About It': The Dilemmas of PowerPoint." *Teaching Sociology* 40 (2012): 242–256, https://doi.org/10.1177/0092055X12444071

Hlynka, Denis and Ralph Mason. "'PowerPoint' in the Classroom: What is the Point?" *Educational Technology* 38 (1998): 45–48.

Holstead, Jenell. "The Impact of Slide-Construction in PowerPoint: Student Performance and Preferences in an Upper-Level Human Development Course." *Scholarship of Teaching and Learning in Psychology* 1 (2015): 337–348, https://doi.org/10.1037/stl0000046

Homa, Donald and Cynthia Viera. "Long-Term Memory for Pictures Under Conditions of Thematically Related Foils." *Memory and Cognition* 16 (1988): 411–421, https://doi.org/10.3758/BF03214221

Horvath, Jared Cooney. "The Neuroscience of PowerPoint." *Mind, Brain, and Education* 8 (2014): 137–143, https://doi.org/10.1111/mbe.12052

Hove, M. Christina and Kevin J. Corcoran. "Educational Technologies: Impact on Learning and Frustration. *Teaching of Psychology* 35 (2008): 121–125, https://doi.org/10.1080/00986280802004578

Howe, Michael J. A. "The Utility of Taking Notes as an Aid to Learning." *Educational Research* 16 (1974): 222–227, https://doi.org/10.1080/0013188740160310

Huxam, Mark. "The Medium Makes the Message: Effects of Cues on Students' Lecture Notes." *Active Learning* in *Higher Education* 11 (2010): 179–188, https://doi.org/10.1177/1469787410379681

Issa, Nabil, Mary Schuller, Susan Santacaterina, Michael Shapiro, Edward Wang, Richard E. Mayer, and Debra A. DaRosa. "Applying Multidmedia Design Principles Enhances Learning in Medical Education." *Medical Education* 45 (2011): 818–826, https://doi.org/10.1111/j.1365-2923.2011.03988.x

Jackson, Maggie. *Distracted: The Erosion of Attention and the Coming Dark Age*. New York: Prometheus Books, 2008.

Jackson, Mary Jo, Marilyn M. Helms, William T. Jackson, and John R. Gum. "Student Expectations of Technology-Enhanced Pedagogy: A Ten-Year Comparison." *Journal of Education for Business* 86 (2011): 294–301, https://doi.org/10.1080/08832323.2010.518648

James, Karen E., Lisa A. Burke, and Holly M. Hutchins. "Powerful or Pointless? Faculty Versus Student Perceptions of PowerPoint Use in Business Education." *Business Communication Quarterly* 69 (2006): 374–396, https://doi.org/10.1177/1080569906294634

James, William. *The Principles of Psychology* Vol. 1. New York: Henry Holt and Company, 1890.

Jandaghi, Gholamreza and Hasan Zarei Matin. "Achievement and Satisfaction in a Computer-Assisted versus a Traditional Lecturing of an Introductory Statistics Course." *Australian Journal of Basic and Applied Sciences* 3 (2009): 1875–1878.

Johnson, Douglas A., and Christensen, Jack. "A Comparison of Simplified-Visually Rich and Traditional Presentation Styles." *Teaching of Psychology* 38 (2011): 293–297, https://doi.org/10.1177/0098628311421333

Kahn, Russell L. "Transforming the Design of Overheads and Their Impact on Learning." *Journal of Educational Technology Systems* 36 (2007): 179–187, https://doi.org/10.2190/ET.36.2.f

Kahraman, Sakip, Ceren Çevik, and Hülya Kodan. "Investigation of University Students' Attitude Toward the Use of Powerpoint According to Some Variables." *Procedia Computer Science* 3 (2011): 1341–1347, https://doi.org/10.1016/j.procs.2011.01.013

Kardes, Seval and Aylin Poroy. "The Effect of PowerPoint Preferences of Students on Their Performance: A Research in Anadolu University." *Turkish Online Journal of Distance Education* 10 (2009): http://tojde.anadolu.edu.tr/tojde33/articles/article_5.htm

Kask, S. "Using Computer-Aided Presentations (CAP) in Teaching: Does it Improve Student Learning?" In *Readings in Teaching and Learning*, 113–124. Littleton, CO: The CIBER Institute, 2004.

Katayama, Andrew D. and Steven M. Crooks. "Online Notes: Differential Effects of Studying Complete or Partial Graphically Organized Notes." The *Journal of Experimental Education* 71 (2003): 293–312,

Kay, Robin H. and Ann LeSage. "Examining the Benefits and Challenges of Using Audience Response Systems: A Review of the Literature." *Computers and Education* 53 (2009): 819–827, https://doi.org/10.1016/j.compedu.2009.05.001

Keller, Julia. "Is PowerPoint the Devil?" *Chicago Tribune*. January 22, 2003, http://faculty.winthrop.edu/kosterj/WRIT465/management/juliakeller1.htm

Kelly, Rebecca. "Getting Everybody Involved: Cooperative PowerPoint Creations Benefit Inclusion Students." *Learning and Leading With Technology* 27 (1999): 10–14.

Keough, Shawn M. "Clickers in the Classroom: A Review and a Replication." *Journal of Management Education* 36 (2012): 822–847, https://doi.org/10.1177/1052562912454808

Kiewra, Kenneth A. "Providing the Instructor's Notes: An Effective Addition to Student Notetaking." *Educational Psychologist* 20 (1985): 33–39.

Kiewra, Kenneth A., Nelson F. DuBois, David Christian, and Anne McShane. "Providing Study Notes: Comparison of Three Types of Notes for Review." *Journal of Educational Psychology* 80 (1988): 595–597, https://doi.org/10.1037/0022-0663.80.4.595

Kinchin, Ian. M. "Concept Mapping, PowerPoint, and a Pedagogy of Access." *Journal of Biological Education* 40 (2006a): 79–83.

---. "Developing PowerPoint Handouts to Support Meaningful Learning." *British Journal of Educational Technology* 37 (2006b): 647–650, https://doi.org/10.1111/j.1467-8535.2006.00536.x

Kinchin, Ian. M and L. B. Cabot. "Using Concept Mapping Principles in PowerPoint." *European Journal of Dental Education* 11 (2007): 194–199.

Kinchin, Ian, Deesha Chadha, and Patricia Kokotailo. "Using PowerPoint as a Lens to Focus on Linearity in Teaching." *Journal of Further and Higher Education* 32 (2008): 333–346, https://doi.org/10.1080/03098770802392923

King, P. "How much of the brain is involved with vision? What percentage of the brain is used for vision? What about hearing? Touch…etc." *Quora*. September 28, 2013. Retrieved June 18, 2015, http://www.quora.com/How-much-of-the-brain-is-involved-with-vision

Kisoglu, M., M. Erkol, R. Dilber, and H. Gurbuz. "Investigation the Effect of Preparing Powerpoint Presentations about Science Topics on Prospective Teachers' Science Achievements and Science Process Skills." *Energy Education Science and Technology Part B: Social and Educational Studies* 4 (2012): 213–222.

Kjeldsen, Jens E. "The Rhetoric of PowerPoint." *Seminar.Net: International Journal of Media, Technology, and Lifelong Learning* 2 (2006): 1–17.

Klemm, W. R. "Computer Slide Shows: A Trap for Bad Teaching." *College Teaching* 55 no. 3 (2007): 121–124.

Klentzin, Jacqueline Courtney, Emily Bounds Paladino, Bruce Johnston, and Christopher Devine. "Pecha Kucha: Using "Lightning Talk" in University Instruction." *Reference Services Review* 38 (2010) 158–167, https://doi.org/10.1108/00907321011020798

Knoblauch, Hubert. *PowerPoint, Communication, and the Knowledge Society*. London: Cambridge University Press, 2012.

Kobayashi, Keiichi. "What Limits the Encoding Effect of Note-Taking? A Meta-Analytic Examination." *Contemporary Educational Psychology* 30 (2005): 242–262, https://doi.org/10.1016/j.cedpsych.2004.10.001

Koeber, Charles. "Introducing Multimedia Presentations and a Course Website to an Introductory Sociology Course: How Technology Affects Student Perceptions of Teaching Effectiveness." *Teaching Sociology* 33 (2005): 285–300.

Kosslyn, Stephen M. "Graphics and Human Information Processing: A Review of Five Books." *Journal of the American Statistical Association* 80 (1985): 499–512.

---. *Clear and to the Point: 8 Psychological Principles for Compelling PowerPoint Presentations.* New York: Oxford University Press, 2007.

Kozma, Robert B. "Will Media Influence Learning? Reframing the Debate." *Educational Technology Research and Development* 42 (1994): 7–19.

Kumar, M. Phani. "Preferences of Undergraduate Medical Students - Electronic and Non-Electronic Teaching Methods in Pathology." *International Journal of Research in Health Sciences* 1 (2013): 239–241.

Kunkel, Karl. R. "A Research Note Assessing the Benefit of Presentation Software in Two Different Lecture Courses." *Teaching Sociology* 32 (2004): 188–196.

Larson, Thomas Donald. *A Comparison of Fifth Grade Children Receiving Both a Traditional and a Technology Based Means of Instruction in Social Studies.* Johnson Bible College (2001): http://www.eric.ed.gov/contentdelivery/servlet/ERICServlet?accno=ED456090

Lavin, Angeline M., Leon Korte, and Thomas L. Davies. "The Impact of Classroom Technology on Student Behavior." *Journal of Technology Research* 2 (2010): 1–13.

Levasseur, David G. and J. Kanan Sawyer. "Pedagogy Meets PowerPoint: A Research Review of the Effects of Computer-Generated Slides in the Classroom." *The Review of Communication* 6 (2006): 101–123, https://doi.org/10.1080/15358590600763383

Levie, W. Howard and Richard Lentz. "Effects of Text Illustrations: A Review of Research." *Educational Communication and Technology* 30 (1982): 195–232.

Levin, Joel R. "On Functions of Pictures in Prose." In *Neuropsychological and Cognitive Processes in Reading*, edited by F. J. Pirozzolo and M. C. Wittrock, 203–228. New York: Academic Press, 1981.

Levin, Joel R., Gary J. Anglin, and Russel N. Carney. "On Empirically Validating Functions of Pictures in Prose." In *The Psychology of Illustration: I. Basic Research*, edited by D. M. Willows and H. A. Houghton, 51–85. New York: Springer, 1987.

Levin, Michael A. and Lori T. Peterson. "Use of Pecha Kucha in Marketing Students' Presentations." *Marketing Education Reviews* 23 (2013): 59–63, https://doi.org/10.2753/MER1052-8008230110

Locke, Edwin. *A Guide to Effective Study*. New York: Springer, 1975.

Locke, Edwin. (1977). An Empirical Study of Lecture Note Taking among College Students." *The Journal of Educational Research* 71 (1977): 93–99, https://doi.org/10.1080/00220671.1977.10885044

Loisel, Meghan and Samantha Galer. "Uses of PowerPoint in the 314L Classroom." *Computer Writing and Research Lab*.

(2004): http://www.dwrl.utexas.edu/sites/www.dwrl.utexas.edu/files/powerpoint314.pdf

Lowerison, Gretchen, Jennifer Sclater, Richard F. Schmid, and Phillip C. Abrami. "Student Perceived Effectiveness of Computer Technology Use in Post-Secondary Classrooms." *Computers and Education* 47 (2006): 465–489, https://doi.org/10.1016/j.compedu.2004.10.014

Lowry, L. B. "Electronic Presentation of Lectures: Effect Upon Student Performance." *University Chemistry Education* 3 (1999): 18–21.

Luna, Carl. J. and Joseph McKenzie. "Testing Multimedia in the Community College Classroom." *THE Journal* 24 (1997): 78–81.

Luttig, Ernest Paul. *Enhancing Student Learning with PowerPoint Presentations*. Michigan: Michigan State University, 1998.

Mackiewicz, Jo. "Audience Perceptions of Fonts in Projected PowerPoint Text Slides." *Technical Communication* 54 (2007a): 295–307.

Mackiewicz, Jo. "Perceptions of Clarity and Attractiveness in PowerPoint Graph Slides." *Technical Communication* 54 (2007b): 145–156.

MacManaway, Lancelot A. "Teaching Methods in Higher Education - Innovation and Research." *Universities Quarterly* 24 (1970): 321–329.

Mahar, Stephen, Ulku Yaylacicegi, and Thomas N. Janicki. "Less is More When Developing PowerPoint Animations." *Information Systems Education Journal* 7 (2009a): 3–11.

---. (2009b). "The Dark Side of Custom Animation." *International Journal of Innovation and Learning* 6 (2009b): 581–592, https://doi.org/10.1504/IJIL.2009.026645

Mandler, George and Billie J. Shebo. "Subitizing: An Analysis of its Component Processes." *Journal of Experimental Psychology: General* 111 (1982): 1–22, https://doi.org/10.1037/0096-3445.111.1.1

Mann, Sandi and Andrew Robinson. "Boredom in the Lecture Theatre: An Investigation into the Contributors, Moderators, and Outcomes of Boredom Amongst University Students." *British Educational Research Journal* 35 (2009): 243–258, https://doi.org/10.1080/01411920802042911

Mantei, Erwin J. "Using Internet Class Notes and PowerPoint in the Physical Geology Lecture." *Journal of College Science Teaching* 29 (2000): 301–305.

Marmienė, A. "The Impact of the Delivery of Prepared PowerPoint Presentations on the Learning Process." *Santalka: Filologija, Edukologija* 2 (2006): 106–109.

Marsh, Elizabeth J. Holli E. Sink. "Access to Handouts of Presentation Slides During Lecture: Consequences for Llearning." *Applied Cognitive Psychology* 24 (2010): 691–706, https://doi.org/10.1002/acp.1579

Mason, Ralph and Denis Hlynka. "'PowerPoint' in the Classroom: Where is the Power?" *Educational Technology* 38 (1998): 42–45.

Massery, L. A. "PowerPoint Technology in the Second Language Classroom." *The International Journal of Technology, Knowledge, and Society* 4 (2008): 139–143.

Maxwell, Alexander. "Ban the Bullet-Point! Content-Based PowerPoint for Historians." *The History Teacher* 41 (2007): 39–54.

Mayer, Richard E. "Systematic Thinking Fostered by Illustrations in Scientific Text." *Journal of Educational Psychology* 81 (1989): 240–246. https://doi.org/10.1037/0022-0663.81.2.240

---. *Multimedia learning.* 2nd ed. New York: Cambridge University Press, 2009.

Mayer, Richard E., Gayle T. Dow, and Sarah Mayer. "Multimedia Learning in an Interactive Self-Explaining Environment: What Works in the Design of Agent-Based Microworlds?" *Journal of Educational Psychology* 95 (2003): 806–812, https://doi.org/10.1037/0022-0663.95.4.806

Mayer, Richard E. and Joan K. Gallini. "When is an Illustration Worth Ten Thousand Words?" *Journal of Educational Psychology* 82 (1990): 715–726, https://doi.org/10.1037/0022-0663.82.4.715

Mayer, Richard E., Julie Heiser, and Steve Lonn. "Cognitive Constraints on Multimedia Learning: When Presenting More Material Results in Less Understanding." *Journal of Educational Psychology* 93 (2001): 187–198, https://doi.org/10.1037//0022-0663.93.1.187

Mayer, Richard E. and Cheryl I. Johnson. "Revising the Redundancy Principle in Multimedia Learning." *Journal of Educational Psychology* 100 (2008): 380–386, https://doi.org/10.1037/0022-0663.100.2.380

Mayer, Richard E. and Roxana Moreno. "A Split-Attention Effect in Multimedia Learning: Evidence for Dual

Processing Systems in Working Memory." *Journal of Educational Psychology* 90 (1998): 312–320, https://doi.org/10.1037/0022-0663.90.2.312

Mayer, Richard E., Andrew Stull, Krista DeLeeuw, Kevin Almeroth, Bruce Bimber, Dorothy Chun, ... Hangjin Zhang. "Clickers in College Classrooms: Fostering Learning with Questioning Methods in Large Lecture Classes." *Contemporary Educational Psychology* 34 (2009): 51–57, https://doi.org/10.1016/j.cedpsych.2008.04.002

McConnell, Davis A. "Using Presentation Software in Large Lecture Classes." *Journal of Geoscience Education* 44 (1996): 164–168.

McKenzie, Jamie. "Scoring Power Points." *From Now On: The Educational Technology Journal* 10 no. 1 (2000): http://www.fno.org/sept00/powerpoints.html

McLuhan, Marshall and Lewis H. Lapham. *Understanding Media: The Extensions of Man.* Cambridge, MA: The MIT Press, 1964.

Medina, J. *Brain Rules: 12 Principles for Surviving and Thriving at Work, Home, and School.* Seattle, WA: Pear Press, 2008.

Meo, Sultan Ayoub, Shaikh Shahabuddin, Abeer A. Al Masri, Shaikh Mujeeb Ahmed, Mansoor Aqil, Muhammad Akmal Anwer and Abdul Majeed Al-Drees. "Comparison of the Impact of PowerPoint and Chalkboard in Undergraduate Medical Teaching: An Evidence-Based Study." *Journal of the College of Physicians and Surgeons Pakistan* 23 (2013): 47–50.

Miller Griffith, Lauren and Brian A. Roberts. "Learning Tool or Distraction: Student Responses to the use of iOS Devices."

In *Increasing Student Engagement and Retention Using Classroom Technologies: Classroom Response Systems and Mediated Discourse Technologies (Cutting-edge Technologies in Higher Education Vol. 6*, edited by C. Wankel & P. Blessinger, 307–336. Emerald Group Publishing Limited, 2013.

Milliken, John and L. Philip Barnes. "Teaching & Technology in Higher Education: Student Perceptions and Personal Reflections." *Journal of Computers in Education* 39 (2002): 223–235, https://doi.org/10.1016/S0360-1315(02)00042-8

Minow, Newton N. *The Vast Wasteland.* Presentation at the National Association of Broadcasters, 1961.

Moreno, Roxana and Richard E. Mayer. "Verbal redundancy in multimedia learning: When Reading Helps Listening." *Journal of Educational Psychology* 94 (2002): 156–163, https://doi.org/10.1037/0022-0663.94.1.156

Morrell, Lesley J. and Domino A. Joyce. "Interactive Lectures: Clickers or Personal Devices?" *F1000Research* (2015): https://doi.org/10.12688/f1000research.6207.1

Morrison, Joline and Doug Vogel. "The Impacts of Presentation Visuals on Persuasion." *Information and Management* 33 (1998): 125–135.

Nathans-Kelly, Traci and Christine G. Nicometo. *Slide rules: Design, Build, and Archive Presentations in the Engineering and Technical Fields.* Hoboken, NJ: IEEE Press; Wiley, 2014.

Nielsen, Jakob. "F-Shaped Pattern for Reading Web Content." *NN* Group, 2006. Retrieved January 3, 2017, https://www.nngroup.com/articles/f-shaped-pattern-reading-web-content/

Noppe, Illene C. "PowerPoint Presentation Handouts and College Student Learning Outcomes." *International Journal for the Scholarship of Teaching and Learning* 1 no. 1 (2007): 1–13, https://doi.org/10.20429/ijsotl.2007.010109

Nouri, Hossein and Abdus Shahid. "The Effect of PowerPoint Presentations on Student Learning and Attitudes." *Global Perspectives on Accounting Education* 2 (2005): 53–73.

---. "The Effects of PowerPoint Lecture Notes on Student Performance and Attitudes." *The Accounting Educators' Journal* 18 (2008): 103–117.

Novelli, Ethel L. B. and Ana Angelica H. Fernandes. "Students' Preferred Teaching Techniques for Biochemistry in Biomedicine and Medicine Courses." *Biochemistry and Molecular Biology Education* 35 (2007): 263–266, https://doi.org/10.1002/bmb.73

O'Dwyer, Aidan. "Responses of Engineering Students to Lectures Using PowerPoint." In *Proceedings of the International Symposium for Engineering Education*, 219–226. Dublin City University, Ireland, 2008.

O'Flaherty, Jacqueline and Craig Phillips. "The Use of Flipped Classrooms in Higher Education: A Scoping Review." *The Internet and Higher Education* 25 (2015): 85–95, https://doi.org/10.1016/j.iheduc.2015.02.002

Ohler, Jason. "The World of Digital Storytelling." *Educational Leadership* 63 (2005): 44–47.

O'Quigley, Margaret. "An Investigation into the Experience of Lectures from the Viewpoint of Lecturers and Students with Particular Emphasis on PowerPoint." *Networks* 14 (2011): 1–7.

Overson, Catherine E. "Applying Multimedia Principles to Slide Shows for Academic Presentation." In *Applying Science of Learning in Education: Infusing Psychological Science into the Curriculum,* edited by V. A. Benassi, C. E. Overson, and C. E. Hakala, (2014): 252–258.

Paivio, Allan. *Mental Representations: A Dual-Coding Approach.* New York: Oxford University Press, 1990.

Paradi, Dave. "Latest Annoying PowerPoint Survey Results." *Think Outsidw the Slidw.* 2017. Retrieved October 21, 2017, http://www.thinkoutsidetheslide.com/free-resources/latest-annoying-powerpoint-survey-results/

Pardini, Eleanor A., Denise P. Domizi, Daniel A. Forbes, and Gretchen V. Pettis. "Parallel Note-Taking: A Strategy for Effective Use of Webnotes." *Journal of College Reading and Learning* 35 (2005): 38–55.

Park, Babette, Terri Flowerday, and Roland Brünken. "Cognitive and Affective Effects of Seductive Details in Multimedia Learning." *Computers in Human Behavior* 44 (2015): 267–278, https://doi.org/10.1016/j.chb.2014.10.061

Parker, Ian. "Absolute PowerPoint: Can a Software Package Edit Our Thoughts?" *New Yorker,* May 28, 2001, 76–87.

Parker, Robyn E., Alison Bianchi, and Tsui Yi Cheah. "Perceptions of Instructional Technology: Factors of Influence and Anticipated Consequences." *Educational Technology and Society* 11 (2008): 274–293.

Parker, Samuel Chester. *A Textbook in the History of Modern Elementary Education: With Emphasis on School Practice in Relation to Social Conditions.* U.S.A: Ginn and Company, 1912.

Parks, Bob. "Death to PowerPoint!" *Bloomberg Businessweek.* August 30, 2012, http://www.bloomberg.com/news/articles/2012-08-30/death-to-powerpoint

Pence, Harry. "PowerPoint and Cooperative Learning: An Ideal Instructional Combination." *The Technology Source*, 1997, http://technologysource.org/article/powerpoint_and_cooperative_learning/

Penney, Catherine G. "Modality Effects and the Structure of Short Term Verbal Memory." *Memory and Cognition* 17 (1989): 398–422, https://doi.org/10.3758/BF03202613

Perry, Robert E. "Audience Requirements for Technical Speakers." *IEEE Transactions on Professional Communication PC-21* 4 no. 3 (1978): 91–96.

Perry, Timothy and Leslie Anne Perry. "University Students' Attitudes Towards Multimedia Presentations." *British Journal of Educational Technology* 29 (1998): 375–377.

Pippert, Timothy D. and Helen A. Moore. "Multiple Perspectives on Multimedia in the Large Lecture." *Teaching Sociology* 27 (1999): 92–109.

Powell, Bonnie Azab. "David Byrne Really Does Love PowerPoint, Berkely Presentation Shows." *Berkeley*, March 8, 2005. Retrieved April 23, 2014, http://www.berkeley.edu/news/media/releases/2005/03/08_byrne.shtml

Prabhu, Rekha, Kirtana M. Pai, Girish Prabhu, and Shrilatha. "A Lecture in Medical Physiology - PowerPoint versus Chalkboard." *South East Asian Journal of Medical Education* 8 (2014): 72–76.

Rankin, Elizabeth L. and David J. Hoaas. "The Use of PowerPoint and Student Performance." *Atlantic Economic Journal* 29 (2001): 113, https://doi.org/10.1007/BF02299936

Rey, Gunter Daniel. "A Review of Research and a Meta-Analysis of the Seductive Detail Effect." *Educational Research Review* 7 (2012): 216–237, https://doi.org/10.1016/j.edurev.2012.05.003

Reynolds, Gnarr. *Presentation Zen: Simple Ideas on Presentation Design and Delivery.* Berkeley, CA: New Riders, 2008.

Ricer, Rick E., Andrew T. Filak, and James Short. "Does a High Tech (Computerized, Animated, PowerPoint) Presentation Increase Retention of Material Compared to a Low Tech (Black on Clear Overheads) Presentation?" *Teaching and Learning in Medicine* 17 (2005): 107–111.

Rickman, Jon and Mike Grudzinski. "Student Expectations of Information Technology Use in the Classroom." *Educause Quarterly* 1 (2000): 24–30.

Rieber, Lloyd P. "Animation as a Distractor to Learning." *International Journal of Instructional Media* 23 (1996): 53–56.

Robin, Bernard R. "Digital Storytelling: A Powerful Technology Tool for the 21st Century Classroom." *Theory Into Practice* 47 (2008): 220–228, https://doi.org/10.1080/00405840802153916

Roehling, Patricia V. and Sonja Trent-Brown. "Differential Use and Benefits of PowerPoint in Upper Level versus Lower Level Courses." *Technology, Pedagogy, and Education* 20 (2011): 113–124, https://doi.org/10.1080/1475939X.2011.55401.8

Rokade, S. A. and B. H. Bahetee. "Shall We Teach Anatomy with Chalk and Board or PowerPoint Presentations? An Analysis of Indian Students' Perspectives and Performance." *Scholars Journal of Applied Medical Sciences* 1 (2013): 837–842.

Roll, Nick. "Communications Crossroads: Many Colleges Continue to Employ Handheld Clickers, but Smartphone Apps are Gaining Ground." *Inside Higher Ed.* August 2, 2017, https://www.insidehighered.com/digital-learning/article/2017/08/02/mobile-apps-gaining-ground-handheld-clickers

Rosenthal, Gary T., Rosenthal, Barlow Soper, Richard R. McKnight, James E. Barr, Lamar V. Wilkinson, Walter C. Buboltz Jr., and C.W. Von Bergen. "Multimedia, It's How You Use It: Reflections on a Selected Computerized Teaching Technology." *Computers in the Schools* 19 (2002): 77–86.

Sambrook, Sally and Jennifer Rowley. "What's the Use of Webnotes? Student and Staff Perceptions." *Journal of Further and Higher Education* 34 (2010): 119–134, https://doi.org/10.1080/03098770903480338

Sammons, Martha C. "Students Assess Computer-Aided Classroom Presentations." *THE Journal* 22 no. 10 (1995): 66–69.

Savoy, April, Robert W. Procter, and Gavriel Salvendy. "Information Rretention from PowerPoint and Traditional Lectures." *Computers and Education* 52 (2009): 858–867, https://doi.org/10.1016/j.compedu.12.005

Schneider, Sascha, Steve Nebel, and Gunter Daniel Rey. "Decorative Pictures and Emotional Design in Multimedia Learning." *Learning and Instruction* 44 (2016): 65–73, https://doi.org/10.1016/j.learninstruc.2016.03.002

Schnider, Armin. *The Confabulating Mind: How the Brain Creates Reality*. New York: Oxford University Press, 2008.

Schrodt, Paul and Paul L. Witt. "Students' Attributions of Instructor Credibility as a Function of Students' Expectations of Instructional Technology Use and Nonverbal Immediacy." *Communication Education* 55 (2006): 1–20, https://doi.org/10.1080/03634520500343335

Schuman, Rebecca. "PowerPointless: Digital Slideshows are the Scourge of Higher Education." *Slate Magazine*. March 7, 2014, http://www.slate.com/articles/life/education/2014/03/powerpoint_in_higher_education_is_ruining_teaching.html

Schweppe, Judith and Ralf Rummer. "Integrating Written Text and Graphics as a Desirable Difficulty in Long-Term Multimedia Learning." *Computers in Human Behavior* 60 (2016): 131–137, https://doi.org/10.1016/j.chb.2016.02.035

Selimoglu, Seval kardes, Aylin Poroy Arsoy, and Ertan Yasemin. "The Effect of PowerPoint Preferences of Students on their Performance: A Research in Anadolu University." *Turkish Online Journal of Distance Education* 10 (2009): 114–129.

Seo, Kay Kyeongju, Rosalyn Templeton, and Debra Pellegrino. "Creating a Ripple Effect: Incorporating Multimedia-Assisted Project-Based Learning in Teacher Education." *Theory Into Practice* 47 (2008): 259–265, https://doi.org/10.1080/00405840802154062

Seth, Vikas, Prerna Upadhyaya, Mushtaq Ahmad, and Virendra Kumar. "Impact of Various Lecture Delivery Methods in Pharmacology." *EXCLI Journal* 9 (2010): 96–101.

Seth, Vikas, Prerna Upadhyaya, Mushtaq Ahmad, and Vijay Moghe. "PowerPoint or Chalk and Talk: Perceptions of Medical Students vs. Dental Students in a Medical College in India." *Advances in Medical Education and Practice* 1 (2010): 11–16, https://doi.org/10.2147/AMEP.S12154

Shackelford, Ray and Kurt Griffis. "Teach Your Students the Power of PowerPoint." *Tech Directions* 66 (2007): 19–21.

Shah, Priti and James Hoeffner. "Review of Graph Comprehension Research: Implications for Instruction." *Educational Psychology Review* 14 (2002): 47–69, https://doi.org/1040-726X/02/0300-0047/0

Shallcross, Dudley E. and Timothy G. Harrison. "Lectures: Electronic Presentations versus Chalk and Talk - A Chemist's View." *Chemistry Education Research and Practice* 8 (2007): 73–79.

Shapiro, Amy M and Leamarie T. Gordon. "Classroom Clickers Offer More than Repetition: Converging Evidence for the Testing Effect and Confirmatory Feedback in Clicker-Assisted Learning." *Journal of Teaching and Learning with Technology* 2 (2013): 15–30.

Shapiro, E. J., J. Kerssen-Griep, B. M. Gayle, and M. Allen "How Powerful is PowerPoint? Analyzing the Educational Effects of Desktop Presentation Programs in the Classroom." In *Classroom Communication and Instructional Processes: Advances Through Meta-Analysis,* edited by B. M. Gayle, R. Preiss, N. Burrell, and M. Allen, 61–75. Malwah, NJ: Lawrence Erlbaum Associates, 2006.

Shaw, Gordon, Robert Brown, and Philip Bromiley. "Strategic Stories: How 3M Is Rewriting Business Planning." *Harvard Business Review* 76 no. 3 (1998): 41–50.

Shittu, Ahmed Tajudeen Kamal Madarsa Basha, Tunku Badariah Tunku Ahmad, and Mukhtar Alhaji Liman. "Analysis of Engineering and Education Students' Experiences and Expectations on PowerPoint Usage for Instruction." *Interdisiciplinary Journal of Contemporary Research in Business* 3 (2011): 1446–1455.

Shuell, Thomas J. and Stacey L. Farber. "Students' Perceptions of Technology Use in College Courses." *Journal of Educational Computing Research* 24 (2001): 119–138, https://doi.org/10.2190/YWPN-H3DP-15LQ-QNK8

Shwom, Barbara L. and Karl P. Keller. "'The Great Man Has Spoken. Now What Do I Do?' A Response to Edward R. Tufte's 'The Cognitive Style of PowerPoint'." *Communication Insight* 1 no. 1 (2003): 2–16.

Sidman, Cara L. and Dianne Jones. "Addressing Students' Learning Styles through Skeletal PowerPoint Slides: A Case Study." *MERLOT Journal of Online Learning and Teaching* 3 (2007): http://jolt.merlot.org/vol3no4/sidman.htm

Siegle, Del and Foster Theresa. "Laptop Computers and Multimedia and Presentation Software: Their Effects on Student Achievement in Anatomy and Physiology." *Journal of Research on Technology in Education* 34 (2001): 29–37.

Simons, Tab. "Does PowerPoint Make You Stupid?" *Presentations.Com*. March 2004, http://www.presentations.

com/presentations/search/article_display.jsp?vnu_content_id=1000482464

Simpson, Claude L., Lissa Pollacia, Jimmy Speers, T. Hillman Willis, and Rick Tarver. "An Analysis of Certain Factors Related to the Use of Powerpoint." *Communications of the International Information Management Association* 3 (2003): 73–83.

Slykhuis, David A., Eric N. Wiebe, and Len A. Annetta. "Eye-Tracking Students' Attention to PowerPoint Photographs in a Science Education Setting." *Journal of Science Education and Technology* 14 (2005): 509–520, https://doi.org/10.1007/s10956-005-0225-z

Smith, Stephen M. and Paul C. Woody. "Interactive Effect of Multimedia Instruction and Learning Styles." *Teaching of Psychology* 27 (2000): 220–223, https://doi.org/10.1207/S15328023TOP2703_10

Snowden, Robert, Peter Thompson, and Tom Troscianko. *Basic Vision: An Introduction to Visual Perception*. Oxford: Oxford University Press, 2012.

Soltan, Margaret. "PowerPoint Pissoff." [Blog]. (2015). Retrieved January 1, 2017, http://www.margaretsoltan.com/?cat=60

Sosin, Kim, Betty J. Blecha, Rajshree Agarwal, Robin L. Bartlett and Joseph I. Daniel. "Efficiency in the Use of Technology in Economic Education: Some Preliminary Results." *The American Economic Review* 94 (2004): 253–258.

Stark-Wroblewski, Kimberly, David S. Kreiner, Chris B. Clause, Jessica Edelbaum, and Shirely B. Ziser. "Does the Generation Effect Apply to PowerPoint Handouts?" *Psychology and Education* 43 (2006): 28–37.

Stewart, Thomas A. "Ban It Now! Friends Don't Let Friends Use PowerPoint." *CNN Money*. February 5, 2001. Retrieved April 8, 2014, http://money.cnn.com/magazines/fortune/fortune_archive/2001/02/05/296173/

Stoloff, Michael. "Teaching Physiological Psychology in a Multimedia Classroom." *Teaching of Psychology* 22 (1995): 138–141, https://doi.org/10.1207/s15328023top2202_15

Stoner, Mark A. "PowerPoint in a New Key." *Communication Education* 56 (2007): 354–382, https://doi.org/10.1080/03634520701342052

Strauss, Judy, Hope Corrigan, and Charles F. Hofacker. "Optimizing Student Learning: Examining the Use of Presentation Slides." *Marketing Education Review* 21 (2011): 151–162, https://doi.org/10.2753/MER1052-8008210205

Stryker, C. "Slideware Strategies for Mathematics Educators." *Journal of Mathematics Education at Teachers College* 1 (2010): 46–50.

Sugahara, Satoshu Sugahara and Gregory Boland. "The Effectiveness of *PowerPoint* Presentations in the Accounting Classroom." *Accounting Education* 15 (2006): 391–403, https://doi.org/10.1080/09639280601011099

Susskind, Joshua E. "PowerPoint's Power in the Classroom: Enhancing Students' Self-Efficacy and Attitudes." *Computers and Education* 45 (2005): 203–215, https://doi.org/10.1016/j.compedu.2004.07.005

---. "Limits of PowerPoint's Power: Enhancing Students' Self-Efficacy and Attitudes, but Not Their Behavior." *Computers and Education* 50 (2008): 1228–1239, https://doi.org/10.1016/j.compedu.2006.12.001

Swati, S. M. C., S. R. T. Suresh, and S. G. D. Sachin. "Student Assessment on Learning Based on Powerpoint versus Chalkboard." *International Journal of Recent Trends in Science and Technology* 13 (2014): 347–351.

Sweller, John, Jeroen J.G. van Merrienboer, and Fred G.W.C. Paas "Cognitive Architecture and Instructional Design." *Educational Psychology Review* 10 (1998): 251–296.

Szabo, Attila and Nigel Hastings. "Using IT in the Undergraduate Classroom: Should We Replace the Blackboard with PowerPoint?" *Computers and Education* 35 (2000): 175–187, https://doi.org/10.1016/S0360-1315(00)00030-0

Tang, Thomas Li-Ping and M. Jill Austin. "Students' Perceptions of Teaching Technologies, Application of Technologies, and Academic Performance." *Computers and Education* 53 (2009): 1241–1255, https://doi.org/10.1016/j.compedu.2009.06.007

Tangen, Jason M., Merryn D. Constable, Eric Durrant, Chris Teeter, Brett R. Beston, and Joseph A. Kim. "The Role of Interest and Images in Slideware Presentations." *Computers and Education* 56 (2011): 865–872, https://doi.org/10.1016/j.compedu.2010.10.028

Taylor, D. "Death by PowerPoint." *Developmental Medicine and Child Neurology* 49 (2007): 395.

Thareja, Priyavrat, Gagandeep Kaur Jayjee, Isha Dhawan, and Preety Singla. "Comparative Analysis of PowerPoint and Blackboard Teaching Methodologies." *Current Trends in Information Technology* 1 (2011): 8–15.

"The Best Video Length for Different Videos on YouTube." *YouTube*. Retrieved January 3, 2017, https://www.minimatters.com/youtube-best-video-length/

Thomas, M. and B. A. Raju. "Are PowerPoint Presentations Fulfilling Its Purpose?" *South-East Asian Journal of Medical Education* 1 (2012): 38–41.

Thompson, Clive. "PowerPoint Makes You Dumb." *The New York Times*. December 14, 2003, http://www.nytimes.com/2003/12/14/magazine/14POWER.html?ex=1072414800&en=1bb908537b11caad&ei=5070

Todorovic, Dejan. "Gestalt principles." *Scholarpedia* 3 (2008): 5345, https://doi.org/10.4249/scholarpedia.5345

Treleven, Mark D., Richard J. Penlesky, Thomas E. Callarman, Charles A. Watts, and Daniel J. Bragg. "Animated PowerPoint Presentations for Teaching Operations and Supply Chain Management: Perceived Value and Electronic Exchange of Files." *American Journal of Business Education* 5 (2012): 763–770.

Treleven, Mark D., Richard J. Penlesky, Thomas E. Callarman, Charles A. Watts, and Daniel J. Bragg. "Using PowerPoint Animations to Teach Operations Management Techniques and Concepts." *Decision Sciences Journal of Innovative Education* 12 (2014): 3–19.

Tufte, Edward R. *Envisioning Information*. Cheshire, CT: Graphics Press LLC, 1990.

---. *Visual Explanations*. Cheshire, CT: Graphics Press LLC, 1997.

---. *The Visual Display of Quantitative Information*. Cheshire, CT: Graphics Press LLC, 2001.

---. "PowerPoint is Evil. Power Corrupts. PowerPoint Corrupts Absolutely." *Wired Magazine*, 2003, https://www.wired.com/2003/09/ppt2/

---. *The Cognitive Style of PowerPoint: Pitching Out Corrupts Within*. 2nd ed. Cheshire, Connecticut: Graphics Press LLC, 2006.

Turkle, Sherry. "How Computers Change the Way We Think." *The Chronicle of Higher Education* 50 no. 21 (2004): B26.

Vallance, Michael and Phillip A. Towndrow. "Towards the 'Informed Use' of Information and Communication Technology in Education: A Response to Adams' 'PowerPoint, Habits of Mind, and Classroom Culture.'" *Journal of Curriculum Studies* 39 no. 2 (2007): 219–227, https://doi.org/10.1080/00220270601105631

van Jole, Francisco. "Het PowerPoint Denken." *FEM Annex New Economy*, 2000, http://www.franciscovanjole.com/archive2/020928.html

van Merriënboer, Jeroen J. G. and John Sweller. "Cognitive Load Theory and Complex Learning: Recent Developments and Future Directions." *Educational Psychology Review* 17 (2005): 147–177, https://doi.org/10.1007/s10648-005-3951-0

Vandehey, Michael A., Crystale M. Marsh, and George M. Diekhoff. "Providing Students with Instructors' Notes: Problems with Reading, Studying, and Attendance." *Teaching of Psychology* 32 (2005): 49–52.

Vickers, Amy. "My Day in PowerPoint Hell with the Bright Sparks from IPC Electric." *The Independent*. September 20, 1999, http://www.independent.co.uk/arts-entertainment/network-new-media-my-day-in-powerpoint-hell-with-the-bright-sparks-from-ipc-electric-1120713.html

Virtanen, Pasi, Jussi Myllärniemi, and Heini Wallander. "Diversifying Higher Education: Facilitating Different Ways of Learning." *Campus-Wide Information Systems* 30 (2013): 201–211, https://doi.org/10.1108/10650741311330384

Weatherly, Jeffrey N., Mark Grabe, and Emily I.L. Arthur. "Providing Introductory Psychology Students Access to Lecture Slides via Blackboard 5: A Negative Impact on Performance." *Journal of Educational Technology Systems* 31 (2002): 463–474.

Wecker, Christof. "Slide Presentations as Speech Suppressors: When and Why Learners Miss Oral Information." *Computers and Education* 59 (2012): 260–273, https://doi.org/10.1016/j.compedu.2012.01.013

Weinraub, Herbert J. "Using Multimedia Authoring Software: The Effects on Student Learning Perceptions and Performance." *Financial Practice and Education* 98 no. 2 (1998): 88–92.

Wertheimer, M. *Productive Thinking*. New York: Harper, 1959.

Wichmann, Felix A., Lindsay T. Sharpe, and Karl R. Gegenfurtner. "The Contributions of Color to Recognition Memory for Natural Scenes." *Journal of Experimental Psychology: Learning, Memory, and Cognition* 28 (2002): 509–520, https://doi.org/10.1037//0278-7393.28.3.509

Williams, Joshua L., Nancy G. McCarley, Jeremy M. Haynes, E.H Williams, T. Whetzel, T. Reilly. . . Lindsey Bailey. "The

Use of Feedback to Help College Students Identify Relevant Information on PowerPoint Slides." *North American Journal of Psychology* 18 (2016): 239–256.

Williams, Joshua L., Nancy G. McCarley, James Parker, Ellen H. Williams, Christiaan Layer, and Dominique Walker. "The Timing of Note Taking and Effects on Lecture Retention." *Delta Journal of Education* 3 (2013): 92–101.

Wilson, Edward O. "The Power of Story." *American Educator* 26 (2002): 8–11.

Wilson, Ian. "Positive PowerPoint: Developing Good Practice Through Practitioner Research." *Teacher Education Advancement Network Journal* 8 (2016): 94–105.

Wilson, Karen and James H. Korn. "Attention During Lectures: Beyond Ten Minutes." *Teaching of Psychology* 34 (2007): 85–89, https://doi.org/10.1177/009862830703400202

Wolfe, Christine, Michael Alley, and Kate C. Sheridan. "Improving Retention of Information from Teaching Slides (p. T2G17-21)." Presentation at the ASEE/IEEE Frontiers in Education Conference, San Diego, CA, 2006.

Wolverton, Lynda, Anna Butler, Carol Martinson, and Courtlann Thomas. "PechaKucha and Ignite: Formats that Improve Student Presentations." *The Teaching Professor* 28 (2014): 3.

Worthington, Debra L. and David G. Levasseur. "To Provide or Not to Provide Course PowerPoint Slides? The Impact of Instructor-Provided Slides on Student Attendance and Performance." *Computers and Education* 85 (2015): 14–22, https://doi.org/10.1016/j.compedu.2015.02.002

Yates, JoAnne. "Graphs as a Managerial Tool: A Case Study of Du Pont's Use of Graphs in the Early Twentieth Century." *Journal of Business Communication* 22 (1985): 5–33.

Yerkes, Robert M. and John D. Dodson. "The Relation of Strength of Stimulus to Rapidity of Habit-Formation." *Journal of Comparative Neurology and Psychology* 18 (1908): 459–482.

Yilmazel-Sahin, Yesim. "A Comparison of Graduate and Undergraduate Students' Perceptions of Their Instructors' Use of Microsoft PowerPoint." *Technology, Pedagogy, and Education* 18 (2009): 361–380, https://doi.org/10.1080/14759390903335866

Young, Jeffrey R. "When Good Technology Means Bad Teaching: Giving Professors Gadgets Without Training can do More Harm than Good in the Classroom, Students Say." *Chronicle of Higher Education* 51 no. 12 (November 12, 2004): A31.

Yue, Carole L., Elizabeth Ligon Bjork, and Robert A. Bjork. "Reducing Verbal Redundancy in Multimedia Learning: An Undesired Desirable Difficulty?" *Journal of Educational Psychology* 105 (2013): 266–278, https://doi.org/10.1037/a0031971

Zacks, Jeff, Ellen Levy, Barbara Tversky, and Diane J. Schiano. "Reading Bar Graphs: Effects of Depth Cues and Graphical Context." *Journal of Experimental Psychology: Applied* 4 (1998): 119–138, https://doi.org/10.1037/1076-898X.4.2.119

Zayac, Ryan M., Thom Ratkos, Jessica E. Frieder, and Amber Paulk. "A Comparison of Active Student

Responding Modalities in a General Psychology Course." *Teaching of Psychology* 43 (2016): 43–47. https://doi.org/10.1177/0098628315620879

www.ingramcontent.com/pod-product-compliance
Lightning Source LLC
Chambersburg PA
CBHW041730300426
44115CB00021B/2964